JUNE 2017

Global Economic Prospects

A Fragile Recovery

WORLD BANK GROUP

ISBN (paper): 978-1-4648-1024-4

ISBN (electronic): 978-1-4648-1026-8

DOI: 10.1596/978-1-4648-1024-4

Cover design: Bill Pragluski (Critical Stages).

The cutoff date for the data used in this report was May 24, 2017.

Table of Contents

Acknowledgments

This World Bank Group Flagship Report is a product of the Prospects Group in the Development Economics Vice Presidency. The project was managed by M. Ayhan Kose and Franziska Ohnsorge, under the general guidance of Paul Romer.

Chapters 1 and 2 were led by Carlos Arteta. Chapter 1 (Global Outlook) was prepared by Carlos Arteta and Marc Stocker, with contributions from Csilla Lakatos and Ekaterine Vashakmadze. Additional inputs were provided by John Baffes, Gerard Kambou, Eung Ju Kim, Hideaki Matsuoka, Bryce Quillin, Yirbehogre Modeste Some, and Dana Vorisek. Research assistance was provide by Xinghao Gong, Liwei Liu, Trang Thi Thuy Nguyen, Collette Wheeler, and Peter Williams.

Box 1.1 was prepared by Gerard Kambou and Boaz Nandwa. Research assistance was provided by Trang Thi Thy Nguyen and Xinghao Gong. Box 1.2 was prepared by Carlos Arteta with contributions from Gerard Kambou, Lei Ye, Boaz Nandwa, Yoki Okawa, Temel Taskin, Ekaterine Vashakmadze, and Dana Vorisek.

The first Special Focus, on debt dynamics in emerging market and developing economies, was prepared by M. Ayhan Kose, Franziska Ohnsorge, and Naotaka Sugawara. The second Special Focus, on arm's-length trade as a source of post-crisis trade weakness, was prepared by Csilla Lakatos and Franziska Ohnsorge.

Chapter 2 (Regional Outlooks) was supervised by Carlos Arteta, Anna Ivanova, and Franziska Ohnsorge. The authors were Ekaterine Vashakmadze (East Asia and Pacific), Yoki Okawa (Europe and Central Asia), Dana Vorisek (Latin America and the Caribbean), Lei Ye with contributions from Ergys Islamaj (Middle East and North Africa), Boaz Nandwa and Temel Taskin (South Asia), and Gerard Kambou (Sub-Saharan Africa). Research assistance was provided by Mai Anh Bui, Xinghao Gong, Liwei Liu, Trang Nguyen, and Shituo Sun.

Modeling and data work were provided by Hideaki Matsuoka, assisted by Mai Anh Bui, Xinghao Gong, Cristhian Javier Vera Avellan, Liwei Liu, Trang Thi Thuy Nguyen, Shituo Sun, Collette Mari Wheeler, and Peter Williams.

The online publication was produced by a team including Graeme Littler, Praveen Penmetsa, and Mikael Reventar, with technical support from Marjorie Patricia Bennington. Phillip Hay and Mark Felsenthal managed media relations and dissemination. The print publication was produced by Maria Hazel Macadangdang, Adriana Maximiliano, and Rosalie Singson Dinglasan, in collaboration with Aziz Gökdemir and Patricia Katayama.

Many reviewers offered extensive advice and comments. These included: Kishan Abeygunawar dana, Magda Adriani, Abebe Adugna Dadi, Kiatipong Ariyapruchya, Luca Bandiera, Rafael Chelles Barroso, Davaadalai Batsuuri, Hans Beck, Robert Beyer, Fabio Sola Bittar, Monika Blaszkiewicz, Elena Bondarenko, Eduardo Borensztein, Cesar Calderon, Kevin Carey, Francisco G. Carneiro, Paloma Anos Casero, Jean-Pierre Christophe Chauffour, Derek Hung Chiat Chen, Ajai Chopra, Ibrahim Saeed Chowdhury, Kevin James Clinton, Fabiano Silvio Colbano, Andrea Coppola, Tito Cordella, Damir Cosic, Barbara Cunha, Stefano Curto, Sudyumna Dahal, Somneuk Davading, Simon Davies, Annette De Kleine-Feige, Agim Demukaj, Allen Curtis Dennis, Shantayanan Devarajan, Tatiana Didier Brandao, Viet Tuan Dinh, Ndiame Diop, Quy-Toan Do, Mariam Dolidze, Jozef Draaisma, Sebastian Eckardt, Kim Alan Edwards, Christian Eigen-Zucchi, Khalid El Massnaoui, Olga Emelyanova, Wilfried Engelke, Marianne Fay, Norbert Matthias Fiess, Fitria

Fitrani, Cornelius Fleischhaker, Samuel Freije-Rodriguez, Roberta V. Gatti, Adnan Ashraf Ghumman, Frederico Gil Sander, Fernando Giuliano, Anastasia Golovach, David M. Gould, Gunjan Gulati, Poonam Gupta, Ricardo Alfredo Habalian, Lea Hakim, Birgit Hansl, Marek Hanusch, Wissam Harake, Fayavar Hayati, Santiago Herrera, Jeremy Hillman, Sandra Hlivnjak, Bert Hofman, Sahar Sajjad Hussain, Zahid Hussain, Elena Ianchovichina, Fernando Gabriel Im, Yoichiro Ishihara, Sheikh Tanjeb Islam, Mohammad Omar Joya, Kamer Karakurum-Ozdemir, Leszek Pawel Kasek, Vera Kehayova, Tehmina S. Khan, Mizuho Kida, Youssouf Kiendrebeogo, David Stephen Knight, Jakob Kopperud, Ewa Joanna Korczyc, Sibel Kulaksiz, Chandana Kularatne, Christoph Kurowski, Kwabena Gyan Kwakye, Jean Pierre Lacombe, Lara Alice Victoria Lambert, Emmanuel K.K. Lartey, Taehyun Lee, Tenzin Lhaden, John Litwack, Gladys Lopez, Acevedo, Sodeth Ly, Sanja Madzarevic-Sujster, Sandeep Mahajan, Facundo S. Martin, Aaditya Mattoo, Kirsten-Anne McLeod, Gianluca Mele, Martin Melecky, Dino Merotto, Elitza Mileva, Deepak K. Mishra, Florian Moelders, Shabih Ali Mohib, Lili Mottaghi, Rafael Munoz Moreno, Nataliya Mylenko, Evgenij Najdov, Nur Nasser Eddin, Claudia Nassif, Antonio Nucifora, Harun Onder, Carlos Orton Romero, Lucy Pan, John Panzer, Catalin Pauna, Keomanivone Phimmahasay, Samuel Pienknagura, Rong Qian, Bryce Quillin, Habib Rab, Martin Rama, Nadir Ramazanov, Luiz Edgard Ramos Oliveira, Sheila Redzepi, Julio Revilla, David John Martin Robinson, Daniel Francisco Barco Rondan, David Rosenblatt, Michele Ruta, Pablo Saavedra, Miguel Eduardo Sanchez Martin, Apurva Sanghi, Ilyas Sarsenov, Julie Saty Lohi, Cristina Savescu, Marc Tobias Schiffbauer, Philip M. Schuler, Claudia Paz Sepulveda, Smriti Seth, Sudhir Shetty, Altantsetseg Shiilegmaa, Emily Sinnott, Gregory Smith, Karlis Smits, Nikola L. Spatafora, Abdoulaye Sy, Congyan Tan, Fulbert Tchana Tchana, Shakira Binti Teh Sharifuddin, Hans Timmer, Emilija Timmis, Yvonne M. Tsikata, Christoph Ungerer, Robert Utz, Ralph Van Doorn, Carlos Vegh, Julio Velasco, Mathew A. Verghis, Muhammad Waheed, Jan Walliser, Pinar Yasar, Ayberk Yilmaz, Hoda Youssef, Albert G. Zeufack, Luan Zhao, May Thet Zin, and Bakhrom Ziyaev.

Regional Projections and write-ups were produced in coordination with country teams, country directors, and the offices of the regional chief economists.

Abbreviations

AE	advanced economies
ASEAN	Association of Southeast Asian Nations
bbl	barrel
BEC	Broad Economic Categories
BIS	Bank for International Settlements
BRICS	Brazil, Russian Federation, India, China, and South Africa
CEMAC	Central African Economic and Monetary Community
CBO	Congressional Budget Office
CY	calendar year
DECPG	Development Economics Prospects Group
EAP	East Asia and Pacific
EBRD	European Bank for Reconstruction and Development
ECA	Europe and Central Asia
ECB	European Central Bank
EECF	enhanced elemental chlorine–free
EM	emerging market economies
EMBI	Emerging Markets Bond Index
EMDE	emerging markets and developing economies
ERR	exchange rate regime
EU	European Union
EPU	economic policy uncertainty
FDI	foreign direct investment
FOMC	Federal Open Market Committee
FSC	Forest Stewardship Council
FTA	free trade agreement
FY	fiscal year
GCC	Gulf Cooperation Council
GDP	gross domestic product
GEP	Global Economic Prospects
GNFS	goods and non-factor services
GNI	gross national income
GSP+	Generalized System of Preferences Plus
GST	goods and services tax
HIPC	Heavily Indebted Poor Countries
IADB	Inter-American Development Bank
IMF	International Monetary Fund
LAC	Latin America and the Caribbean
LIC	low-income country
MDRI	multilateral debt relief initiative
NAICS	North American Industry Classification System
MENA or MNA	Middle East and North Africa
NAFTA	North American Free Trade Agreement

ODA	official development assistance
OECD	Organisation for Economic Co-operation and Development
OPEC	Organization of the Petroleum Exporting Countries
PCF	processed chlorine–free
PMI	purchasing managers' indexes
PPP	purchasing power parity
QQE	quantitative and qualitative monetary easing
RHS	right-hand side (in figures)
SAR	South Asia
SF	Special Focus
SSA	Sub-Saharan Africa
TCF	totally chlorine-free
TFP	total factor productivity
TPP	Trans-Pacific Partnership
UNCTAD	United Nations Conference on Trade and Development
UNIDO	United Nations Industrial Development Organization
VIX	Chicago Board Options Exchange (CBOE) Volatility Index
VAT	value-added tax
WAEMU	West African Economic and Monetary Union
WEO	World Economic Outlook
WTO	World Trade Organization

CHAPTER 1

GLOBAL OUTLOOK

A Fragile Recovery

Global activity is firming broadly as expected. Manufacturing and trade are picking up, confidence is improving, and international financing conditions remain benign. Global growth is projected to strengthen to 2.7 percent in 2017 and 2.9 percent in 2018-19, in line with January forecasts. In emerging market and developing economies (EMDEs), growth is predicted to recover to 4.1 percent in 2017 and reach an average of 4.6 percent in 2018-19, as obstacles to growth in commodity exporters diminish, while activity in commodity importers continues to be robust. Risks to the global outlook remain tilted to the downside. These include increased trade protectionism, elevated economic policy uncertainty, the possibility of financial market disruptions, and, over the longer term, weaker potential growth. A policy priority for EMDEs is to rebuild monetary and fiscal space that could be drawn on were such risks to materialize. Over the longer term, structural policies that support investment and trade are critical to boost productivity and potential growth.

Summary

Global growth is firming, contributing to an improvement in confidence. A recovery in industrial activity has coincided with a pickup in global trade, after two years of marked weakness (Figure 1.1). In emerging market and developing economies (EMDEs), obstacles to growth among commodity exporters are gradually diminishing, while activity in commodity importers remains generally robust. As a result, and despite substantial policy uncertainty, global growth is projected to accelerate to 2.7 percent in 2017, up from a post-crisis low of 2.4 percent in 2016, before strengthening further to 2.9 percent in 2018-19, broadly in line with January projections.

Activity in advanced economies is expected to gain momentum in 2017, supported by an upturn in the United States, as previously anticipated. In the Euro Area and Japan, growth forecasts have been upgraded, reflecting strengthening domestic demand and exports. Investment across advanced economies has firmed, while private consumption growth has moderated. As actual growth continues to exceed potential growth, increasing inflation and narrowing output gaps have raised the prospects of less accommodative monetary policy. Advanced economy growth is expected to accelerate to 1.9 percent in 2017, before moderating gradually in 2018-19. As usual, the

outlook is predicated only on legislated fiscal and trade policies.

The recovery in global trade coincides with strengthening investment, which is more import-intensive than other components of aggregate demand. Nevertheless, structural headwinds, including slower trade liberalization and value chain integration, as well as elevated policy uncertainty, continue to weigh on the outlook for trade.

Global financing conditions have been benign and benefited from improving market expectations about growth prospects. Financial market volatility has been low despite elevated policy uncertainty, reflecting investor risk appetite and, perhaps, some level of market complacency. Renewed risk appetite has supported EMDE financial markets and led to a narrowing of corporate bond spreads globally. Capital inflows to EMDEs were robust in the first half of 2017, partly in a rebound from late-2016 weakness. Over time, however, a gradual tightening of international financing conditions may weigh on capital flows to EMDEs. Commodity prices have continued to rise moderately, although prospects for increased U.S. shale oil production are weighing on the outlook for oil prices.

Against an improving international backdrop, growth in EMDEs has strengthened from a post-crisis low of 3.5 percent in 2016. It is projected to reach 4.1 percent in 2017 and 4.5 percent in 2018. In commodity exporters, firming commodity prices, recovering industrial activity, stabilizing investment, and improving confidence are supporting a gradual recovery, following near-stagnation in the past couple of years. This

---

Note: This chapter was prepared by Carlos Arteta and Marc Stocker, with contributions from Csilla Lakatos and Ekaterine Vashakmadze. Additional inputs were provided by John Baffes, Gerard Kambou, Eung Ju Kim, Hideaki Matsuoka, Bryce Quillin, Yirbehogre Modeste Some, and Dana Vorisek. Research assistance was provided by Xinghao Gong, Liwei Liu, Trang Thi Thuy Nguyen, Collette Wheeler, and Peter Williams.

TABLE 1.1 Real GDP[1]
(percent change from previous year)

	2014	2015	2016	2017	2018	2019	2016	2017	2018	2019
			Estimates	Projections			Percentage point differences from January 2017 projections			
World	2.8	2.7	2.4	2.7	2.9	2.9	0.1	0.0	0.0	0.0
Advanced economies	1.9	2.1	1.7	1.9	1.8	1.7	0.1	0.1	0.0	0.0
United States	2.4	2.6	1.6	2.1	2.2	1.9	0.0	-0.1	0.1	0.0
Euro Area	1.2	2.0	1.8	1.7	1.5	1.5	0.2	0.2	0.1	0.1
Japan	0.3	1.1	1.0	1.5	1.0	0.6	0.0	0.6	0.2	0.2
Emerging and developing economies (EMDEs)	4.3	3.6	3.5	4.1	4.5	4.7	0.1	-0.1	-0.1	0.0
Commodity-exporting EMDEs	2.2	0.3	0.4	1.8	2.7	3.0	0.1	-0.5	-0.3	-0.1
Other EMDEs	6.0	6.0	5.7	5.7	5.7	5.8	0.1	0.1	0.0	0.0
Other EMDEs excluding China	4.5	5.0	4.5	4.6	4.9	5.1	0.2	0.0	-0.1	0.0
East Asia and Pacific	6.8	6.5	6.3	6.2	6.1	6.1	0.0	0.0	0.0	0.0
China	7.3	6.9	6.7	6.5	6.3	6.3	0.0	0.0	0.0	0.0
Indonesia	5.0	4.9	5.0	5.2	5.3	5.4	-0.1	-0.1	-0.2	-0.1
Thailand	0.9	2.9	3.2	3.2	3.3	3.4	0.1	0.0	0.0	0.0
Europe and Central Asia	2.3	1.0	1.5	2.5	2.7	2.8	0.3	0.1	-0.1	-0.1
Russia	0.7	-2.8	-0.2	1.3	1.4	1.4	0.4	-0.2	-0.3	-0.4
Turkey	5.2	6.1	2.9	3.5	3.9	4.1	0.4	0.5	0.4	0.4
Poland	3.3	3.9	2.8	3.3	3.2	3.2	0.3	0.2	-0.1	-0.2
Latin America and the Caribbean	0.9	-0.8	-1.4	0.8	2.1	2.5	0.0	-0.4	-0.2	-0.1
Brazil	0.5	-3.8	-3.6	0.3	1.8	2.1	-0.2	-0.2	0.0	-0.1
Mexico	2.3	2.6	2.3	1.8	2.2	2.5	0.3	0.0	-0.3	-0.3
Argentina	-2.5	2.6	-2.3	2.7	3.2	3.2	0.0	0.0	0.0	0.0
Middle East and North Africa	3.4	2.8	3.2	2.1	2.9	3.1	0.5	-1.0	-0.4	-0.3
Saudi Arabia	3.7	4.1	1.4	0.6	2.0	2.1	0.4	-1.0	-0.5	-0.5
Iran, Islamic Rep.	4.3	-1.8	6.4	4.0	4.1	4.2	1.8	-1.2	-0.7	-0.3
Egypt, Arab Rep.[2]	2.9	4.4	4.3	3.9	4.6	5.3	0.0	-0.1	-0.1	-0.1
South Asia	6.7	6.9	6.7	6.8	7.1	7.3	-0.1	-0.3	-0.2	-0.1
India[3]	7.2	7.9	6.8	7.2	7.5	7.7	-0.2	-0.4	-0.3	-0.1
Pakistan[2]	4.0	4.0	4.7	5.2	5.5	5.8	0.0	0.0	0.0	0.0
Bangladesh[2]	6.1	6.6	7.1	6.8	6.4	6.7	0.0	0.0	-0.1	0.0
Sub-Saharan Africa	4.6	3.1	1.3	2.6	3.2	3.5	-0.2	-0.3	-0.4	-0.2
South Africa	1.6	1.3	0.3	0.6	1.1	2.0	-0.1	-0.5	-0.7	0.2
Nigeria	6.3	2.7	-1.6	1.2	2.4	2.5	0.1	0.2	-0.1	0.0
Angola	4.8	3.0	0.0	1.2	0.9	1.5	-0.4	0.0	0.0	0.6
Memorandum items:										
Real GDP[1]										
High-income countries	1.9	2.2	1.7	1.9	1.9	1.7	0.1	0.1	0.1	0.0
Developing countries	4.4	3.6	3.6	4.3	4.7	4.9	0.1	-0.1	-0.1	0.0
Low-income countries	6.3	4.7	4.4	5.4	5.8	5.8	-0.3	-0.2	-0.2	-0.3
BRICS	5.1	3.9	4.2	5.0	5.2	5.4	-0.1	-0.1	-0.2	-0.1
World (2010 PPP weights)	3.5	3.3	3.1	3.4	3.6	3.7	0.1	-0.1	-0.1	0.0
World trade volume[4]	4.1	2.7	2.5	4.0	3.8	3.8	0.0	0.4	-0.2	-0.1
Commodity prices										
Oil price[5]	-7.5	-47.3	-15.6	23.8	5.7	5.4	-0.5	-4.4	-2.7	0.8
Non-energy commodity price index	-4.6	-15.0	-2.6	4.0	0.7	1.0	0.0	2.6	-1.5	-1.1

Source: World Bank.

Notes: PPP = purchasing power parity. World Bank forecasts are frequently updated based on new information. Consequently, projections presented here may differ from those contained in other World Bank documents, even if basic assessments of countries' prospects do not differ at any given moment in time. Country classifications and lists of emerging market and developing economies (EMDEs) are presented in Table 1.2. BRICS include: Brazil, Russia, India, China, and South Africa.

1. Aggregate growth rates calculated using constant 2010 U.S. dollars GDP weights.

2. GDP growth values are on a fiscal year basis. Aggregates that include these countries are calculated using data compiled on a calendar year basis. Pakistan's growth rates are based on GDP at factor cost. The column labeled 2017 refers to FY2016/17.

3. The column labeled 2016 refers to FY2016/17.

4. World trade volume of goods and non-factor services.

5. Simple average of Dubai, Brent, and West Texas Intermediate.

For additional information, please see www.worldbank.org/gep.

recovery will be broad-based, impacting nearly 70 percent of commodity exporters in 2017. However, lingering fiscal and external adjustment needs dampen growth prospects in a number of countries. As a result, growth in commodity exporters is projected to rise from 0.4 percent in 2016 to 1.8 percent in 2017 and 2.7 percent in 2018—somewhat below January forecasts, reflecting longer-than-expected adjustment to low commodity prices in some countries and, to a lesser degree, slightly lower oil price projections.

Growth continues to be robust among commodity importers. Windfalls from the recent decline in commodity prices is waning, but accommodative policies are supporting domestic demand and export growth is being bolstered by a recovery in global trade. The forecast for growth in commodity importers remains stable, at an average of 5.7 percent in 2017-19.

In low-income countries, growth is rebounding, as rising metals prices lift production in metals exporters and infrastructure investment continues in non-resource-intensive economies. However, some low-income countries are still struggling with declining oil production, conflict, drought, and security and political challenges. Growth in low-income countries is expected to strengthen during 2017-19, as activity firms in commodity exporters.

A number of factors weigh on longer-term EMDE growth prospects, including structural headwinds to global trade, worsening demographics, slowing productivity growth, and governance and institutional challenges. Even if the expected modest rebound in investment across EMDEs materializes, slowing capital accumulation in recent years may already have reduced potential growth.

Substantial risks cloud this outlook, despite the possibility of fiscal stimulus in some major advanced economies, particularly the United States (Figure 1.2). Escalating trade restrictions could derail a fragile recovery in trade and undo gains from past liberalization efforts. A further increase in policy uncertainty from already high levels could dampen confidence and investment and trigger financial market stress, after a period of

FIGURE 1.1 Global prospects

Growth is projected to gain strength in both advanced economies and emerging market and developing economies (EMDEs). Global trade growth has firmed and is expected to outpace GDP growth after two years of marked weakness. The pickup in global trade partly reflects a bottoming out of global investment, which is relatively import-intensive. Global financing conditions remain benign. The projected recovery in EMDEs is largely driven by expectations of diminishing obstacles to activity in commodity exporters.

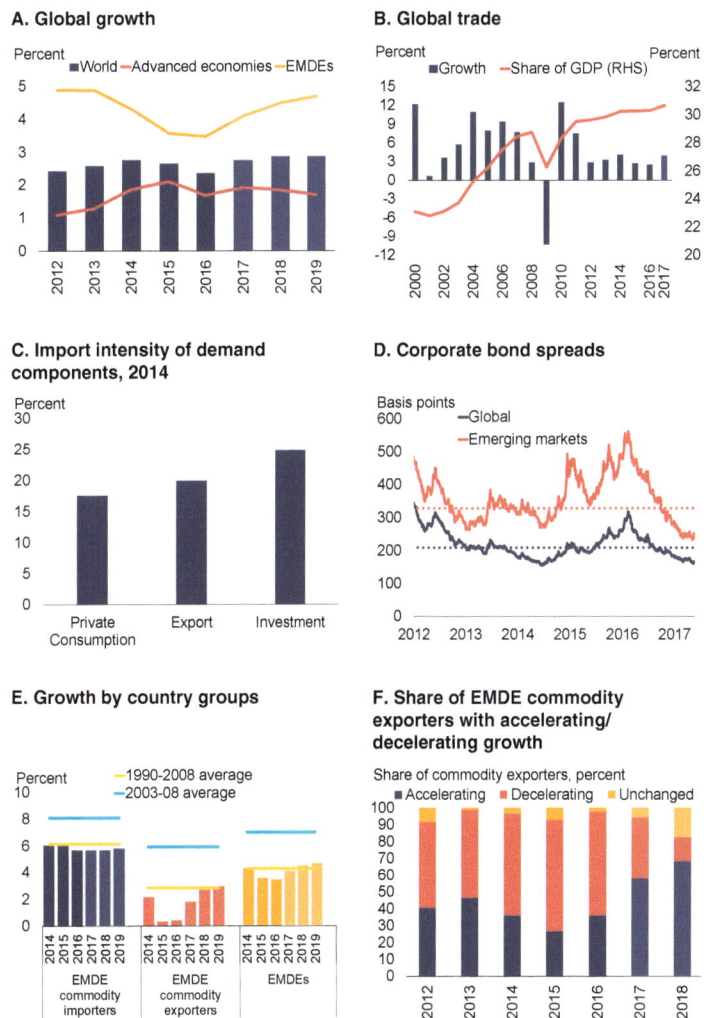

A. Global growth

B. Global trade

C. Import intensity of demand components, 2014

D. Corporate bond spreads

E. Growth by country groups

F. Share of EMDE commodity exporters with accelerating/ decelerating growth

Sources: Bloomberg, World Bank, World Input-Output Database.
A.B.E.F. Shaded areas indicate forecasts.
A. Aggregate growth rates calculated using constant 2010 U.S. dollars GDP weights.
B. Global trade is measured as volume of goods and services.
C. Import intensity for each GDP component computed from input-output tables based on Hong et al. (2016). GDP-weighted average of 25 advanced economies and 7 EMDEs.
D. Spread between yields on non-sovereign debt with at least 18 months to final maturity and U.S. Treasury yields of equivalent maturity. Individual bonds are weighted by market capitalization. Dotted lines indicate the median values since 2005. Last observation is May 24, 2017.
E. Aggregate growth rates calculated using constant 2010 U.S. dollars GDP weights.
F. Accelerating / decelerating growth are changes of at least 0.1 percentage point in growth rates from the previous year. Sample includes 86 commodity-exporting EMDEs.

unusually low financial market volatility. Market reassessment of advanced-economy monetary policy, or disorderly exchange rate developments, could contribute to swings in EMDE asset prices

FIGURE 1.2 Global risks and policy challenges

Downside risks to global growth include rising protectionism, high policy uncertainty, and the possibility of financial market disruptions. U.S. monetary policy has tightened gradually so far, but a faster pace would impact global financing conditions. Inflation has eased among EMDE commodity exporters, allowing room for cuts in policy interest rates. With deficits prevailing across EMDEs, and debt on a rising path, especially in commodity exporters, fiscal space remains constrained.

A. Probability of a 1-percentage-point deviation from one-year ahead global growth forecasts

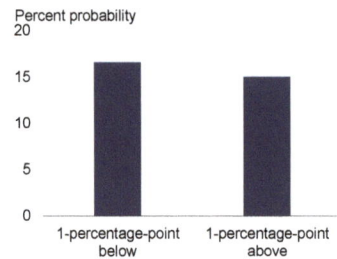

B. Global trade and tariffs

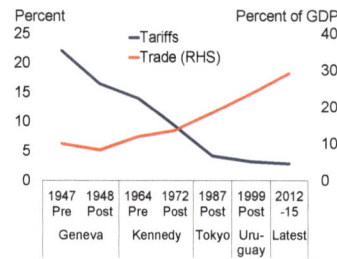

C. Economic policy uncertainty (EPU) and financial market volatility (VIX)

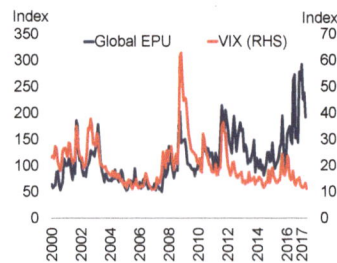

D. U.S. policy interest rates around tightening cycles

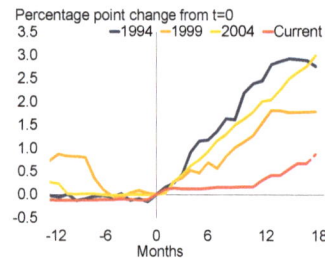

E. Consumer price inflation in EMDEs

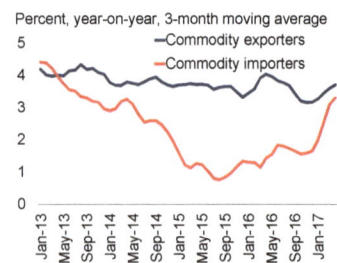

F. Fiscal sustainability gap

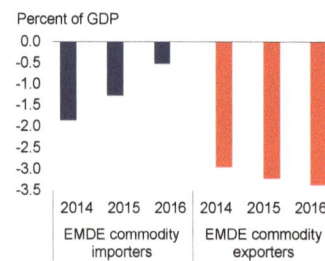

Sources: Baker, Bloom, and Davis (2015); Bloomberg; Bown and Irwin (2015); Federal Reserve Board; Haver Analytics; International Monetary Fund WEO; World Bank.

A. Probabilities computed from forecast distribution of 18-month ahead oil price futures, S&P500 equity price futures, and term spread forecasts. Last observation is April 2017.

B. Global trade is defined as the average of exports and imports in percent of GDP. Applied tariff rates based on weighted mean for all products.

C. VIX is the implied volatility of option prices on the U.S. S&P 500. EPU is the Economic Policy Uncertainty index computed by Baker, Bloom, and Davis (2015). Last observation is April 2017 for EPU and May 24, 2017 for VIX.

D. t=0 refers to the start of U.S. monetary policy tightening cycles (January 1994, June 1999, June 2004, and December 2015 ("current"). Dashed lines show market implied changes. Last observation is May 24, 2017.

E. Sample includes 75 commodity-exporting and 54 commodity-importing EMDEs and shows the median in each respective group. Last observation is April 2017.

F. Sustainability gap is measured as the difference between the primary balance and the debt-stabilizing primary balance, assuming historical average (1990–2016) interest rates and growth rates. A negative gap indicates that government debt is on a rising trajectory; a positive gap indicates government debt is on a falling trajectory. Figure shows median in each country group. Sample includes 44 commodity-exporting and 28 commodity-importing EMDEs.

and capital flows, potentially amplified by vulnerabilities in some countries. Over the longer term, persistent weakness in productivity and investment growth would erode potential growth.

Policymakers face the challenge in nurturing the recovery, confronting downside risks, and fostering longer-term growth. Central banks in advanced economies will gradually normalize monetary policy as inflation increases and economic slack diminishes. While the U.S. tightening cycle is well ahead of other major advanced economies, it is proceeding at a substantially slower pace than in the past. Expansionary fiscal policy could help support the recovery, as long as it is consistent with medium-term fiscal sustainability. Policy priorities include measures to support workers most affected by sectoral shifts in employment through better training and job search programs, and to share the dividends of growth and gains from globalization more widely.

Inflation rates in EMDE commodity exporters and importers are converging. Easing inflation among commodity exporters since mid-2016 has allowed a more accommodative monetary policy stance in some countries. Although the impact of the earlier drop in commodity prices on the government budgets of commodity exporters is dissipating, fiscal space remains constrained in many EMDEs, suggesting the need for continued fiscal adjustment. EMDEs will need to continue to pursue structural reforms to improve their longer-term growth prospects, diversify their economies, and develop domestic as well as foreign markets. These efforts include policies to improve the business climate, support investment in human and physical capital, and enhance regional and global trade integration of EMDEs.

Major economies: Recent developments and outlook

Growth in major advanced economies has strength-ened, and their short-term outlook has improved, despite elevated policy uncertainty. A modest recovery should continue, with output gaps narrowing and inflation gradually converging toward central bank targets. U.S. monetary policy normalization is expect-ed to proceed at a measured pace. China's policy-guided gradual transition to slower but more sustainable growth continues as expected.

Advanced economies started the year on a solid note, with investment and exports regaining momentum after subdued growth in 2016. Private consumption decelerated somewhat in early 2017, but has been supported by labor market improvements. Import demand has strengthened, further contributing to a recovery in global trade. In 2017, growth is expected to pick up in the United States and Japan, and to remain broadly stable in the Euro Area (Figure 1.3). Forecasts for several major economies have been upgraded. Economic slack continues to diminish, and inflation expectations are rising, albeit at different rates.

United States

Following a slowdown in 2016 that reflected investment and export weakness, growth is expected to recover this year. At the start of 2017, activity was temporarily held back by a deceleration in consumer spending, largely due to one-off factors and despite high consumer confidence (Figure 1.4). This was partly offset by an appreciable pickup in private investment, after subdued gains in 2016. Capital expenditure in the energy sector showed signs of bottoming out, following two years of heavy retrenchment and productivity gains in the shale oil sector. Labor market conditions have continued to improve in 2017, but wage and productivity growth remain sluggish. Stagnant productivity partly reflects diminished firm entry rates, including a decline in the startup rate in key innovative sectors, as well as lower job flows (Haltiwanger 2015; Decker et al. 2017). Economic slack remains, as reflected in underemployment and unused capacity in manufacturing above levels of earlier cyclical peaks (Yellen 2017). However, slack is diminishing, and the unemployment rate is close to its estimated long-run equilibrium (FOMC 2017). Following its March 2017 policy rate hike, the U.S. Federal Reserve is expected to continue to tighten monetary policy—but at a more gradual pace than in the past three tightening cycles, reflecting

FIGURE 1.3 Advanced economies

Growth in the United States is expected to recover in 2017 and to continue at a moderate pace in 2018, as previously envisaged. The forecasts for the Euro Area and Japan have been revised upward, reflecting robust growth at the start of 2017. Inflation expectations have increased from 2016, albeit from low levels in the Euro Area and Japan.

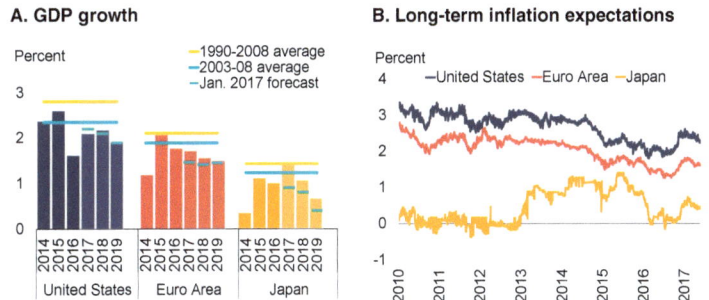

A. GDP growth

B. Long-term inflation expectations

Sources: Bloomberg, World Bank.
A. Shaded areas indicate forecasts.
B. Long-term inflation expectations are derived from 5-year/5-year forward swap rates. Last observation is May 24, 2017.

FIGURE 1.4 United States

Private consumption moderated in early 2017, despite strong consumer confidence. Private investment strengthened, whereas capital expenditures in the energy sector showed signs of bottoming out. Economic slack is diminishing, but unused capacity remains above pre-crisis levels. Over the long run, net migration is expected to account for the bulk of population growth, assuming no policy change.

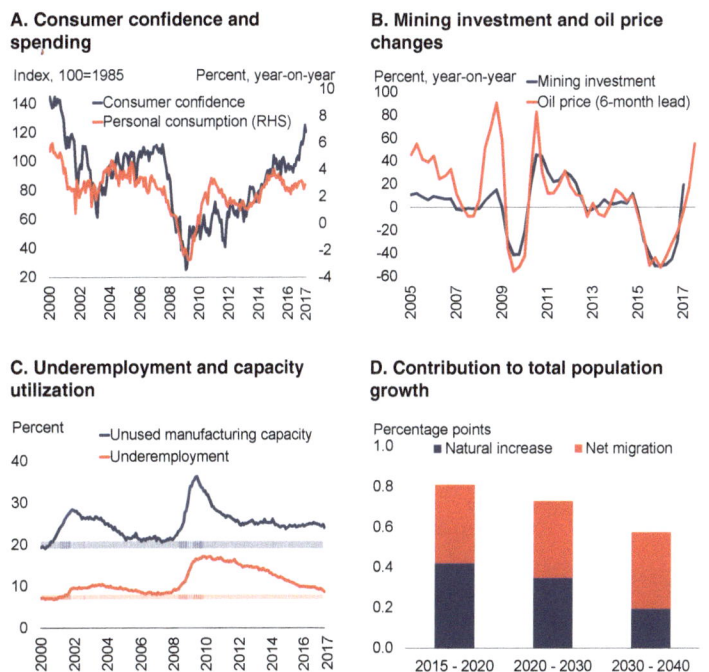

A. Consumer confidence and spending

B. Mining investment and oil price changes

C. Underemployment and capacity utilization

D. Contribution to total population growth

Sources: Board of Governors of the Federal Reserve System, Haver Analytics, U.S. Bureau of Labor Statistics, U.S. Census Bureau, World Bank.
A. Last observation is April 2017 for consumer confidence and March for real personal consumption.
B. Last observation is 2017Q1.
C. Underemployment is the sum of unemployed, people marginally attached to the labor market, and involuntary part-time workers, in percent of the labor force. Ranges denote values of each data series at cycle peaks. Shaded areas denote U.S. recessions. Last observation is April 2017.
D. Net migration includes the international migration of both native and foreign-born populations. Based on the 2014 U.S. Census Bureau population projections.

FIGURE 1.5 **Euro Area**

Unemployment fell rapidly throughout 2016, but remains slightly above structural levels. Actual and expected inflation increased somewhat since the start of the year. Investment is recovering, but remains on a lower trajectory than in previous upturns. The United States and the United Kingdom remain the single largest destination of extra-Euro Area exports.

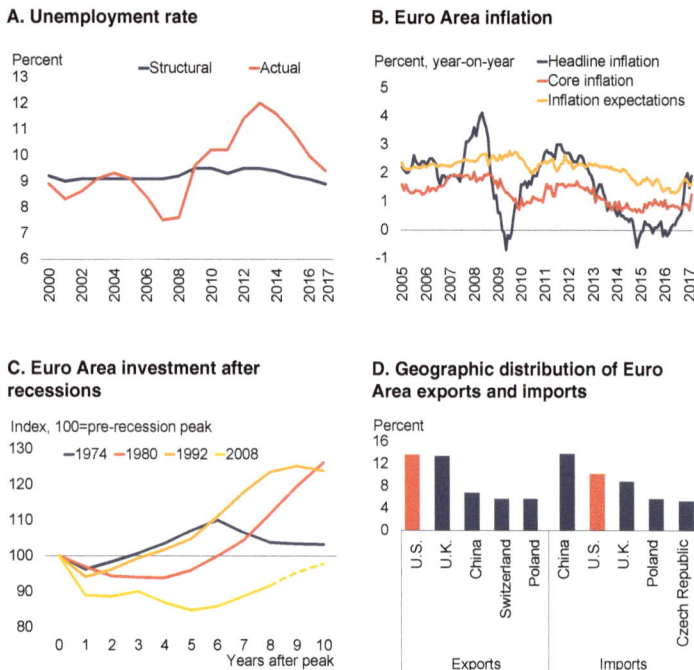

A. Unemployment rate

B. Euro Area inflation

C. Euro Area investment after recessions

D. Geographic distribution of Euro Area exports and imports

Sources: Bloomberg, European Commission, Eurostat, Haver Analytics, World Bank.
A. Structural unemployment is the non-accelerating wage inflation rate of unemployment (NAWRU) estimated by the European Commission.
B. Long-term inflation expectations are derived from 5-year/5-year forward swap rates. Last observation is April 2017.
D. Share of extra-Euro Area exports and imports in 2016.

significant additional policy changes presents upside as well as downside risks to the U.S. growth forecast for 2018-19. Tax cuts and infrastructure programs could lead to stronger-than-expected growth in the short term, but also to a more rapid increase in policy interest rates (World Bank 2017a). In contrast, should substantial changes in trade policies emerge, they might trigger retaliatory measures, damaging activity in both the United States and its trading partners. U.S. multinationals are tightly interconnected in regional and global supply chains and account for a substantial share of exports, domestic sales, and employment in the United States (Kose et al. 2017a). The impact on trade and activity of border tax adjustments in corporate taxation would largely depend on the reaction of the exchange rate and on associated policy uncertainties (Auerbach and Holtz-Eakin 2016). Over time, more restrictive immigration rules could reduce potential output growth. Net migration contributes to both employment and productivity growth, and is expected to account for the bulk of population growth in coming decades (Alesina, Harnoss, and Rapoport 2013; Borjas 2013; Jaumotte, Koloskova, and Saxena 2016; Peri 2012).[1]

Euro Area

Growth was robust in 2016 and continued at a sustained pace at the start of 2017. Manufacturing activity and goods exports have been lifted by strengthening global trade and investment. The unemployment rate fell throughout 2016 to reach 9.5 percent in the first quarter of 2017, about 2.5 percentage points below its peak in 2013. However, the jobless rate remains above structural levels, indicating that some labor market slack persists (Figure 1.5). Headline inflation has risen as the energy price decline of early 2016 has unwound, but core inflation and inflation expectations remain below the European Central Bank (ECB) target, pointing to prospects of continued monetary policy accommodation.

persistent legacies from the financial crisis and lower equilibrium interest rates. Thus far, financial markets have been resilient despite rising U.S. policy interest rates, possibly because rate increases were interpreted as a recognition of strengthening U.S. growth prospects (Arteta et al. 2015). As a result, financing conditions remain accommodative and broadly supportive of a continued recovery.

Overall, a moderate expansion in activity is expected to continue. Growth is projected to rise from 1.6 percent in 2016 to 2.1 percent in 2017 and 2.2 percent in 2018, before slowing to 1.9 percent in 2019 as it moves closer to potential. The remaining output gap could close by 2018 and become positive in 2019. The possibility of

---

[1]The global implications of possible U.S. policy changes are discussed in greater detail in the risks and policy challenges sections.

Accommodative monetary policy is expected to help sustain domestic demand in the near term. Unconventional measures undertaken by the ECB since 2014 have helped stimulate credit growth, lift inflation expectations, and foster a gradual recovery (Arteta et al. 2016; Andrade et al. 2016). Fiscal policy is expected to be broadly neutral to growth in 2017 (European Commission 2017). The recovery in private investment and export growth is projected to continue, while private consumption decelerates on receding tailwinds from low energy prices. On balance, growth is projected to remain at 1.7 percent in 2017, better than anticipated in January. In 2018-19, growth is expected to moderate to 1.5 percent, as economic slack diminishes and the ECB gradually unwinds exceptional policy measures. Nevertheless, growth should remain well above potential growth, currently estimated at about 1.2 percent (European Commission 2017). Prospects remain clouded by elevated policy uncertainties, including election outcomes, the direction of Brexit negotiations, and financial sector fragilities such as high levels of non-performing bank loans in some economies. Policy changes in the United States, the single largest destination of Euro Area exports, also remain a source of uncertainty.

Japan

Growth has picked up in 2017, supported by a recovery in external demand. Exports have strengthened, especially for information technology-related products and capital goods (Figure 1.6). Business investment has gained momentum, as reflected by a gradual shift from foreign to domestic machinery orders. The pickup in capital spending has been supported by elevated corporate profits as well as preparations for the 2020 Tokyo Olympics (Osada et al. 2016; Brückner and Pappa 2015). Despite some strengthening, consumption continues to be on a subdued trend, and wage increases have been weak despite a tight labor market. While headline inflation has been positive in 2017, inflation expectations remain low, despite a steady increase since the introduction of quantitative easing measures in 2013 (Bank of Japan 2016). Administered prices, as well as some services prices, appear unresponsive to tighter labor market conditions (Shintani et al. 2016).

FIGURE 1.6 Japan

Exports have picked up, especially for information technology-related products and capital goods. A relative increase in domestic versus foreign machinery orders is consistent with strengthening investment. Inflation expectations have risen, but remain below the central bank's target. The Bank of Japan policy shift to targeting long-term interest rates around zero slowed its asset purchases.

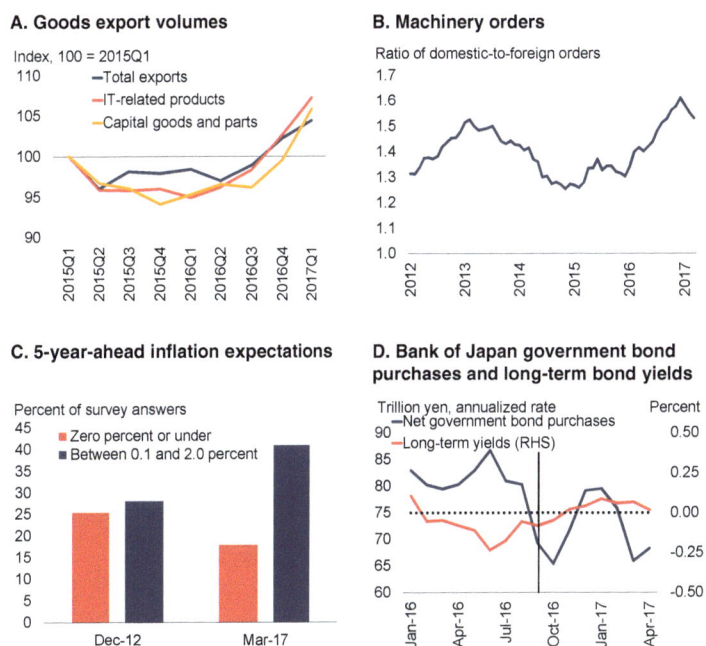

A. Goods export volumes

B. Machinery orders

C. 5-year-ahead inflation expectations

D. Bank of Japan government bond purchases and long-term bond yields

Sources: Bank of Japan, Haver Analytics, Japan Cabinet Office, World Bank.
A. Last observation is 2017Q1.
B. Data represent a 12-month moving average. Last observation is March 2017.
C. Percent of surveyed households.
D. Data for asset purchases are 3-month moving averages. Last observation is April 2017. The vertical line denotes the start of the Bank of Japan policy of adjusting asset purchases to stabilize 10-year government bond yields at zero.

Continued accommodative monetary and fiscal policies should support growth, which is projected to edge up to 1.5 percent in 2017, a significant upgrade from previous forecasts. Growth is expected to moderate to 1.0 percent in 2018—a rate that remains somewhat above estimated potential growth, which has been upgraded following the release of revised capital stock and national accounts data (Kawamoto et al. 2017). The Bank of Japan's policy shift in 2016 to targeting long-term interest rates around zero is expected to keep interest rates at low levels throughout 2017. Supplementary public spending, amounting to 1.2 percent of GDP, is expected to support activity throughout 2017, and to a lesser degree in 2018. In 2019, growth is forecast to slow to 0.6 percent, as a planned consumption tax hike is implemented.

FIGURE 1.7 China

Domestic rebalancing from investment to consumption resumed in 2017, reflecting strengthening consumer spending and the waning effect of state-driven infrastructure spending. Import and export growth have rebounded. Consumer price inflation remains below target, while producer price inflation has increased sharply, reflecting higher commodity prices and reduced overcapacity in heavy industry. Reserves remain at around $3 trillion, helped by a tightening of capital controls and measures to encourage FDI.

A. Contribution to GDP growth

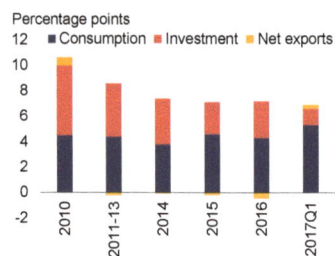

B. Export and import growth

C. Inflation

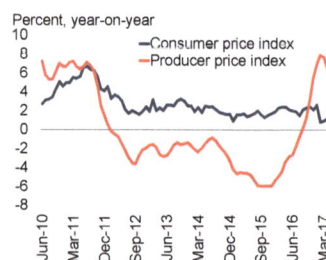

D. Foreign currency reserves

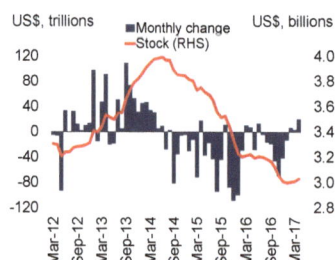

Sources: China National Bureau of Statistics, Haver Analytics, World Bank.
A. Investment refers to gross capital formation, which includes change in inventories.
B.-D. Last observation is April 2017.

China

GDP expanded 6.7 percent in 2016, as expected. Domestic rebalancing from investment to consumption slowed toward the end of 2016, as infrastructure spending by state-owned companies and the public sector accelerated, more than offsetting a sharp slowdown in private sector investment (Lardy and Huang 2017). However, rebalancing from industry to services and from exports to domestic sources of demand continued (Figure 1.7). The current account surplus narrowed to 1.8 percent of GDP in 2016, reflecting stronger import demand and declining exports.

Steady growth continued in early 2017. Easing state-driven investment growth was offset by strengthening export growth against the backdrop of robust consumption growth and still-weak private sector investment growth. Despite monetary tightening, credit growth still outpaces nominal GDP growth. A housing market correction in the largest (Tier 1 and Tier 2) cities is unfolding alongside stable growth of both sales and prices in smaller (Tier 3) cities (Chen and Wen 2017; World Bank 2017b). While consumer price inflation remains below target, producer price inflation has increased sharply, reflecting higher commodity prices and reduced overcapacity in heavy industry. Exchange rate pressures have eased from late 2016, partly as a result of a tightening of capital controls and measures to encourage inward foreign direct investment (FDI), which are also helping maintain reserves at around US$3 trillion.

Growth is projected to slow to 6.5 percent in 2017, in line with January expectations. This forecast envisages strengthening trade this year, with a moderate recovery of imports, amid robust domestic demand, and a gradual acceleration of exports, reflecting firming external demand. Intermittent fiscal support will continue to be used to calibrate growth as monetary policy tightens further. Growth is expected to moderate to 6.3 percent on average in 2018-19, as simulative policies are slowly withdrawn. Key downside risks to the outlook stem from financial sector vulnerabilities and increased protectionist policies in advanced economies.

Global trends

Global trade has strengthened in 2017, as manufacturing activity firmed and investment growth bottomed out, especially in advanced economies. Appetite for EMDE assets has returned, reflecting market expectations of strengthening growth and still favorable international financing conditions. Moderate increases in commodity prices are expected to continue, although oil price projections have been revised slightly down, reflecting the prospect of increased U.S. shale oil production.

Global trade

Global trade growth has rebounded from a post-crisis low of 2.5 percent in 2016, despite rising trade policy uncertainty. The recovery, which began in the second half of 2016, has been supported by stronger industrial activity (Figure 1.8). Just as a slowdown in global investment growth was an important factor behind the deceleration of global goods trade, strengthening investment may support trade in 2017 (Freund 2016; Boz et al. 2015; Bussière et al. 2013; World Bank 2015a). Investment growth in advanced economies is firming, and the post-crisis deceleration in capital spending observed in EMDEs appears to be easing as the earlier terms-of-trade shock for commodity exporters wanes. A recovery in goods trade is supporting an upturn in China's exports, which in turn boosts imports of intermediate products across regional and global value chains. Policy-induced infrastructure spending in China has also supported demand for industrial commodities, benefiting countries exporting raw materials.

Services trade was resilient throughout 2016, supported by robust global consumer spending, particularly in major advanced economies. The ongoing recovery in goods trade may also boost services exports embodied in traded products (Lanz and Maurer 2015). Overall, trade in services continues to play a stabilizing role, being less volatile and pro-cyclical than goods trade (Borchert and Mattoo 2009; Ariu 2016; World Bank 2016a).

Global trade growth is expected to rebound to 4 percent in 2017, a faster pace than previously forecast. The recovery in trade growth in 2017 is supported by stronger import demand from major advanced economies, increased trade flows to and from China, and a diminished drag from weak import demand from commodity-exporting EMDEs. Nevertheless, trade growth will continue to be held back by structural impediments, such as maturing global value chains and a slower pace of trade liberalization (World Bank 2015a; ECB 2016).

Protectionist measures do not appear to have been a significant factor behind weak trade since the global financial crisis. According to the WTO, the number of new trade restrictions in 2016 was broadly in line with previous years. And although the use of non-tariff restrictions appears to have increased recently (Evenett and Fritz 2016), their dampening effect has been limited so far (Ghodsi,

FIGURE 1.8 Global trade

Global goods trade growth has rebounded since mid-2016, supported by a recovery in manufacturing activity, and remained strong in the first quarter of 2017. The improvement coincided with the bottoming out of global investment, which is relatively trade-intensive. Services trade continued to play a stabilizing role, outperforming goods trade during a period of marked weakness in the first half of 2016. The number of newly adopted protectionist measures has generally been in line with past years.

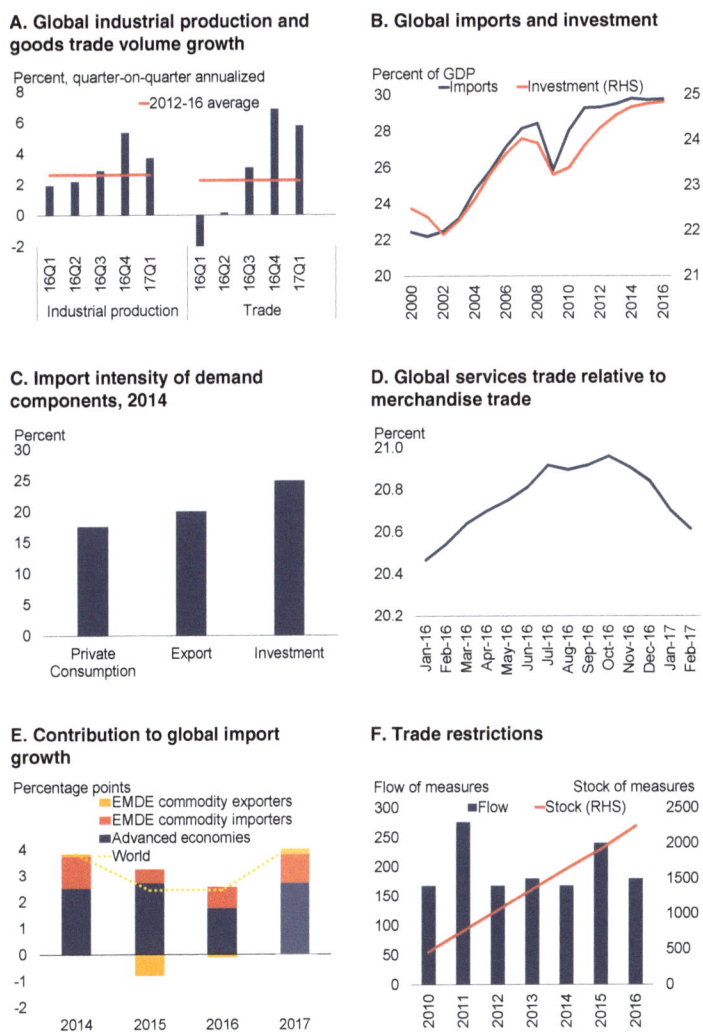

A. Global industrial production and goods trade volume growth

B. Global imports and investment

C. Import intensity of demand components, 2014

D. Global services trade relative to merchandise trade

E. Contribution to global import growth

F. Trade restrictions

Sources: CPB Netherlands Bureau for Economic Policy Analysis, World Bank, World Input-Output Database, World Trade Organization.
A. Last observation is 2017Q1.
B. World investment, imports, and GDP calculated using constant 2010 U.S. dollars weights.
C. Import intensity for each GDP component computed from input-output tables based on Hong et al. (2016). GDP-weighted average of 25 advanced economies and 7 EMDEs.
D. 12-month moving average of global import and export values. Last observation is February 2017.
E. Aggregate imports calculated using constant 2010 U.S. dollar weights. Shaded area indicates forecasts.
F. Trade restrictions include trade remedy measures. 2016 data as of October.

Jokubauskaite, and Stehrer 2015). Nevertheless, an expanding stock of restrictions and growing uncertainty about the direction of trade policy in some major economies could at some point have a material negative impact.

FIGURE 1.9 Financial markets

U.S. long-term yields have stabilized since the start of 2017, following a marked increase around the November 2016 elections. Long-term yields in core Euro Area countries remain low, helping to maintain favorable global financing conditions. Improved growth prospects and increased investor risk appetite have led to a benign reaction of emerging-market assets to rising U.S. yields, especially when compared with the mid-2013 Taper Tantrum. Capital inflows and bond issuance in EMDEs continue to be robust.

A. 10-year bond yields around 2016 elections and 2013 Taper Tantrum

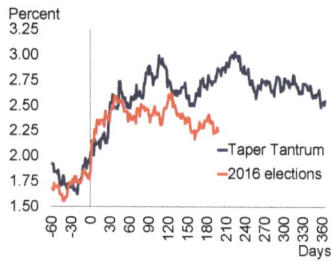

B. U.S. and German 5-year bond yields

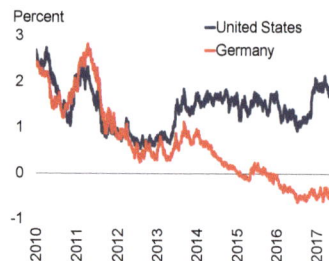

C. Change in EMDE bond spreads around 2016 U.S. elections and Taper Tantrum in 2013

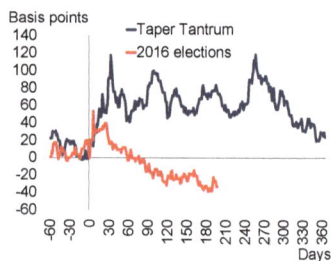

D. Commodity-exporting EMDE bond spreads and exchange rates

E. Portfolio flows to EMDEs

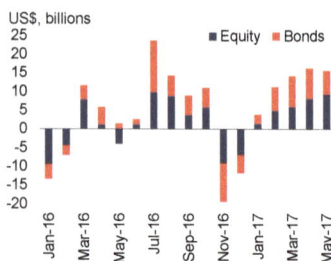

F. Cumulative EMDE bond issuance

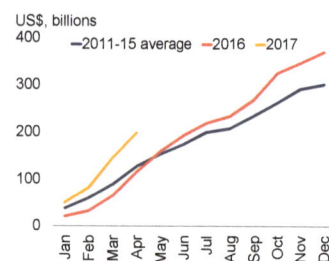

Sources: Bloomberg, Dealogic, Haver Analytics, J.P. Morgan, World Bank.
A. Day 0 refers to May 22, 2013, and November 8, 2016. Last observation is May 24, 2017.
B. Last observation is May 24, 2017.
C. EMDE bond spreads are market-value weighted spreads between U.S. dollar-denominated EMDE sovereign bonds and U.S. Treasury bonds. Last observation is May 24, 2017.
D. Medians of a nine-country group of EMDE commodity exporters are shown. Exchange rates are bilateral against the U.S. dollar, with upward movement showing an appreciation. Last observation is May 24, 2017.
E. Net flows into EMDE bond and equity funds. Last observation is May 24, 2017.
F. Data include both international sovereign and corporate issuances. Last observation is April 2017.

Financial markets

Global financing conditions have been benign since the start of 2017. Shortly after the U.S. elections of November 2016, U.S. long-term yields rose sharply, similar to their surge during the mid-2013 Taper Tantrum (Figure 1.9). Unlike the Taper Tantrum, the late-2016 increase reflected market expectations of strengthening growth and higher inflation in the United States, and was not accompanied by a sudden and sustained re-pricing of risk, including of emerging market assets. Since early 2017, U.S. long-term yields have plateaued, even as the Federal Reserve has continued to raise short-term rates.

Euro Area bond yields have remained exceptionally low, supported by continued monetary policy accommodation by the ECB (Mojon 2017). The decoupling of Euro Area and U.S. long term yields is expected to help maintain low global interest rates, even as the Federal Reserve pursues policy normalization. In some Euro Area countries, however, upcoming political events and renewed banking sector concerns have contributed to a rise in risk premiums (De Santis 2017).

In an environment characterized by low market volatility and robust investor risk appetite, emerging market bond spreads have narrowed and equity prices have recovered. This provides another sharp contrast with the Taper Tantrum, which was accompanied by a substantial deterioration in financing conditions for EMDEs. Bond spreads have narrowed most notably among commodity exporters, while their currencies have generally regained ground. Overall, capital inflows to EMDEs have been robust in the first half of 2017, with EMDE bond issuance activity increasing at a record pace. Corporate bond issuance has been particularly buoyant, notably in Latin America, as companies aimed at extending maturity and lowering interest costs. Amid rising fiscal deficits, the Middle East and North Africa region has accounted for about half of total EMDE sovereign bond issuances since the start of 2017. Fewer credit downgrades and improving growth prospects have supported a recovery in capital flows to some commodity-exporting EMDEs, despite continued weak FDI in resource sectors.

Capital flows are expected to remain steady in 2017 and 2018, reflecting the offsetting effects of gradually tighter international financing conditions and strengthening growth prospects in EMDEs (Eichengreen, Gupta, and Masetti 2017).

Commodities

After averaging $53 per barrel (bbl) during the first quarter of 2017, oil prices dropped below $50/bbl in early May, amid stubbornly high OECD stocks and rising Libyan production (Figure 1.10). Global oil consumption is expected to grow at a moderate 1.4 percent in 2017-18 despite global growth gathering momentum. Oil production declined in early 2017 as a result of the implementation of cuts agreed in November 2016 by some Organization of the Petroleum Exporting Countries (OPEC) and non-OPEC oil producers. However, these cuts were partly offset by stronger-than-expected shale oil production in the United States, following steep productivity improvements. A rebound in drilling activity doubled the U.S. oil rig count from its 2016 low. As a result, oil inventories remain high, particularly in the United States—a key factor behind persistent weakness in oil prices.

Oil prices are expected to average $53/bbl in 2017, up 24 percent from 2016, but $2/bbl less than January forecasts. Large stocks are expected to unwind during the second half of the year. This will support an increase in oil prices to $56/bbl on average in 2018, down $4/bbl from January projections. These forecasts reflect expectations of increased U.S. shale oil production following productivity gains that have reduced costs considerably, as well as an extension of production cuts by OPEC and non-OPEC producers until March 2018. Downside risks for oil prices arise mainly from the resilience of the U.S. shale oil industry or weak compliance to the production cuts. Conversely, further disruptions among politically stressed producers (e.g., Iraq, Libya, Nigeria, República Bolivariana de Venezuela), as well as commitments to additional production cuts into 2018, could temporarily lift prices.

Metals prices continue to increase from their late-2015 lows, partly due to China's policy-driven increase in infrastructure investment. In addition,

FIGURE 1.10 Commodity markets

Oil prices weakened in March and April, reflecting an improved production outlook in the United States. The resilience of the U.S. shale oil industry presents a considerable downside risk for oil prices. Metals prices, which are largely influenced by fluctuations in demand from China, are projected to rise 16 percent in 2017. Agricultural prices are expected to remain stable, with global stocks of the three key grains at 15-year highs.

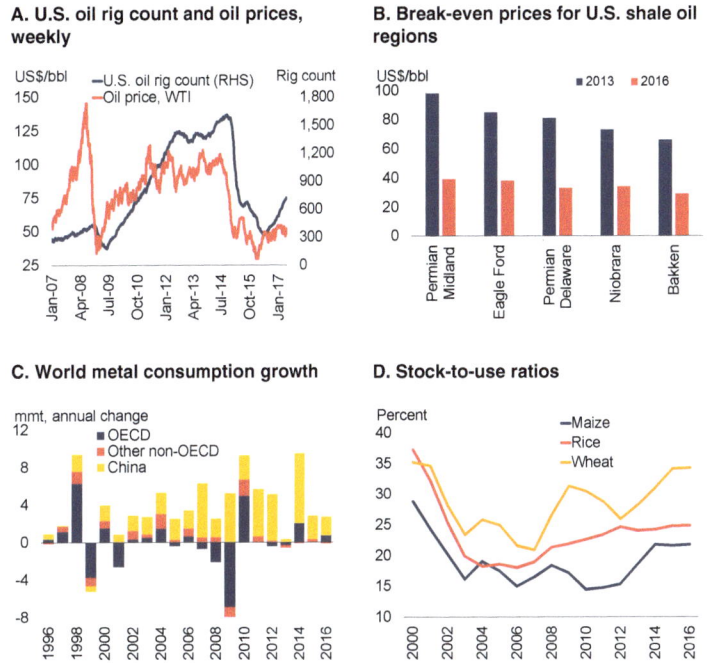

A. U.S. oil rig count and oil prices, weekly

B. Break-even prices for U.S. shale oil regions

C. World metal consumption growth

D. Stock-to-use ratios

Sources: Baker Hughes, Bloomberg, Rystad Energy, U.S. Department of Agriculture, World Bank, World Bureau of Metal Statistics.
A. Last observation is May 19, 2017 for rig count and May 24, 2017 for WTI.
C. 2016 data are estimates.
D. Stock-to-use ratios denote the ratio of ending stocks to domestic consumption and represent a measure of how well supplied the market is. The data reflect the April 2017 U.S. Department of Agriculture update.

prices rose on supply constraints, including wage negotiations in large copper mines in Chile, planned shutdowns of nickel mines in the Philippines, and aluminum capacity reductions in China. Exhaustion of zinc deposits in Australia and Canada also played a role. Average annual metals and mineral prices, which declined 6 percent in 2016, are projected to rise 16 percent in 2017 and decline marginally in 2018 as some of the temporary supply constraints are resolved. Price forecasts have been lifted from January projections due to stronger-than-expected demand in China and some unexpected supply constraints.

Agricultural prices are projected to remain broadly stable in 2017 and 2018. Improved growing conditions have pushed stocks-to-use ratios of key grains to 15-year highs. Fears of supply disruptions in the Southern Hemisphere, which boosted soybean prices earlier in the 2016-17 crop year, have diminished. Since agricultural production is energy intensive, lower energy prices (compared to pre-2015 levels) continue to dampen grain and oilseed prices. In addition, lower energy prices reduce the incentive to divert land use away from food to biofuel commodities. Indeed, biofuel production has changed very little in the past two years and is forecast to increase 5 percent in 2017, compared with an annual average rate of expansion of 15 percent during the preceding 10 years (World Bank 2017c).

Emerging market and developing economies: Recent developments and outlook

From a post-crisis low in 2016, growth is strengthening in EMDEs. A recovery in commodity exporters is being led by some large economies where adjustment to the earlier decline in commodity prices is well advanced. However, some other economies still face longer-than-expected adjustment needs, suggesting that this recovery will be somewhat softer than previously envisioned. In commodity importers, growth is projected to remain solid, as stronger exports offset the impact of diminishing policy support. Despite an easing of short-term macroeconomic pressures in many EMDEs, the longer-term EMDE outlook is constrained by structural headwinds to world trade and slowing productivity growth.

Recent developments

Growth in EMDEs reached a post-crisis low of 3.5 percent in 2016, as commodity exporters continued to stagnate and idiosyncratic factors held back growth in some large commodity-importing EMDEs (e.g., India, Turkey). Activity firmed toward the end of 2016 and into 2017 (Figure 1.11), reflecting a recovery in commodity exporters, where the contraction in investment is easing and import growth is bottoming out. This trend was broad-based across energy, metals, and agricultural commodity exporters. Some large commodity exporters are beginning to emerge

from recession (e.g., Argentina, Brazil, Nigeria, Russia), while growth in commodity importers continues to generally be robust.

Industrial production and manufacturing purchasing managers' indexes have increased in 2017. This increase has been most pronounced among commodity exporters, where PMIs reached their highest levels since early 2015. In commodity importers, industrial production remains robust, with PMIs well into expansionary territory.

Domestic demand is leading the upturn in 2017, amid improving confidence and, in a number of commodity exporters, diminishing drag from earlier policy tightening. This is mirrored in rising import demand, which bottomed out in late 2016. Stronger external demand is also supporting the recent improvement in EMDE conditions, albeit unevenly.

Commodity-exporting EMDEs

Growth appears to be bottoming out, to varying degrees, in many of the large commodity exporters that were in recession or stagnation in 2016 (e.g., Angola, Argentina, Brazil, Kazakhstan, Nigeria, Russia). Activity remains solid in a number of diversified, or non-resource-intensive, economies (e.g., Costa Rica, Ethiopia, Indonesia, Malaysia, Rwanda, Senegal, Sri Lanka, Tanzania). However, remaining adjustment needs, particularly related to fiscal sustainability, are holding back economic activity in some economies, especially in those that have significant domestic vulnerabilities and political challenges (IMF 2017a).

In general, currencies in commodity exporters have strengthened and inflation has retreated as commodity prices have stabilized, allowing monetary policy to be eased in some countries (e.g., Brazil, Chile, Colombia, Ghana, Kazakhstan, Russia, Ukraine). Fiscal policy adjustment to low commodity prices is easing in countries where such adjustment started early and is well advanced (e.g., Honduras, Indonesia, Malaysia). Confidence is generally improving, although it remains fragile (e.g., Argentina, Brazil, Kazakhstan, Nigeria, Russia, Ukraine). While private consumption growth appears to have bottomed out, impaired household balance sheets continue to weigh on consumption in some countries (e.g., Brazil, Kazakhstan, Russia, Ukraine). In resource sectors, corporate profits have picked up and companies have made progress in repairing their balance sheets.

Russia is emerging from recession, with a diminishing contraction of consumer demand amid increasing price and currency stability, and a positive contribution from exports (World Bank 2017d). Growth in other large commodity exporters is firming, supported by higher commodity prices and gradual monetary policy easing (e.g., Indonesia, Kazakhstan), as well as improved confidence (e.g., Malaysia, Ukraine). In Nigeria, recent indicators point to a recovery in the manufacturing and non-manufacturing sectors. Brazil is expected to slowly emerge from recession in 2017 (Banco Central do Brasil 2017). Activity indicators have improved, including a resumption of industrial output growth and a pickup in export growth, as well as gains in confidence and manufacturing. However, the country continues to struggle with rising unemployment and still sizable fiscal adjustment needs.

In general, growth in energy exporters lags that of metal and agriculture exporters. Energy exporters face more recent, and deeper, adjustment needs. In addition, they have enacted policy measures later than other exporters. Oil production cuts and protracted fiscal consolidation has weighed on growth of Gulf Cooperation Council (GCC) countries and other affected energy exporters (e.g., Algeria, Angola, Ecuador, Iraq, Kuwait, Qatar, Saudi Arabia, United Arab Emirates). Real exchange rate appreciation in economies pegged to the U.S. dollar has curtailed current account improvements (Werner, Adler, and Magud 2017).

In contrast to the generally improving trend across EMDE commodity exporters, activity was weak in early 2017 in some countries in Sub-Saharan Africa (e.g., Burundi, Chad, Equatorial Guinea), Latin America and the Caribbean (e.g., Ecuador, República Bolivariana de Venezuela), Europe and Central Asia (e.g., Azerbaijan), and East Asia and Pacific (e.g., Mongolia, Papua New Guinea). This generally reflects sizable and protracted policy adjustment to low commodity prices. Country-

FIGURE 1.11 EMDE activity

EMDE growth is strengthening, led by commodity exporters, where the contraction of investment is easing and imports are bottoming out. The recovery is broad-based among energy, metals, and agricultural commodity exporters. Industrial production and manufacturing PMIs are rising. EMDE domestic demand is firming, amid improved confidence.

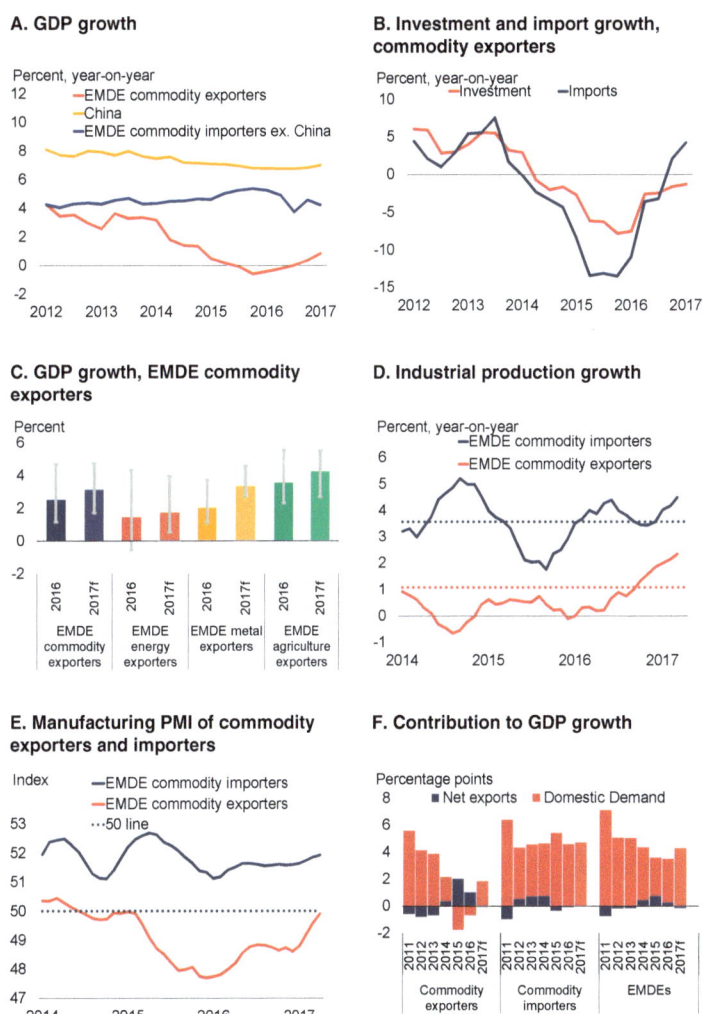

A. GDP growth

B. Investment and import growth, commodity exporters

C. GDP growth, EMDE commodity exporters

D. Industrial production growth

E. Manufacturing PMI of commodity exporters and importers

F. Contribution to GDP growth

Sources: Haver Analytics, World Bank.
A. B. Aggregate growth rates calculated using constant 2010 U.S. dollars weights. Last observation is 2017Q1.
C. Simple average of GDP growth. EMDE commodity exporter groups exclude BRICS countries. Gray line indicates interquartile ranges of growth in each group. Shaded areas indicate forecasts.
D. 6-month moving average of year-on-year industrial production growth. EMDE commodity importers excludes China. Last observation is March 2017. Dotted lines indicate median values from 2012-16.
E. 6-month moving average of country sample. Index values above 50 indicate expansion. EMDE commodity importers excludes China. Sample includes 5 EMDE commodity exporters (Brazil, Russia, Indonesia, Malaysia, South Africa) and 7 EMDE commodity importers ex. China (India, Poland, Philippines, Thailand, Vietnam, Mexico, Turkey). Last observation is April 2017.
F. Shaded areas indicate forecasts. Commodity importers excludes China.

specific domestic challenges have added to the difficulties, including domestic and external imbalances, exchange rate misalignments, social tensions, political challenges, security issues, and droughts. Recent activity in some metals exporters has been held back by special factors, including production bottlenecks (e.g., Papua New Guinea), policy uncertainty (e.g., Armenia, South Africa), and mining sector disruptions and natural disasters (e.g., Chile, Peru).

Commodity-importing EMDEs

Growth in commodity importers remains generally robust. In East Asia and Pacific and in South Asia, solid domestic demand, strong infrastructure spending, FDI-led investment into highly competitive manufacturing sectors and services, and rising global demand are benefiting many countries (e.g., Bangladesh, Cambodia, India, the Philippines, Vietnam; World Bank 2017b). Asian EMDE economies are also helped by increased intra-regional trade and investment flows, which may receive a further boost from China's "One Belt, One Road" initiative (World Bank 2016b).

Robust domestic demand and stronger imports from the Euro Area has favored commodity importers in Europe and Central Asia (e.g., Bulgaria, Romania, Serbia). Accelerated implementation of EU-funded projects is lifting other regional economies (e.g., Hungary, Poland), while adverse spillovers from recession in Russia and Ukraine are fading, benefiting neighboring countries (e.g., Belarus, Georgia, Moldova) (World Bank 2017e). Activity in commodity importers in the Middle East and North Africa is improving as reforms are implemented, as political conditions normalize, and as harvest conditions recover (e.g., Jordan, Lebanon, Tunisia).

Despite an overall solid performance among commodity importers, special factors are weighing on growth in some large economies. In Mexico, uncertainty about U.S. trade policy appears to be discouraging investment. In Turkey, lingering effects from the failed coup last year and high inflation stemming from a substantial currency depreciation have hurt confidence. Growth in Thailand remains below its long-term trend, as policy uncertainty and competitiveness challenges are dampening investment and exports.

Low-income countries

Growth in low-income countries is rebounding after a slowdown in 2016, supported by both global and domestic factors (Box 1.1). Improving metals prices are stimulating production in metals exporters (e.g., Democratic Republic of Congo, Guinea). In many non-resource-intensive low-income countries, solid growth achieved in 2016 is continuing, driven by infrastructure investment. In countries hit by drought in 2016, above-average rainfalls are boosting agricultural production. Elsewhere, reconstruction efforts following natural disasters (e.g., the earthquake in Nepal) are picking up pace. However, some low-income countries remain under significant economic stress due to declining oil production (e.g., Chad), conflict (e.g., South Sudan), drought (e.g., South Sudan), security threats (e.g., Afghanistan), or political instability (e.g., Burundi).

Outlook

EMDE growth is projected to strengthen from 3.5 percent in 2016 to 4.1 percent in 2017 and reach an average of 4.6 percent in 2018-19, reflecting a recovery in commodity exporters and steady growth in commodity importers (Figure 1.12). Commodity prices are expected to rise moderately from low 2016 levels, although oil prices are projected to rise slightly less than forecast in January. A rebound in global trade is expected to offset the negative effects associated with a gradual tightening of global financing conditions.

Growth in commodity exporters is expected to pick up from 0.4 percent in 2016 to 1.8 percent in 2017, and to reach 2.8 percent on average in 2018-19. The improvement is expected to be broad-based, with an acceleration of activity predicted in the majority of commodity exporters both in 2017 and in 2018. Aggregate growth in commodity exporters will be supported by improved confidence and rising commodity prices, and will solidify as the adjustment to the earlier terms-of-trade shock runs its course, as exports rebound and domestic demand firms.

Nevertheless, the expected recovery in commodity exporters is weaker than envisioned in January, mainly reflecting longer-than-expected adjustment to low commodity prices in some countries and, to a lesser degree, weaker energy price prospects. Special factors contributing to downward revisions include slowing oil sector growth in the Islamic

BOX 1.1 Low-income countries: Recent developments and outlook

Growth in low-income countries slowed to 4.4 percent in 2016 but is projected to pick up to 5.4 percent in 2017. Output in oil and metals-exporting countries will recover gradually, reflecting improvements in commodity prices and global trade, and reforms to remove constraints to growth. Average growth in non-resource-intensive countries is expected to remain solid, supported by domestic demand and, in particular, public investment. The main downside risks to the outlook include a weaker-than-expected recovery in commodity prices, a delay in necessary fiscal adjustments, and a deterioration in security and political conditions.

Growth rebound. Growth in low-income countries is rebounding in 2017 from the 2016 slowdown.[1] The increase in metals prices is stimulating production in metals exporters (e.g., Democratic Republic of Congo, Niger). In many non-resource-intensive countries, including in the West African Economic and Monetary Union (WAEMU), the rebound is led by infrastructure investment (IMF 2017b).[2] Investor risk appetite for low-income countries' assets has improved. In May, Senegal tapped the Eurobond market to finance its investment projects. In countries that were hit by an El Niño-related drought in 2016 (e.g., Malawi, Mozambique), above average rainfalls are boosting agricultural production. Elsewhere, reconstruction efforts following natural disasters (e.g., the earthquake in Nepal) are picking up pace. However, a number of low-income countries remain under significant economic stress on account of declining oil production (e.g., Chad), conflict (e.g., South Sudan), drought (e.g., Somalia, South Sudan), security threats (e.g., Afghanistan), or political instability (e.g., Burundi).

Elevated current account deficits. Current account positions remain weak across low-income countries (Figure 1.1.1). Although current account deficits in oil and metals exporters are declining, they are still elevated. For oil exporters, the improvement mainly reflects the recent increase in the price of oil and a decline in imports resulting from cuts in public investment. In metals exporters, exports are gradually increasing as production expands from existing and new mining projects. Among non-resource-intensive countries (e.g., Rwanda, Uganda), rising fuel prices and large public investment programs are keeping current

account deficits high. Foreign reserves remain under pressure in many countries, reflecting continued weakness of current account balances and lower-than-expected external financing. Reserve levels were less than two months of imports of goods and services in several countries at end-2016 (e.g., Chad, Democratic Republic of Congo, South Sudan) (IMF 2016a).

Stabilizing exchange rates, high inflation. The currencies of commodity exporters are stabilizing, following sharp depreciations in 2016, although they continue to weaken in some cases (e.g., Democratic Republic of Congo). Large exchange rate depreciations, compounded by the impact of drought on food prices, contributed to a rapid increase in inflation in some metals exporters. Inflation in Mozambique exceeded 20 percent in the first quarter of 2017. In non-resource-intensive countries, inflationary pressures are intensifying across East Africa, where a drought has reduced agricultural production, causing a spike in food prices (e.g., Ethiopia, Rwanda). Other cases of high inflation reflect domestic supply disruptions from natural disasters (e.g., Haiti). In Chad and WAEMU low-income countries, inflation has remained generally low, reflecting the stable peg to the euro. In some countries where inflation has stabilized, central banks have reduced policy rates (e.g., Tanzania, Uganda).

Improving fiscal positions. Fiscal positions have improved somewhat across low-income countries, reflecting fiscal consolidation efforts. Large drops in oil revenues have forced sharp spending cuts in Chad. Some metals exporters (e.g., Mozambique, Sierra Leone) have revised their spending plans to stabilize their economies. However, in others (e.g., Liberia, Niger), fiscal balances remain under pressure, reflecting delayed fiscal consolidation. Fiscal deficits widened in several non-resource-intensive countries (e.g., Togo, Uganda) due to the continued expansion in public infrastructure. As a result, government debt ratios in low-income countries have continued to rise (e.g.,

---

Note: This box was prepared by Gerard Kambou and Boaz Nandwa. Research assistance was provided by Trang Thi Thy Nguyen and Xinghao Gong.

[1] For the 2017 fiscal year, low-income countries are defined as those with a gross national income (GNI) per capita, calculated using the World Bank Atlas method, of $1,025 or less.

[2] The WAEMU low-income countries are Benin, Burkina Faso, Guinea-Bissau, Mali, Niger, Senegal, and Togo.

BOX 1.1 Low-income countries: Recent developments and outlook *(continued)*

FIGURE 1.1.1 Recent developments

Growth slowed markedly in several low-income countries toward the end of 2016. The impact of low commodity prices was the dominant factor, although drought and conflict also played a role. Inflationary pressures increased at the start of the year, reflecting large currency depreciations and the effect of drought on food prices in some countries. While current account and fiscal deficits remain elevated across low-income countries, they are narrowing in oil and metals exporters as commodity prices improve.

A. GDP growth

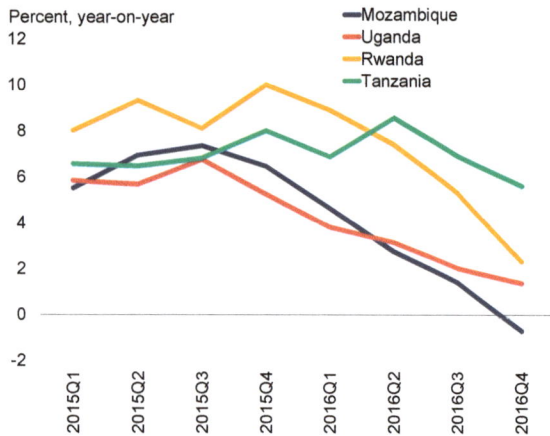

B. Consumer price inflation

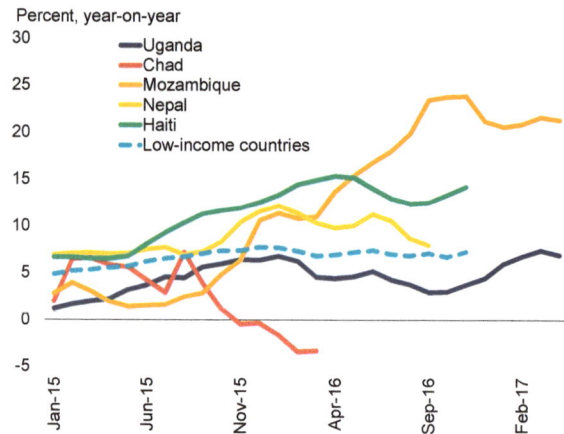

C. Current account balance

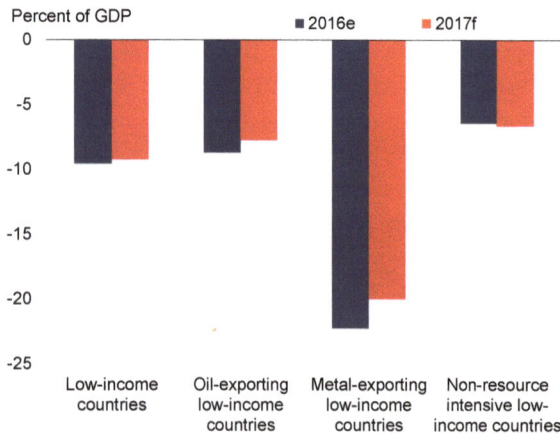

D. Fiscal balance

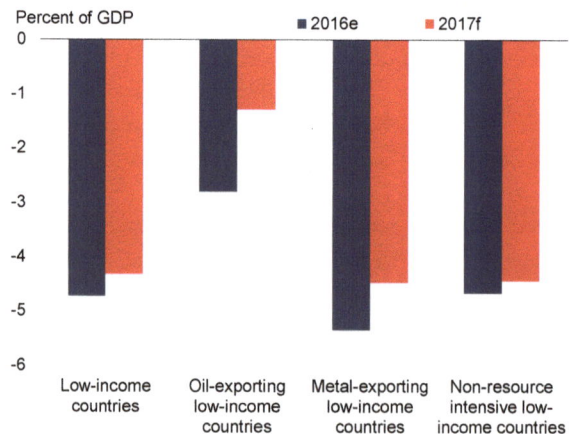

Sources: Haver Analytics, International Monetary Fund, Tanzania Bureau of Statistics, World Bank.
A. Last observation is 2016Q4.
B. Last observation is March 2016 for Chad, September 2016 for Nepal, November 2016 for Haiti and low-income countries, and April 2017 for Mozambique and Uganda.
C.D. Non-resource-intensive countries include agricultural-based economies and commodity importers.

Ethiopia, Liberia, Togo), or stayed elevated (e.g., Mozambique, Senegal), exceeding in most cases 50 percent of GDP at end-2016. The rising government debt levels indicate a need for low-income countries to improve debt management capacity to manage rollover risks (World Bank 2017f).

Weaker-than-expected growth outlook. Growth in low-income countries is projected to reach 5.4 percent in 2017 and strengthen to 5.8 percent by 2019 (Figure 1.1.2). The turnaround is predicated on a continued recovery of commodity prices, as well as on policy actions to reduce macroeconomic imbalances. These

BOX 1.1 Low-income countries: Recent developments and outlook *(continued)*

FIGURE 1.1.2 Outlook

GDP growth in low-income countries is projected to recover to 5.4 percent in 2017 and to 5.8 percent in 2018-19. This reflects a moderate recovery in oil and metals exporters toward their long term average growth. Growth in non-resource-intensive countries is projected to remain robust.

A. GDP growth: Low-income country groups

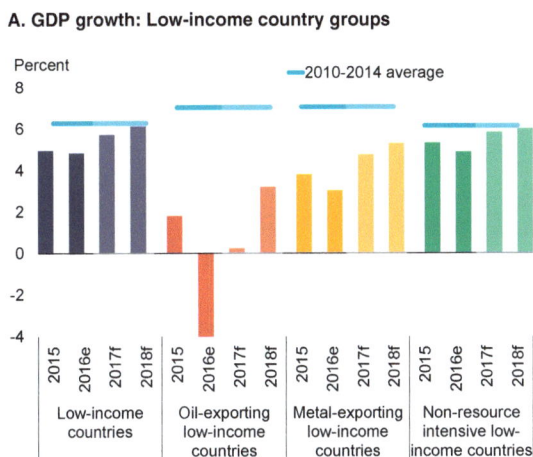

B. GDP growth: Selected countries

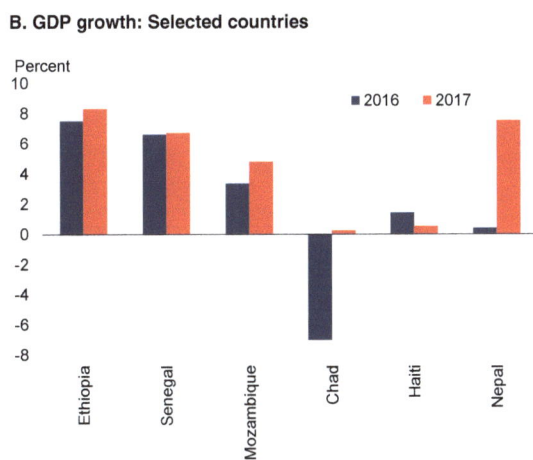

Source: World Bank.

forecasts are slightly weaker than those in January, with a more moderate recovery among oil and metals exporters, where growth will remain well below its 2010-2014 average. The factors underlying the modest recovery vary. Maturing oil fields (e.g., Chad) or

conflict (e.g., South Sudan) will dampen the growth of oil production. Among metals exporters, inflation and fiscal tightening will be a greater drag on growth than expected.

In non-resource-intensive countries, growth should remain robust. Large low-income countries in Sub-Saharan Africa (e.g., Ethiopia, Tanzania) will expand at a rapid pace, helped by buoyant service sectors, infrastructure investment, and a rebound in agriculture. However, with elevated debt levels, these countries will need to increase public savings, contain debt accumulation, and rebuild policy buffers. Fragile states (e.g., Burundi, Haiti, Zimbabwe) will continue to expand at a slower pace.

Risks tilted to the downside. External risks include the possibility of weaker-than-expected growth in advanced economies. This could reduce demand for low-income countries' exports, depress commodity prices, and curtail foreign direct investment in mining and infrastructure. Low-income countries in SSA are particularly vulnerable to this risk because of their dependence on commodity exports. Other major risks are a sharp reduction in foreign aid, particularly in view of the cuts proposed by the U.S. administration; larger declines in remittances due to stricter immigration policies (e.g., Haiti); and border closures (e.g., Afghanistan). The materialization of these risks would dampen investment, consumption, and regional trade in many low-income countries.

There are also a number of domestic downside risks. Failure to implement appropriate macroeconomic policies, especially in countries where large fiscal adjustments are needed, would further weaken macroeconomic stability. Adjustment needs are particularly large in several low-income countries in SSA, including Chad and Mozambique. In addition, rising security threats (e.g., Afghanistan), heightened political uncertainty (e.g., Democratic Republic of Congo, Burundi), intensification of conflict (e.g., South Sudan), and worsening drought conditions (e.g., Somalia, South Sudan) would severely affect economic conditions in fragile countries.

BOX 1.1 Low-income countries: Recent developments and outlook *(continued)*

TABLE 1.1.1 Low-income country forecasts[a]
(Real GDP growth at market prices in percent, unless indicated otherwise)

	2014	2015	2016	2017	2018	2019	2016	2017	2018	2019
			Estimates	Projections			Percentage point differences from January 2017 projections			
Low Income Country, GDP[b]	6.3	4.7	4.4	5.4	5.8	5.8	-0.3	-0.2	-0.2	-0.3
Afghanistan	1.3	1.1	2.2	2.6	3.4	3.1	1.0	0.8	0.4	-0.5
Benin	6.4	2.1	4.0	5.5	6.0	6.3	-0.6	0.3	0.7	1.0
Burkina Faso	4.0	4.0	5.4	6.1	6.3	6.3	0.2	0.6	0.3	0.3
Burundi	4.7	-3.9	-0.6	1.5	2.0	2.6	-0.1	-1.0	-1.5	-0.9
Chad	6.9	1.8	-7.0	0.2	3.2	3.1	-3.5	0.5	-1.5	-3.2
Comoros	2.1	1.0	2.2	3.3	4.0	4.0	0.2	0.8	1.0	1.0
Congo, Dem. Rep.	9.0	6.9	2.2	4.7	4.9	4.9	-0.5	0.0	-0.1	-0.1
Ethiopia[c]	10.3	9.6	7.5	8.3	8.0	7.9	-0.9	-0.6	-0.6	-0.7
Gambia, The	0.9	4.1	2.1	2.5	3.8	4.0	1.6	1.7	1.2	1.4
Guinea	0.4	0.1	4.6	4.4	4.6	4.6	-0.6	-0.2	0.0	0.0
Guinea-Bissau	2.5	4.8	4.9	5.1	5.1	5.1	0.0	0.0	0.0	0.0
Haiti[c]	2.8	1.2	1.4	0.5	1.7	2.3	0.2	1.1	0.2	0.3
Liberia	0.7	0.0	-1.2	3.0	5.3	5.7	-3.7	-2.8	0.0	0.4
Madagascar	3.3	3.8	4.4	3.5	6.4	4.7	0.3	-1.0	1.6	-0.1
Malawi	5.7	2.8	2.5	4.4	4.9	5.3	0.0	0.2	0.4	0.8
Mali	7.0	6.0	5.6	5.3	5.2	5.1	0.0	0.2	0.2	0.1
Mozambique	7.4	6.6	3.3	4.8	6.1	6.7	-0.3	-0.4	-0.5	0.1
Nepal[c]	6.0	3.3	0.4	7.5	5.5	4.5	-0.2	2.5	0.7	-0.2
Niger	7.0	3.6	4.7	5.2	5.5	5.5	-0.3	-0.1	-0.5	-0.5
Rwanda	7.0	6.9	5.9	6.0	6.8	7.0	-0.1	0.0	-0.2	0.0
Senegal	4.3	6.5	6.6	6.7	6.9	7.0	0.0	-0.1	-0.1	0.0
Sierra Leone	4.6	-20.6	5.0	5.4	5.6	5.9	1.1	-1.5	-0.3	0.0
Tanzania	7.0	7.0	6.9	7.2	7.2	7.4	0.0	0.1	0.1	0.3
Togo	5.9	5.4	5.0	4.6	5.5	5.5	-0.4	-0.4	0.0	0.0
Uganda[c]	5.6	5.6	4.8	4.6	5.2	5.6	0.2	-1.0	-0.8	-0.4
Zimbabwe	3.8	0.5	0.7	2.3	1.8	1.7	0.3	-1.5	-1.6	-1.7

Source: World Bank.
World Bank forecasts are frequently updated based on new information and changing (global) circumstances. Consequently, projections presented here may differ from those contained in other Bank documents, even if basic assessments of countries' prospects do not significantly differ at any given moment in time.
a. Central African Republic, Democratic People's Republic of Korea, and Somalia are not forecast due to data limitations.
b. GDP at market prices and expenditure components are measured in constant 2010 U.S. dollars.
c. GDP growth based on fiscal year data. For Nepal, the year 2017 refers to FY2016/17, which runs from July 16 to July 15 of the following year.
For additional information, please see www.worldbank.org/gep.

Republic of Iran, the protracted effects of restricted access to international financial markets in Russia, deeper-than-expected oil production cuts in Saudi Arabia, and a deterioration of investor confidence in South Africa amid two recent sovereign rating downgrades to sub-investment grade. More generally, the subdued long-term outlook for commodity prices is expected to keep investment rates in commodity exporters well below the high rates achieved during the pre-2014 commodity boom. In this context, growth in regions with large numbers of commodity exporters will strengthen in 2017, but at a slower-than-expected pace (Box 1.2).

Growth in commodity importers is projected to remain broadly stable, at around 5.7 percent on average in 2017-19. In general, stronger exports are expected to offset the impact of diminishing policy support and waning windfalls from earlier commodity price declines. A gradual slowdown in China will be partly offset by a modest pickup in the rest of the group. Excluding China, growth in commodity importers will accelerate from 4.6 percent in 2017 to an average of 5.0 percent in 2018-19, partly reflecting the diminishing role of idiosyncratic factors holding back activity in some large economies (e.g., Mexico, Turkey). Relative to January projections, the outlook for commodity importers is little changed. In particular, a downgrade to India's fast pace of expansion, mainly reflecting a softer-than-expected recovery in private investment, is accompanied by an upward revision to Turkey, partly due to signs of less severe effects of last year's failed coup and a reassessment of potential growth.

In low-income countries, growth is projected to rebound to 5.4 percent in 2017, helped by a pickup in metals exporters, and strengthen to 5.8 percent in 2018-19, as activity improves in oil exporters. This turnaround is predicated on policy actions to tackle macroeconomic imbalances, as well as on moderately rising commodity prices. These forecasts are slightly lower than in January. In oil exporters, oil production will increase at a slower pace than previously projected due to maturing oil fields (Chad) or conflict (South Sudan). In metals exporters, high inflation and tight fiscal policy will be a greater drag on activity than previously thought in several countries. Growth should remain robust in non-resource-intensive countries as they continue to benefit from infrastructure investment (e.g., Ethiopia, Senegal) and buoyant services sectors (e.g., Tanzania).

While the easing of macroeconomic pressures is a positive development in the short term for many EMDEs, structural obstacles continue to impede the longer-term outlook. These include structural headwinds to world trade, such as slower trade liberalization and value chain integration; persistently low commodity prices; worsening demographics in most developing regions; slowing productivity growth; and governance and institutional challenges. In addition, many economies have experienced trend slowdowns in investment growth in recent years (World Bank

FIGURE 1.12 EMDE growth outlook

EMDE growth is projected to pick up to 4.1 percent in 2017 and accelerate further in 2018-19. Amid strengthening global trade, EMDE exports and imports are expected to firm. The strengthening EMDE outlook mainly reflects a recovery in commodity exporters, while growth in commodity importers is projected to remain robust. However, EMDE investment is likely to remain subdued, with investment recoveries concentrated in a few large EMDEs.

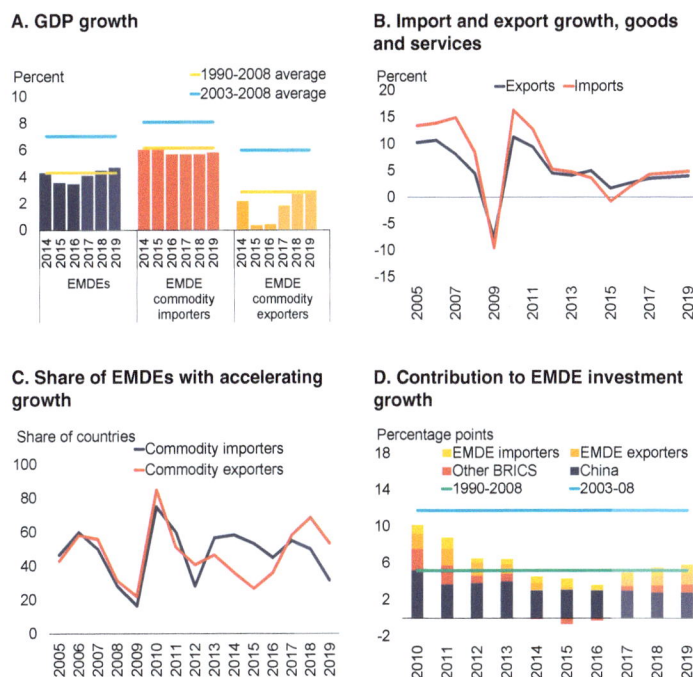

A. GDP growth

B. Import and export growth, goods and services

C. Share of EMDEs with accelerating growth

D. Contribution to EMDE investment growth

Source: World Bank.
A.-D. Shaded areas indicate forecasts.
A. Aggregate growth rates calculated using constant 2010 U.S. dollars GDP weights.
B. Export and import volumes include goods and non-factor services.
C. Share of countries in EMDE commodity exporters and importers whose GDP growth is at least 0.1 percentage point higher than the previous year. Sample includes 60 commodity importers and 86 commodity exporters.
D. Averages for 1990-2008 and 2003-08 include all EMDEs.

2017a). Even if the expected modest recovery in investment materializes, the slower rate of capital accumulation in previous years, and the associated loss of embodied technological progress, may have already set back potential output growth. Moreover, the overall EMDE investment recovery is expected to be concentrated in a few large economies.

Risks to the outlook

Despite the possibility of more expansionary fiscal policies than currently assumed in major economies, the balance of risks remains titled to the downside, although slightly less so than at the start of the year.

BOX 1.2 Regional perspectives: Recent developments and outlook

Growth in most EMDE regions with a substantial number of commodity exporters is projected to strengthen in 2017, amid modestly rising commodity prices and growing trade. However, this acceleration is weaker than previously envisioned, mainly due to longer-than-expected adjustment to the weak commodity price outlook and, to a lesser degree, a minor downward revision to oil price forecasts. EMDE regions with large numbers of commodity importers are expected to continue to experience solid growth.

East Asia and Pacific. Regional growth is projected to inch down from 6.2 percent in 2017 to 6.1 percent on average in 2018-19, in line with previous forecasts (Figure 1.2.1). A gradual slowdown in China will be partly offset by a modest pickup in the rest of the region. Domestic demand is projected to remain robust. Firming exports are expected to offset the negative impact of gradual policy tightening. Downside risks include heightened policy uncertainty, increased protectionism in key advanced economies, and an abrupt tightening of financing conditions. A sharper-than-expected slowdown in China could have adverse consequences for the rest of the region and continues to be a low-probability risk.

Europe and Central Asia. Regional activity has picked up since the end of 2016, and the 2017 growth forecast of 2.5 percent is in line with January projections. Both commodity exporters and importers are recovering. The region is benefiting from modestly rising oil prices, benign global financing conditions, and solid growth in the Euro Area. Regional growth is expected to edge up to an average of 2.8 percent in 2018-19, as activity in Russia and other commodity exporters firms and growth in Turkey recovers. The main downside risks include renewed declines in oil and other commodity prices, policy uncertainty and geopolitical risks, and international financial market disruptions. Domestic banking system weaknesses are a vulnerability and could amplify internal and external shocks.

Latin America and the Caribbean. Regional output contracted 1.4 percent in 2016, pulled down by recessions in Argentina, Brazil, and República Bolivariana de Venezuela. Although recent data suggest that the regional economy is stabilizing after two years of contraction, the recovery is expected to be subdued in the short term. Growth is projected to reach 0.8

FIGURE 1.2.1 Regional growth

Growth in most EMDE regions with a substantial number of commodity exporters is projected to pick up in 2017; however, this acceleration is weaker than previously envisioned. EMDE regions with large numbers of commodity importers are expected to continue to experience solid growth.

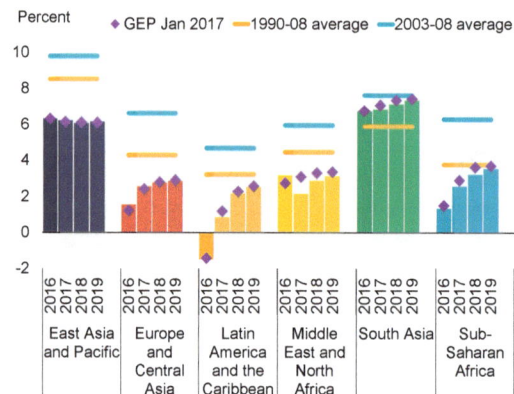

A. Regional growth (weighted average)

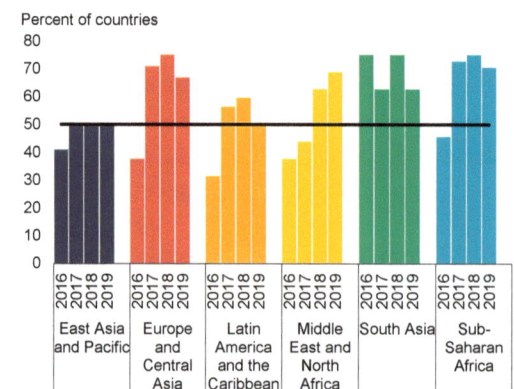

B. Share of countries with increasing growth

Source: World Bank.
A.B. Average for 1990-08 is constructed depending on data availability. For ECA, data for 1995-2008 are used to exclude the immediate aftermath of the collapse of the Soviet Union.
A. Bars denote latest forecast; diamonds denote previous forecasts. Since the largest economies of each region account for almost 50 percent of regional GDP in some regions, weighted average predominantly reflects the development in the largest economies in each region.
B. Share of countries that GDP growth exceeds that of the previous year out of total countries in the region. Horizontal black line denotes 50 percent.

Note: This box was prepared by Carlos Arteta with contributions from Gerard Kambou, Lei Ye, Boaz Nandwa, Yoki Okawa, Temel Taskin, Ekaterine Vashakmadze, and Dana Vorisek. Research assistance was provided by Trang Thi Thy Nguyen.

BOX 1.2 Regional perspectives: Recent developments and outlook *(continued)*

percent in 2017, supported by strengthening private consumption and an easing contraction in investment, despite a slowdown in Mexico as uncertainty about U.S. economic policy dents confidence. Regional growth is expected to accelerate to an average of 2.3 percent in 2018-19, as the recoveries in Brazil and other commodity exporters advance. The main downside risks to the outlook arise from domestic political and policy uncertainty and from possible policy changes in the United States.

Middle East and North Africa. Regional growth is projected to decline from 3.2 percent in 2016 to 2.1 percent in 2017. The deceleration reflects slowdowns in oil-exporting economies, resulting from OPEC-led oil production cuts agreed in November 2016. In oil importers, growth is expected to improve this year, aided by reforms and supply-side factors such as weather-induced recoveries in agricultural output. Regional growth is expected to pick up to an average of 3 percent in 2018-19, amid modestly rising oil prices. The need for additional fiscal consolidation by both oil exporters and importers remains an important headwind over the medium term. Key risks include a weaker-than-expected rise in oil prices, continued geopolitical conflicts, and social tensions that may delay implementation of key structural reforms.

South Asia. Regional growth is projected to remain strong, at 6.8 percent in 2017. India is recovering from the temporary adverse effects of the end-2016 withdrawal of large-denomination currency notes. Elsewhere in the region, growth in Pakistan is accelerating this year, largely driven by robust domestic demand and improved foreign direct investment, while activity in Bangladesh is moderating, reflecting a pullback in domestic demand and in industrial production. Regional growth is expected to firm in 2018-19, reaching an average of 7.2 percent, supported by robust domestic demand, an uptick in exports, and strong foreign direct investment. The regional outlook has been slightly revised down from January, reflecting a more protracted recovery in private investment in India than previously expected. Risks to the outlook are tilted to the downside and include reforms setbacks, geopolitical tensions, and policy uncertainty.

Sub-Saharan Africa. Regional growth is projected to recover in 2017 to 2.6 percent, reflecting a modest rise in commodity prices, strengthening external demand, and the end of drought in several countries. The recovery is proceeding at a slightly more moderate pace than anticipated in January, reflecting in part the longer-than-expected adjustment among some large commodity exporters to low commodity price prospects, as well as heightened political uncertainty in South Africa. Solid growth in non-resource-intensive countries is continuing into 2017, as expected. However, in some countries, drought continues to weigh on agricultural production. Growth is projected to pick up to 3.4 percent in 2018-19. Downside risks to the outlook include insufficient adjustment to low commodity prices, weaker improvements in commodity prices, stronger-than-expected tightening of global financing conditions, and political uncertainty.

Increased protectionism, persistent policy uncertainty, geopolitical risks, or renewed financial market turbulence could derail an incipient recovery. Financial market stress could be amplified by vulnerabilities in some EMDEs. Over the longer term, a protracted slowdown in productivity and investment growth could further deteriorate the growth potential of advanced economies and EMDEs.

Baseline forecasts point to strengthening momentum throughout 2017, with global growth reaching 2.7 percent in 2017, helped by a moderate investment-led recovery in advanced economies and diminishing headwinds among commodity-exporting EMDEs. In 2018 and 2019, global growth is predicted to average 2.9 percent, as recoveries in commodity-exporting EMDEs gain traction.

In particular, aggregate growth in the largest seven EMDEs (Brazil, China, India, Indonesia, Mexico, the Russian Federation, and Turkey) is expected to pick up throughout the forecast horizon, surpassing its long-term average by 2018 (Figure 1.13). Over time, this group has come to play an

FIGURE 1.13 Role of the largest EMDEs in the global outlook

Aggregate growth in the largest seven EMDEs is expected to pick up throughout the forecast horizon. Over time, this group has come to play an increasingly important role in the global economy. Recovering activity in the largest EMDEs should have notable positive effects for growth in other EMDEs as well as globally.

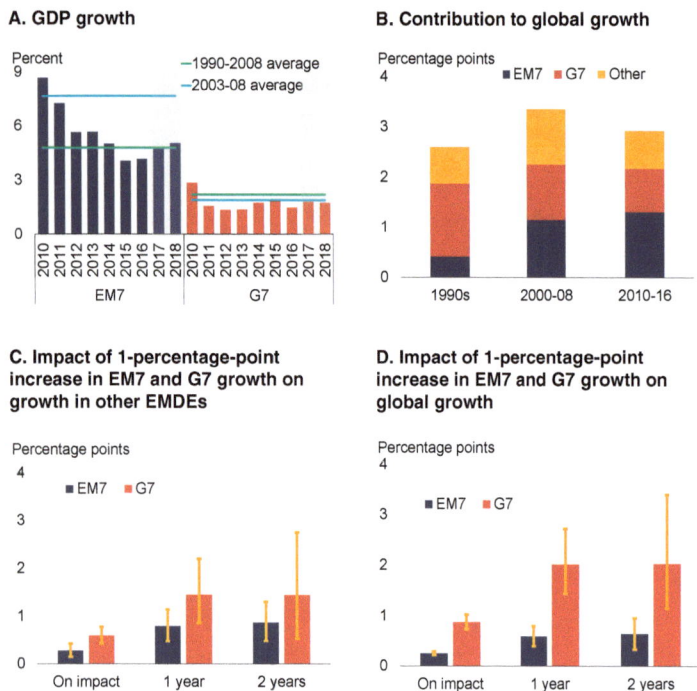

A. GDP growth

B. Contribution to global growth

C. Impact of 1-percentage-point increase in EM7 and G7 growth on growth in other EMDEs

D. Impact of 1-percentage-point increase in EM7 and G7 growth on global growth

Source: World Bank.
A.-D. EM7 includes Brazil, China, India, Indonesia, Mexico, the Russian Federation, and Turkey. G7 includes Canada, France, Germany, Italy, Japan, the United Kingdom, and the United States.
A. Aggregate growth rates calculated using constant 2010 U.S. dollars GDP weights. Shaded areas denote forecasts.
C. Cumulative impulse responses of a 1-percentage-point increase in EM7 and G7 growth on growth in other EMDEs. Solid bars represent medians, and error bars represent 16-84 percent confidence intervals.
D. Cumulative impulse responses of a 1-percentage-point increase in EM7 and G7 growth on global growth. The impact is the GDP-weighted average of the responses of EM7, other EMDEs, and G7 countries. Solid bars represent medians, and error bars represent 16-84 percent confidence intervals.

increasingly important role in the global economy. Accordingly, recovering activity in the largest EMDEs should have notable positive effects for growth in other EMDEs as well as globally—even if the largest advanced economies continue to be the main source of global spillovers (Huidrom, Kose, and Ohnsorge 2017).

The benign global outlook is little changed since January 2017, after a sequence of forecast downgrades in previous years (Figure 1.14). While a more expansionary fiscal stance in advanced economies—particularly the United States—could lead to stronger-than-expected growth, downside

risks continue to dominate. Policy uncertainty is likely to remain high in 2017, and there is a risk that financial market volatility could increase from current low levels. This could be triggered by unexpected changes in monetary, trade, or other policies in major economies; heightened financial sector concerns; electoral outcomes; or rising geopolitical risks. Over the longer term, a more prolonged slowdown in investment could further erode the growth potential and resilience of both advanced economies and EMDEs.

Against this backdrop, downside risks remain above historical averages. This implies a continued downward skew in the distribution of possible forecast errors. At present, the estimated 50-percent probability range for global growth in 2018 is 2.2-3.6 percent. The probability that global growth could be more than 1 percentage point below baseline over the next year is currently estimated at 17 percent. The probability of global growth being more than 1 percentage point above the baseline next year is estimated at 15 percent.

Upside risk: fiscal stimulus in advanced economies

While the baseline forecast assumes that fiscal policy in major advanced economies will be broadly neutral to growth, a more expansionary fiscal stance could eventually materialize over the forecast period, particularly in the United States. Fiscal stimulus could provide a boost to U.S. growth, depending on the nature of the measures (World Bank 2017a). Although this would have positive effects on global growth, its benefits for trading partners could be dampened by countervailing forces—in particular, changes in U.S. trade policy.

The proposed tax cuts and measures to boost U.S. infrastructure spending are not included in baseline projections due to insufficient details and the unclear timeframe. Suggested tax reforms include a reduction in marginal tax rates for corporations and individuals, a simplification of the tax code, and measures to improve international tax competitiveness. Large cuts to corporate and personal income taxes could have a positive short-term effect on growth, but could also lead to a substantial increase in fiscal deficits.[2] Immediate expensing of business investments could provide particularly strong support to capital expenditures, and help spur U.S. growth above current projections (Auerbach et al. 2017). Infrastructure investment programs could also lead to stronger-than-expected U.S. growth in the short-term, and increase potential output over the medium term (Bivens 2014; Whalen and Reichling 2015). However, the U.S. economy is already close to full employment, which could limit the short-term lift from fiscal stimulus, and lead to earlier, and ultimately larger, policy interest rate increases (Auerbach and Gorodnichenko 2012; Christiano, Eichenbaum, and Rebelo 2011).

In the Euro Area, fiscal stimulus could boost growth in view of still-high unemployment and low equilibrium interest rates (European Commission 2016). Given the high trade intensity of Euro Area activity, positive spillovers of Euro Area stimulus for the rest of the world, and for EMDEs in particular, could be substantial (World Bank 2017a). In Japan, additional stimulus measures in the short term, and further delays in planned consolidation measures over the medium term, could lead to a slightly higher growth trajectory in coming years.

Downside risk: increased protectionism and trade retaliation

Despite the recent improvement in world trade, the possibility of rising trade protectionism has become a major source of concern (Figure 1.15). Over the medium term, additional erosion of the multilateral rules-based system that has been built since the mid-1940s could put downward pressure on economic integration, and ultimately on growth and job creation.

While the widespread imposition of trade barriers remains a tail risk in the short term, unilateral restrictions may be met with retaliatory measures.

---

[2]Simulations suggest that a reduction in the statutory corporate tax rate from 35 percent to 15 percent, along with a reduction in marginal personal income tax rates by an average of 2.5 percentage points, could increase GDP by about 1.2 to 1.9 percent above baseline after 2 years, but also widen fiscal deficits by 1.9 to 2.4 percent of GDP over the same period (World Bank 2017a).

FIGURE 1.14 Global risks

Global growth forecasts have stabilized following sequential downgrades in previous years. However, downside risks remain above historical averages. The probability that global growth could be more than 1 percentage point below the baseline next year is currently estimated at 17 percent. The probability of global growth being more than 1 percentage point above the baseline next year is 15 percent.

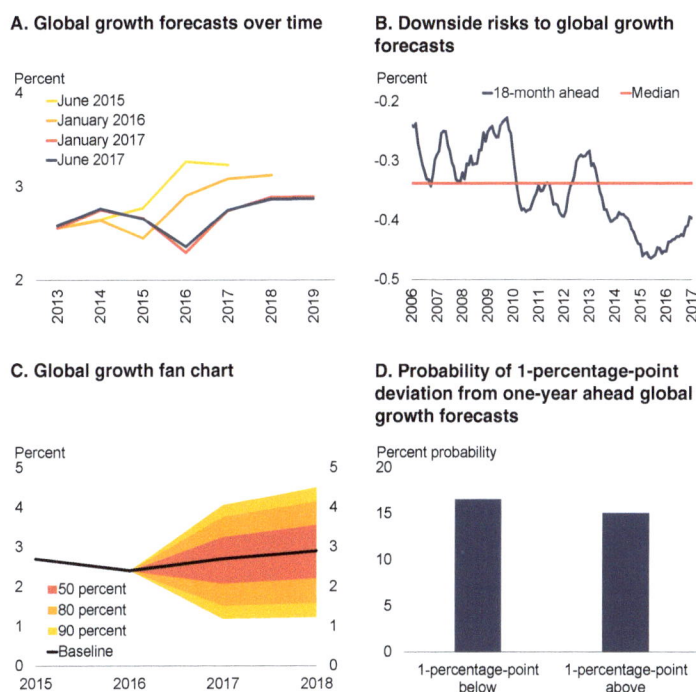

A. Global growth forecasts over time

B. Downside risks to global growth forecasts

C. Global growth fan chart

D. Probability of 1-percentage-point deviation from one-year ahead global growth forecasts

Sources: Bloomberg, Consensus Economics, World Bank.
A. The dates indicate the editions of *Global Economic Prospects*.
B. Downside risks measured as the time-varying skewness of global growth forecasts, computed from the forecast distribution of the three underlying risk factors (oil price futures, the S&P 500 equity price futures, and term spread forecasts). Each of the three risk factors' weight is estimated using the variance decomposition of global growth forecasts derived from the vector autoregression model described in Ohnsorge, Stocker, and Some (2016).
C.D. The fan chart and the corresponding probabilities are constructed based on the recovered standard deviation and skewness, assuming a two-piece normal distribution. Values for 2017 are computed from the forecast distribution of 6-month ahead oil price futures, S&P500 equity price futures, and term spread forecasts. Values for 2018 are based on 18-month ahead forecast distributions. Last observation is April 2017.

A non-cooperative rise in trade restrictions could result in retaliatory measures, eventually leading to substantial increases in tariffs worldwide (Ossa 2014; Tabakis and Zanardi 2016). This could result in large income losses for all countries involved (Broda, Limao, and Weinstein 2008; Perroni and Whalley 2000).

An upward spiral in beggar-thy-neighbor protectionist measures would put into reverse the process of trade liberalization that has been a major contributor to deepening trade in past decades. For example, new preferential trade agreements, and a rising number of WTO

FIGURE 1.15 **Risk of protectionism**

Protectionism has become an important source of concern. A spiral of retaliatory trade restrictions could undo gains from past trade liberalization.

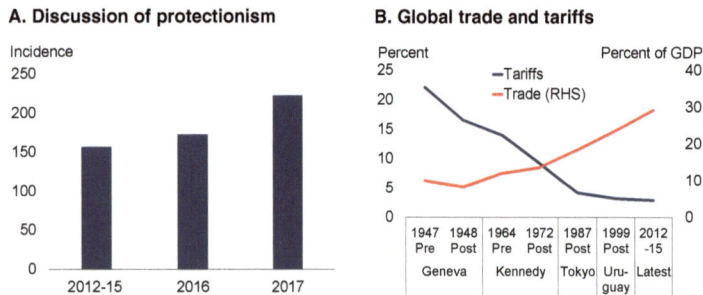

A. Discussion of protectionism

B. Global trade and tariffs

Sources: Bown and Irwin (2015), Google Trends, World Bank.
A. Weekly average Google Trend search for "protectionism," "trade restrictions," "trade war," and "import tariffs." 2017 average is year-to-date. Latest observation is May 21, 2017.
B. Global trade is defined as the average of exports and imports in percent of global GDP. Applied tariff rates based on the weighted mean for all products.

members, appear to have increased global trade growth by an average of more than 1 percentage point per year (Mattoo, Mulabdic, and Ruta 2017). The unwinding of such agreements would likely put downward pressure on trade prospects and jeopardize the effectiveness and viability of the multilateral trading system. Past experiences with protectionist policies warn of considerable unintended damage.

In turn, rising protectionism and declining trade integration would harm growth. Trade—particularly vertical specialization—tends to boost productivity, and hence activity (Constantinescu, Mattoo, and Ruta 2017). In the presence of complex value chain integration, tariffs and other barriers to trade are cumulative, as intermediate goods cross borders multiple times through the stages of production. An increase in barriers to trade may result in cascading trade costs along the supply chain (Diakantoni et al. 2017; Rouzet and Mirodout 2013). Consumers would ultimately bear these costs, resulting in widespread welfare losses. Deteriorating trade relationships between major economies could also increase the risk of geopolitical tensions and conflict (Copeland 2014).

Downside risk: policy uncertainty and geopolitical risks

Global economic policy uncertainty has been particularly elevated since mid-2016. If this

uncertainty persists, it could weigh on confidence and derail the ongoing recovery in global growth. Increased uncertainty about policy direction can delay investment and hiring decisions (Fernández-Villaverde et al. 2011; Born and Pfeifer 2014; Kose et al. 2017b). Policy uncertainty can also constrain the supply of credit to the economy, which can prolong or amplify economic downturns (Bordo, Duca, and Koch 2016; Karnizova and Li 2014). The threat of increased trade tariffs, even in the absence of actual changes in trade policies, could negatively impact investment and trade as well (Crowley, Song, and Meng 2016). Elevated policy uncertainty is negatively associated with firms' entry into foreign markets, and the decision to undertake costly and irreversible investments associated with exporting. Overall, a 10-percent increase in global policy uncertainty is associated with a 0.2 percentage-point reduction in trade growth (Constantinescu, Mattoo, and Ruta 2017).

The potential sources of economic policy uncertainty are extensive. In the United States, the new administration has suggested major shifts in fiscal, trade, and immigration policies. These changes could affect investment and hiring decisions by companies, as well as capital and remittance flows to EMDEs. Even without concrete changes, uncertainty about the direction and scope of U.S. policies could affect prospects for the U.S. economy and its main trading partners (Kose et al. 2017a; World Bank 2017a). These effects could be exacerbated by political uncertainty. In Europe, the rising influence of populist parties could impact policies and affect economic integration in the European Union. Negotiation around the exit of the United Kingdom from the European Union also carries risks.

Geopolitical risks have also steadily increased, and fragile security conditions could set back activity in a number of regions. The risk of large-scale conflict in the Middle East continues, reflecting persistent unrest in Iraq, the Syrian Arab Republic, and the Republic of Yemen, as well as sectarian divisions in the region. A flare-up of geopolitical risks in the Middle East could lead to disruptions in global oil supplies and a resurgence of refugee flows, posing additional challenges for host countries (Adhikari 2013). Water scarcity and food insecurity could also contribute to instability in the Middle East and Sub-Saharan Africa. Droughts and conflict have already led to intensifying risks of famine in Nigeria, Somalia, South Sudan, and the Republic of Yemen and contributed to further unrest in Syria. Finally, the threat of conflict in the Korean peninsula represents a significant source of regional and global risk.

Downside risk: financial market stress

A disorderly tightening of financing conditions or a sharp increase in financial market volatility from current low levels represent significant risks. These could be triggered by a number of factors.

Repricing of policy-related risks

Since the start of 2017, financial market volatility has been low, despite elevated policy uncertainty. This divergence is unusual (Figure 1.16). A sudden reassessment of policy-related risks could lead to abrupt adjustments in asset prices and safe-haven flows, with adverse consequences for higher-yielding assets, including those from EMDEs. In general, high policy uncertainty is associated with higher risk premiums as investors seek to hedge against negative outcomes (Brogaard and Detzel 2015; Pastor and Veronesi 2013). Economic policy uncertainty is generally a weak predictor of financial market volatility. However, specific events, such as the U.S. debt ceiling negotiations in 2011, have provoked bouts of volatility and sudden repricing of risks on international markets (Hamilton 2017). In turn, both volatility and policy uncertainty shocks can lead to adverse short-term effects on activity, with the former generally having a larger impact (Alexopoulos and Cohen 2015; Baker, Bloom, and Davis 2015; Jurado, Ludvigson, and Ng 2015). Countries with large exposures to international financial markets could be particularly susceptible to these negative effects (Adrian, Stackman, and Vogt 2016).

Sudden increase in borrowing costs

Changes in monetary policy expectations, including a faster-than-expected normalization in U.S. policy, or signals of an earlier-than-anticipated exit from exceptional easing measures

FIGURE 1.16 Financial market risks

A sudden reassessment of policy-related risks could trigger financial market volatility and set back global activity. An uptick in the U.S. term premium from current low levels could raise long-term yields, and worsen financing conditions for EMDEs. Given elevated private sector debt, some countries remain vulnerable to a sharp increase in borrowing costs. Some countries also remain vulnerable to risks associated with further U.S. dollar appreciation, but foreign reserves are ample and external debt is manageable in most cases.

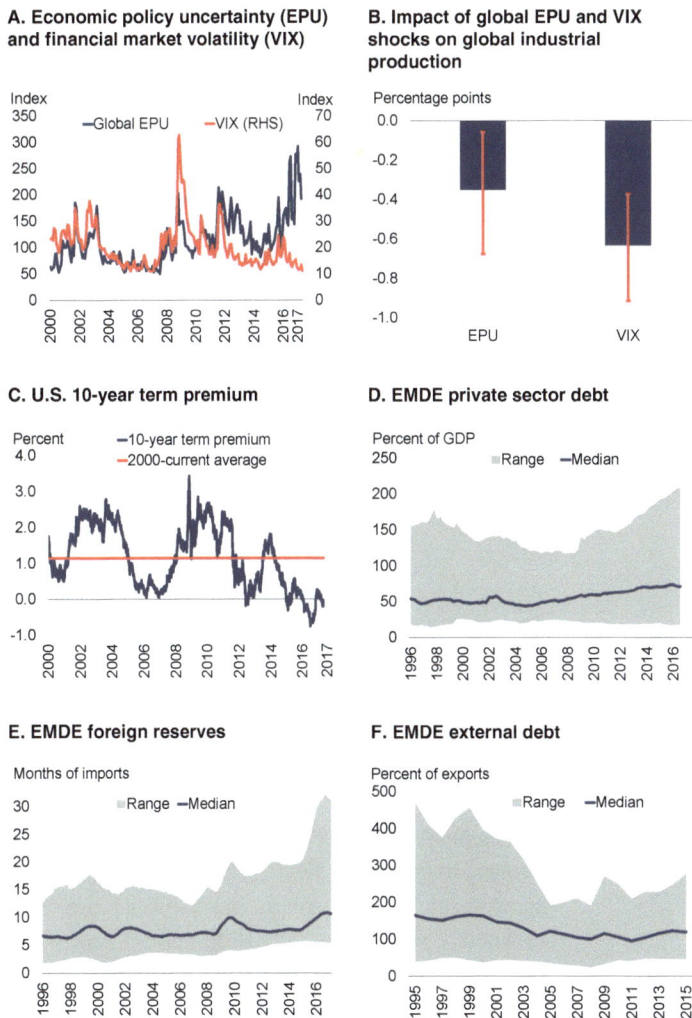

A. Economic policy uncertainty (EPU) and financial market volatility (VIX)

B. Impact of global EPU and VIX shocks on global industrial production

C. U.S. 10-year term premium

D. EMDE private sector debt

E. EMDE foreign reserves

F. EMDE external debt

Sources: Baker, Bloom, and Davis (2015); Board of Governors of the Federal Reserve System; Bloomberg; Bank for International Settlements; Federal Reserve Bank of New York; Haver Analytics; World Bank.
A. VIX is the implied volatility of option prices on the U.S. S&P 500. EPU is the Economic Policy Uncertainty index computed by Baker, Bloom, and Davis (2015). Last observation is April 2017 for EPU and May 24, 2017 for VIX.
B. Cumulative impulse response of global industrial production growth after 12-months to a one-standard-deviation shock in global Economic Policy Uncertainty (EPU) and VIX. Data are in deviation from mean and scaled by the standard deviation. Estimation based on a Bayesian vector autoregression of global EPU, VIX, and global industrial production growth rate. Blue bars denote median responses and lines denote 16th-84th percentile confidence intervals. The sample period is 2000M1-2017M2.
C. Term premium estimates from the model in Adrian, Crump, and Moench (2013). Last observation is May 24, 2017.
D.-F. Range indicates minimum to maximum of country sample.
D. Country sample includes Argentina, Brazil, Chile, China, Colombia, Czech Republic, Hungary, India, Indonesia, Malaysia, Mexico, Russia, Saudi Arabia, South Africa, Thailand, and Turkey. Last observation is 2016Q3.
E. F. Country sample includes Brazil, Bulgaria, China, Colombia, Mexico, Peru, India, Indonesia, Malaysia, Philippines, Thailand, Romania, South Africa, and Turkey. Last observation is April 2017 for foreign reserves and 2015 for external debt.

in the Euro Area and Japan, could trigger a sudden increase in borrowing costs. A build-up of inflation fears or the perception of increased macroeconomic risks could lead to an uptick in term premiums from current exceptionally low levels. Such events could trigger an abrupt deterioration in financing conditions for EMDEs and a slowing of capital inflows—particularly if higher yields do not reflect improved advanced-economy prospects (Arteta et al. 2015). Sizable external financing needs, limited levels of foreign reserves, and elevated domestic debt expose various EMDEs to a sudden rise in borrowing costs. Rapid deleveraging could potentially intensify slowdowns—including in China, where private indebtedness and financial sector vulnerabilities remain elevated (Bernardini and Forni 2017; World Bank 2016a; World Bank 2017b). While vulnerabilities have somewhat diminished in EMDEs in recent years, the dispersion of vulncrabilities across countries widened in 2016 as commodity exporters faced continued challenges.

Further U.S. dollar appreciation

Diverging monetary policies, with the U.S. Federal Reserve raising policy rates well ahead of other major central banks, has already contributed to a significant U.S. dollar appreciation. Fiscal stimulus measures in the United States could intensify this trend. Safe-haven flows triggered by increased investor risk aversion, or unexpected changes in trade or fiscal policies in the United States, could also push up the value of the U.S. currency. Broad-based U.S. dollar appreciation has been associated historically with tighter global financing conditions and balance sheet pressures for countries with large U.S. dollar debt exposure (Bruno and Shin 2015). Debt levels in foreign currency have increased in recent years, particularly among EMDE corporates. A sudden strengthening of the U.S. dollar could contribute to rollover and currency risks for companies with unhedged foreign exchange exposures. For companies in commodity-related sectors, such pressures can be amplified by the negative correlation between the U.S. dollar and commodity prices (Baffes et al. 2015).

However, there are several mitigating factors. The bulk of EMDE credit growth over the last decade has been in domestic currency. The number of countries with currency pegs to the U.S. dollar has declined. The ratio of external debt to exports remains in most cases markedly lower than in the early 2000s, despite some recent increases, and foreign reserves are generally ample. High vulnerability to currency risks is confined to those countries that still have elevated short-term foreign-currency-denominated debt (Chow et al. 2015; Chui, Kuruk, and Turner 2016).

Downside risk: impact of renewed sharp slide in oil prices on oil exporters

A faster-than-expected rise in unconventional oil supplies, such as U.S. shale production, or faltering commitment of OPEC and non-OPEC producers to additional cuts in output, could keep oil markets oversupplied. This could lead to an abrupt slide in oil prices.

For many oil-exporting EMDEs, a renewed sharp decline in oil prices, after two years of difficult adjustments to the previous plunge, could substantially weigh on growth prospects. Financially constrained exporters with depleted fiscal buffers could be forced into additional consolidation measures, while deteriorating current account positions could increase external financing pressures. This could lead to renewed currency depreciation and trigger a re-pricing of credit and sovereign risks (Baffes et al. 2015). As highlighted by the early-2016 oil price drop, which heightened concerns about default risks in oil and gas companies, an abrupt decline in oil prices could also intensify corporate balance sheet pressures among energy companies, which are among the most leveraged in EMDEs (IMF 2016b, Bank for International Settlements 2016, World Bank 2016a). Although banking systems in most oil-exporting EMDEs have become more resilient to oil price changes, financial strains could intensify in the face of persistently depressed prices.

In principle, these negative effects on oil producers would be accompanied by real income gains for oil importers, offsetting the overall impact on global growth. This offsetting effect is most likely when oil price declines are due to abundant supply, as opposed to weakening demand (Cashin, Mohaddin, and Raissi 2014; Cerdeiro and Plotnikov 2017). However, renewed weakness and financial stress in large oil-exporting EMDEs could have adverse contagion effects on other economies through trade, financial market, and remittance flows (Huidrom, Kose, and Ohnsorge 2017; World Bank 2016c). Moreover, oil price movements could have asymmetric effects—with declines having a smaller positive effect on oil importers than increases having a negative one—due, for instance, to frictions associated with the relocation of activity across sectors (Engemann, Kliesen, and Owyang 2011; Hamilton 2011; Jo 2014).

Downside risk: slowdown in potential output growth

Potential output growth has softened appreciably in both advanced economies and EMDEs in recent years, reflecting the combined deceleration in productivity and investment growth, albeit to different degrees. While baseline projections for both advanced economies and EMDEs assume some cyclical recovery in productivity and investment, risks to long-term growth remain predominantly on the downside.

The trend deceleration in total factor productivity growth largely predated the global financial crisis, and it has been particularly pronounced in EMDEs since 2010 (Figure 1.17). This pattern has been broad-based and is seen in more than 60 percent of EMDEs. Weak productivity trends could be associated with a slower rate of innovation among companies and countries operating at the technological frontier, and a slower pace of diffusion to companies and countries operating below that frontier (Buera and Oberfield 2016; Andrews, Criscuolo, and Gal 2015; Gordon 2014).

The anticipation of lower future growth may lead to a decrease in current investment, depressing aggregate demand in the short term and slowing capital accumulation over the longer term (Blanchard, L'Huillier, and Lorenzoni 2013).

FIGURE 1.17 Risks linked to weak productivity and investment growth

A key factor behind the slower growth potential in both advanced economies and EMDEs has been a deceleration in total factor productivity. Investment growth slowed considerably in EMDEs, reducing the contribution of capital accumulation to growth.

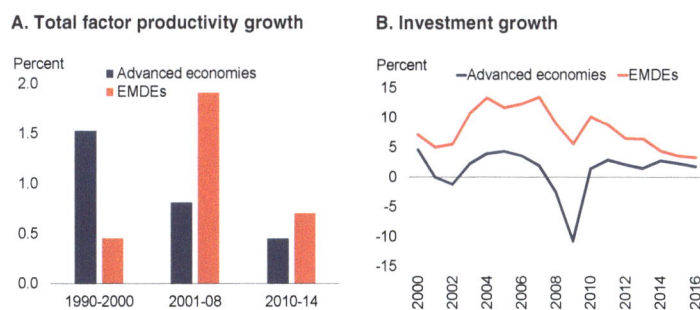

Sources: Penn World Table, World Bank.
A. TFP growth measured at constant national prices and aggregated using 2011 U.S. dollars GDP weights. Sample includes 28 advanced economies and 68 EMDEs.
B. Aggregate growth rates calculated using constant 2010 U.S. dollars gross fixed investment weights.

Demographic pressures in advanced economies, and in some large EMDEs, could also contribute to a lower rate of return on capital (Baker, De Long, and Krugman 2005; Rachel and Smith 2015). Over time, capital deepening, which has been an important engine of growth in EMDEs over the last two decades, could further decelerate, adding downward pressure to productivity and potential output growth.

Policy challenges

Challenges in major economies

Advanced economies have begun to shift away from a mix of exceptionally supportive monetary policy and restrictive fiscal policy. Central banks in major advanced economies face the challenge of normalizing monetary policy without disrupting a fragile recovery or triggering financing market disruptions. Expansionary fiscal policy would be appropriate in a number of economies, provided it is complemented with measures to bolster medium-term fiscal sustainability. Globalization and technological progress have changed the demand for jobs and skills; accordingly, there is a need to support the adjustment process for workers that are adversely affected. In China, avoiding a sharp slowdown and a disorderly unwinding of financial vulnerabilities will require a careful balancing of policy objectives.

FIGURE 1.18 Monetary policy challenges in advanced economies

U.S. monetary policy normalization has been significantly slower than in past tightening episodes. Large central bank balance sheets might constrain monetary policy actions in the case of a renewed downturn.

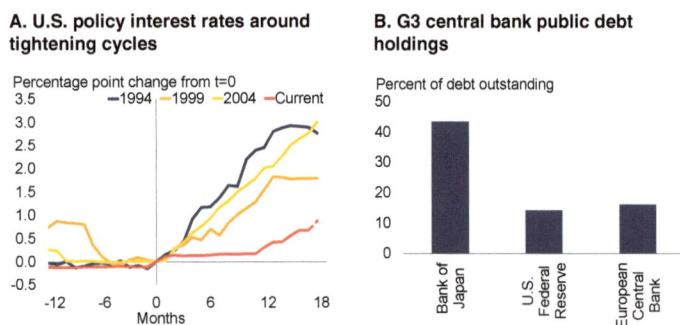

A. U.S. policy interest rates around tightening cycles

B. G3 central bank public debt holdings

Sources: Bank of Japan, Bloomberg, European Commission, Federal Reserve Bank of St. Louis, Federal Reserve Board, Haver Analytics, World Bank.
A. t=0 refers to the start of U.S. monetary policy tightening cycles. Percentage point change from t=0 in monthly effective federal funds rates. Previous tightening cycles refer to those beginning in January 1994, June 1999, and June 2004, with the current cycle having begun in December 2015. Dashed lines show market implied changes in the given rates over the next four months. Last observation is May 24, 2017.
B. Public debt held by the European Central Bank is calculated as the ratio of the Eurosystem's holdings of general government debt to general government debt outstanding. The Federal Reserve's debt holding is in percent of publicly held U.S. Treasury securities. Data as of December 31, 2016.

Monetary policy in advanced economies

A gradual pickup in inflation across advanced economies has raised the prospects of less accommodative monetary policy. In the United States, inflation and employment are already near central bank objectives, justifying continued policy normalization (Yellen 2017). A more expansionary fiscal policy stance could accelerate the pace of interest rate increases, but the materialization of downside risks to growth, due to policy changes or other factors, could have the opposite effect. Historically low equilibrium interest rates will likely result in a lower terminal point for policy rates during this tightening cycle compared with previous episodes (Figure 1.18). Over the longer term, this could increase the frequency and duration of periods when nominal policy interest rates are constrained by the zero lower bound (Kiley and Roberts 2017). Such constraints have led to calls for higher central bank inflation targets, which would create additional space for interest rate cuts in the future (Ball 2014; Ball et al. 2016).

In the Euro Area and Japan, large-scale unconventional policies continue to be in operation and are helping to maintain supportive borrowing conditions. In the Euro Area, quantitative easing is expected to be gradually unwound, as economic slack narrows and inflation moves toward policy objectives. However, a prolonged period of low inflation has made expectations more susceptible to negative shocks, encouraging the ECB to maintain a highly accommodative stance over a sustained period of time (Ciccarelli et al. 2017). The Bank of Japan has so far been successful in stabilizing long-term interest rates around zero, but this policy may only deliver a slow increase in inflation (Cecchetti and Schoenholtz 2016). Looking forward, the exceptionally large balance sheets and elevated government bond holdings of major central banks might constrain their ability to undertake further unconventional policies in case of a renewed downturn. Fiscal policy would need to stand ready to implement counter-cyclical measures in the event of future growth setbacks.

Fiscal policy in advanced economies

Fiscal policy in advanced economies stopped being a drag on growth in 2016, for the first time since 2010 (Figure 1.19). This shift was visible in the United States, Euro Area, and Japan, and it is expected to continue to a lesser degree in 2017. In the United States, where fiscal stimulus is under consideration, a priority could be infrastructure spending in view of large unmet needs and of the elevated fiscal multipliers of such spending (Bivens 2014). Improving public sector efficiency, regulation, and private sector participation could also increase economic returns from infrastructure investment. As the U.S. economy is already operating close to full capacity, growth windfalls from fiscal stimulus measures could be short lived and might be offset over time by pressures associated with deteriorating public finances. Under unchanged policies, public debt is already expected to significantly increase over the next decade (CBO 2017). Unfunded tax cuts could add to the upward trajectory (Page 2017). In contrast, tax and spending reforms that enhance productivity and are consistent with medium-term fiscal sustainability could deliver lasting benefits.

In the Euro Area, a more expansionary fiscal policy stance to absorb remaining slack would be appropriate for the region as a whole (European

Commission 2016). However, countries with fiscal space are generally not those in the greatest need of stimulus. The absence of a more centralized fiscal capacity and strong coordination makes it more difficult to implement supportive fiscal policies in a monetary union (Eyraud, Gaspar, and Poghosyan 2017; European Commission 2014; Bańkowski et al. 2017). In Japan, the government is debating whether fiscal consolidation should be implemented before the inflation target is reached, with some arguing that fiscal policy should help complement monetary policy in stabilizing inflation (Sims 2016).

Structural policy in advanced economies

In advanced economies, rising income inequality and stagnant median wages have fueled the political debate on the benefits of globalization and trade liberalization, amid a trend decline in the share of manufacturing jobs. This has led to calls for unwinding past trade liberalization efforts, and for increased protection for domestic industry.

The last three decades have seen a decline of manufacturing employment across most advanced economies (Wood 2017). For instance, the share of manufacturing jobs in total private employment in the United States, Germany, and Japan has fallen by 10 percentage points since 1985 (Figure 1.20). Over that period, the United States accumulated large goods trade deficits, but Japan and especially Germany registered substantial trade surpluses. Since 2000, the drop in manufacturing jobs has accelerated, particularly in the United States, but productivity gains have more than offset the decline, leading to a continued rise in output. These common trends highlight complex interactions between technological change and globalization. Automation, shifts in production patterns, and trade policies all played a role in driving labor market outcomes (Wood 2017; De Long 2017; Felipe and Mehta 2016; Autor, Dorn, and Hanson 2016).

Measures to support workers directly affected by sectoral shifts in employment, and to more widely spread the benefits of technological progress and globalization, should be reinforced. This includes vocational training, life-long learning, better

FIGURE 1.19 Fiscal policy challenges in advanced economies

Fiscal policy in advanced economies was no longer a drag on growth in 2016, a first since 2010. A more expansionary fiscal stance in the Euro Area would be warranted, but countries with fiscal space are generally not those in most need of stimulus.

A. Change in structural fiscal balance and growth in advanced economies

B. Structural fiscal balance and unemployment across Euro Area countries

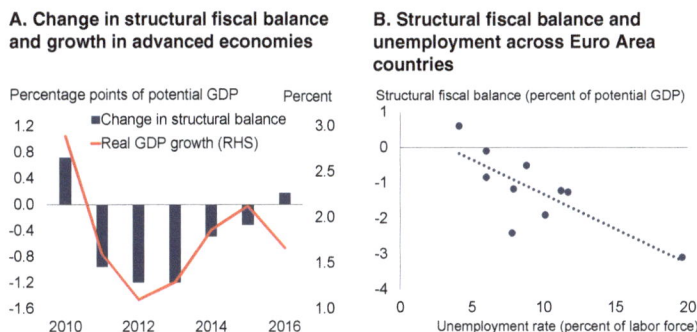

Sources: Eurostat, International Monetary Fund WEO, World Bank.
A. Structural fiscal balance is the cyclically-adjusted primary balance in percent of potential GDP.
B. Last observation is 2016.

FIGURE 1.20 Structural policy challenges in advanced economies

The last three decades have seen a decline in the share of manufacturing employment across major advanced economies. Since 2000, this decline has accelerated, particularly in the United States. Productivity gains, nevertheless, resulted in rising manufacturing output.

A. Manufacturing as a share of total employment

B. Advanced economies manufacturing productivity and employment

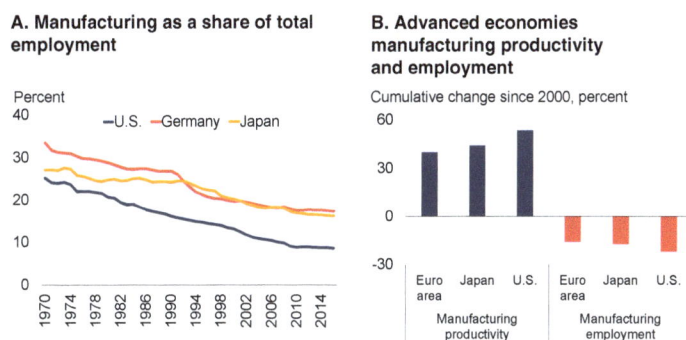

Sources: Federal Reserve Bank of St. Louis, Haver Analytics, Organisation for Economic Co-operation and Development, U.S. Bureau of Labor Statistics.
A. U.S. data measures total employment on nonfarm payrolls. Last observation is 2016.
B. Cumulative changes from 2000 to 2015. Manufacturing productivity is the gross value added per person employed.

employment services, and effective social protection systems.

Challenges in China

The key policy challenge for China remains to manage a gradual deceleration to a sustainable growth rate in the medium term. Avoiding a sharp slowdown and a disorderly unwinding of financial

FIGURE 1.21 EMDE monetary policy

Inflation rates in commodity exporters and importers are converging. Declining inflation has enabled some central banks in commodity-exporting EMDEs to reduce policy rates.

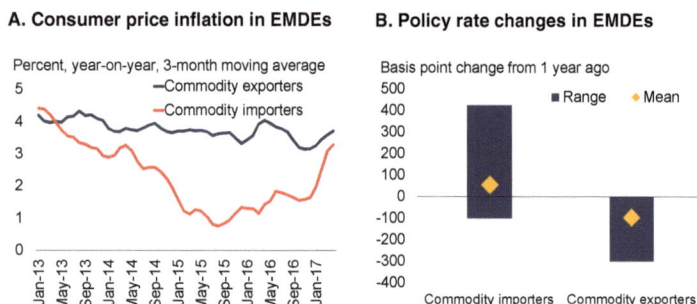

A. Consumer price inflation in EMDEs

B. Policy rate changes in EMDEs

Sources: Haver Analytics, National central banks, World Bank.
A. Sample includes 75 commodity-exporting and 54 commodity-importing EMDEs and shows median in each respective group. Last observation is April 2017.
B. Commodity importers include China, Hungary, India, Mexico, Philippines, Poland, Romania, Thailand, and Turkey. Commodity exporters include Brazil, Chile, Colombia, Indonesia, Malaysia, Peru, Russia, and South Africa. Last observation is April 2017.

vulnerabilities accumulated during years of rapid credit growth will require a careful balancing of policy objectives.

China has initiated a wide range of reforms in recent years. Efforts have focused on excess capacity reduction and re-employment of affected workers. Measures to improve the viability of state-owned enterprises include the promotion of stronger participation of the private sector, more market discipline, and competition. In the oil and gas sector, these efforts are being accompanied by a reorganization of the industry to separate functions in the value chains. Considerable progress has been made in household registration reforms. Fiscal reform initiatives have focused on addressing imbalances in revenue and expenditure responsibilities across different levels of government, the conversion of business taxes to value-added tax (VAT), tax cuts for small and high-tech firms, and reform of the personal income tax system. In addition, measures to improve local-government debt management have been implemented, such as revisions of the budget law, market-based conversion of debt to bonds, and more effective monitoring and classification of local government debt. Financial regulation has been tightened to contain financial sector vulnerabilities, including through broader regulatory oversight of off-balance sheet items

such as wealth management products. Exchange rate flexibility has been enhanced, with the use of a basket of currencies rather than the U.S. dollar to determine the reference rate. The relaxation of foreign institutional investor rules and the opening of the bond and currency derivatives market should help promote foreign participation (IMF 2016c).

Despite considerable progress, there is a need to further contain financial and fiscal vulnerabilities, including rapid credit growth and high levels of debt. Financial and corporate sector reforms, including appropriate budget constraints on state-owned enterprises, could improve the allocation of capital. They would also help reallocate factors of production toward more productive sectors and away from stagnating sectors with excess capacity, which would spur productivity.

Additional structural reforms could help China shift its growth model from manufacturing to services, from investment to consumption, and from exports to domestic spending. China has significant potential for rapid urban development and technological transformation. Land and hukou (labor market) reforms could significantly lift urban growth and employment. Productivity in rural areas could be bolstered by reorienting subsidy and price support programs toward the development of more efficient and sustainable agricultural production systems. During the reform period, counter-cyclical fiscal measures to support consumption and private investment could smooth the transition, as long as they are consistent with medium-term fiscal sustainability. The economic and social dislocations that might arise from enterprise restructuring could be addressed by targeted temporary income support and by robust social protection programs.

Challenges in emerging and developing economies

Inflation rates in commodity exporters and importers are converging. Easing inflation is allowing policymakers in some commodity exporters to adopt a more accommodative policy stance. Although the impact of the drop in commodity prices on government revenues in commodity exporters is beginning to wane, fiscal space remains generally constrained across EMDEs. Policies that improve the business climate and support investment are critical to boost long-term growth. In addition, policies that promote trade integration and address structural impediments to trade will help counteract the negative effects of trade policy uncertainty and rising protectionism.

Monetary and financial policies

Headline inflation in commodity exporters and importers is converging (Figure 1.21). Stabilizing or appreciating exchange rates account for much of the decline in inflation in commodity exporters since mid-2016, and inflation is already within the target bands in some countries (e.g., Brazil, Indonesia, Russia). In commodity importers, the more recent increase in inflation reflects the lagged impact of rising energy prices in 2016. Easing inflation and subdued growth have led monetary policymakers in several major commodity exporters to cut policy rates (e.g., Brazil, Colombia, Kazakhstan), despite rising interest rates in the United States (IMF 2017c). Meanwhile, some commodity importers facing currency pressures have tightened policy amid rising inflation (e.g., Mexico, Turkey).

Market concerns about financial stability in EMDEs have receded relative to late 2016, when a tightening of global financing conditions led to market volatility. This highlights the need to shore up buffers of liquidity and capital to mitigate future encounters with financial stress. In the event of bouts of financial market stress, depending on country-specific circumstances, appropriate policy actions could include providing liquidity support to markets or implementing macro-prudential measures (e.g., Israel in August 2013; the Republic of Korea in July 2014; IMF 2014a). In conjunction with other appropriate monetary and financial policies, there could be a role in some countries for the temporary and targeted use of capital controls (e.g., Colombia's unremunerated reserve requirements during 2007-08), if needed and transparently implemented (Baba and Kokenyne 2011; Baffes et al. 2015; IMF 2014b).

FIGURE 1.22 EMDE fiscal policy

The impact of the sharp drop in commodity prices on government revenues in commodity-exporting EMDEs is beginning to fade. But with fiscal space still constrained across EMDEs, consolidation will need to continue to set debt on a sustainable path, particularly in commodity exporters.

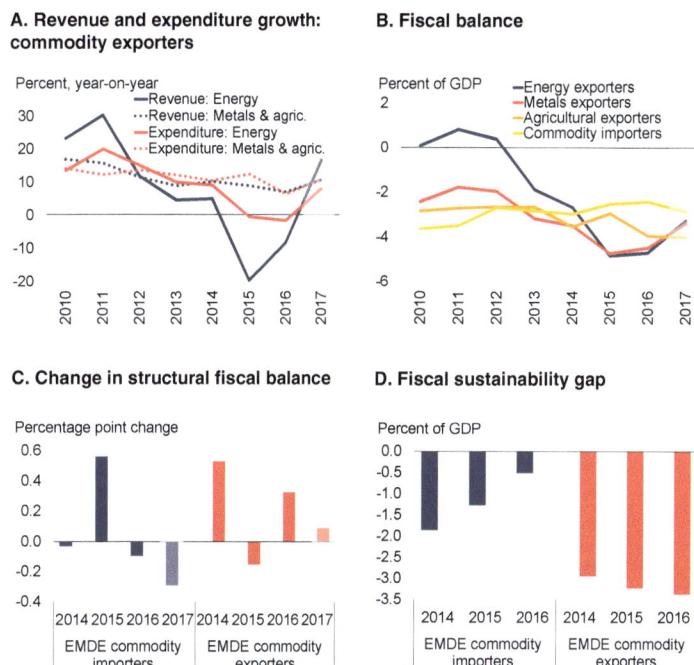

A. Revenue and expenditure growth: commodity exporters

B. Fiscal balance

C. Change in structural fiscal balance

D. Fiscal sustainability gap

Sources: International Monetary Fund, World Bank.
A. Figure shows median in each country group. Sample includes 35 energy exporters and 56 metal and agricultural product exporters. Shaded areas indicate forecasts.
B. Figure shows median in each country group. Sample includes 35 energy exporters, 34 agricultural product exporters, 20 metals exporters, and 62 commodity importers.
C. Structural balance is the fiscal balance adjusted for the economic cycle and for one-off effects. Figure shows median in each country group. Sample includes 17 commodity exporters and 22 commodity importers. Shaded areas indicate forecasts.
D. Sustainability gap is measured as the difference between the primary balance and the debt-stabilizing primary balance, assuming historical average (1990–2016) interest rates and growth rates. A negative gap indicates that government debt is on a rising trajectory; a positive gap indicates government debt is on a falling trajectory. Figure shows median in each country group. Sample includes 44 commodity-exporting and 28 commodity-importing EMDEs.

Fiscal policy

Fiscal consolidation continues in commodity-exporting EMDEs. Revenue losses from the sharp drop in commodity prices since 2014 deepened already large deficits in some countries (e.g., Mongolia, República Bolivariana de Venezuela) and turned large surpluses into large deficits in others (e.g., Oman, Saudi Arabia). More generally, many commodity exporters still face substantial consolidation needs to ensure fiscal sustainability in the medium term (Figure 1.22). In energy exporters, slowing expenditure growth and strengthening oil revenues in the second half of 2016 have helped stabilize deficits (e.g., Algeria,

FIGURE 1.23 EMDE structural domestic policy challenges

Policies directed at improving the overall business environment are critical to boosting investment, productivity, and long-term growth of output and employment. Well-managed public investment raises aggregate investment directly and can crowd-in private investment.

A. Factors influencing foreign investors' location choice

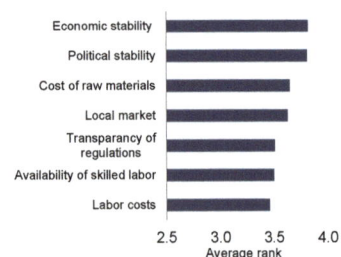

B. Cumulative impact on private investment of a 1 percent increase in public investment

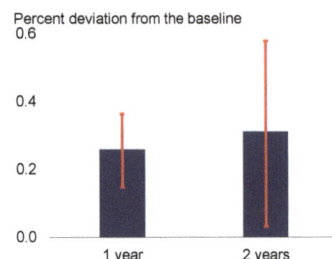

Sources: UNIDO (2011), World Bank.
A. Average rankings according to a business survey of 7,000 companies in 19 Sub-Saharan African countries conducted from 2010-2011.
B. Cumulative impulse responses of private investment to a positive shock to public investment, based on a sample of 8 EMDEs for the period 1998Q1-2016Q2. The model includes, in this order, real public investment, real GDP, real private investment, current account balance, and real effective exchange rate. The shock size is such that public investment increases by 1 percent from the base-line on impact. Blue bars represent median values and red error bars 16-84 percent confidence intervals.

Azerbaijan, Iraq, Kazakhstan). Among commodity-importing EMDEs, slowing revenue growth in 2016 contributed to a modest worsening of fiscal balances (e.g., China, Dominican Republic, Egypt, Turkey).

With average oil and metals prices expected to rise in 2017, and amid ongoing fiscal consolidation, deficits in most commodity exporters are expected to narrow this year. Structural budget balances in this group are projected to improve only marginally. With deficits predominating across EMDEs, and debt on a rising path, especially in commodity exporters, fiscal space remains constrained (Special Focus 1). In such an environment, careful consideration of revenue and expenditure reforms needed to support both activity and long-term fiscal sustainability is key (Cordes et al. 2015). In particular, reallocating spending toward investment would help reduce the trade-off between the need for fiscal consolidation and the goal of boosting growth. EMDE policymakers could also take advantage of still benign financing conditions to lengthen the maturity and duration of public debt as a precaution against a further tightening of borrowing conditions. Countries with elevated

foreign-currency debt could consider shifting to domestic currency financing, if feasible, to reduce the risks from currency depreciation.

Building credibility—for instance, by setting achievable fiscal targets and implementing them consistently, or establishing fiscal councils—will continue to be a policy priority (Debrun and Kinda, forthcoming). Replenishing or establishing stabilization funds, and improving tax administration, will help rebuild fiscal space and increase resilience to shocks (World Bank 2015a).

Structural policy

Despite signs of pickup in EMDE activity in the near term, these economies continue to face various structural challenges to boost growth over the longer run. On the domestic front, potential output growth in EMDEs is likely to further decline as a result of weak productivity growth and demographic pressures (IMF 2015). As the current global context illustrates, notable structural challenges to trade growth and growing protectionist pressures are likely to weigh on the recovery in global trade flows. This highlights the importance of efforts to further promote trade integration.

Domestic policy challenges

Modest growth rates in advanced economies, structural impediments to trade, and increasing protectionist sentiment suggest that EMDEs may need to become less reliant on external demand. Addressing domestic bottlenecks would help boost growth prospects in EMDEs. Policy measures that improve infrastructure, encourage innovation, promote labor market and education reform, and deepen within-country integration will foster potential growth (OECD and World Bank 2017; World Bank 2017g). EMDEs can reap substantial benefits from upgrading institutions and improving the overall business environment through more efficient regulations.

In light of the sharp investment growth slowdown in recent years across EMDEs, structural policies to boost fixed capital formation are crucial. Policies that reduce economic and political uncertainty, improve the transparency of regulations through the elimination of bureaucratic obstacles, streamline regulatory practices, and increase the availability of skilled labor are critical to enhance a country's attractiveness for investors (Figure 1.23). Measures directed at enhancing the overall business environment through improved access to credit, fewer obstacles to start a business, and enhanced contract enforcement would encourage greater market entry for new firms, job creation, and investment (World Bank 2017h; Dabla-Norris, Ho, and Kyobe 2016). In addition, reforms that help level the playing field between private and state-owned enterprises and promote the participation of private investors in public-private partnerships can play an important role in fostering capital formation (G20 2015).

Under the right circumstances—including the presence of economic slack and a strong institutional and legal environment—well-managed public investment directly raises aggregate investment and also crowds-in private investment. This effect can be boosted by accommodative financial conditions, as well as reforms that reduce barriers to trade and foreign investment and strengthen property rights (World Bank 2017a; Bruno, Campos, and Estrin 2017).

Trade policy challenges

Trade has been a catalyst for economic growth and stability. It boosts aggregate demand, enhances productivity, and fosters job creation. However, rising protectionist pressures, coupled with economic and trade policy uncertainty and various structural factors, are weighing on the outlook for trade growth (Constantinescu, Mattoo, and Ruta 2017).

Economic policy uncertainty is negatively associated with trade growth as it impacts exporters' entry into foreign markets and the decision to undertake costly investments associated with exporting (Special Focus 2). Exporting firms in EMDEs—in particular, low-income countries—are likely to be disproportionately affected, as they rely more on imports of capital equipment and intermediate goods, and their costs associated with exporting account for a larger share of total costs.

FIGURE 1.24 EMDE structural trade policy challenges

Deep trade agreements—those that contain substantial provisions beyond the mere liberalization of border measures—have become more common in recent years, although they still lag behind in EMDEs.

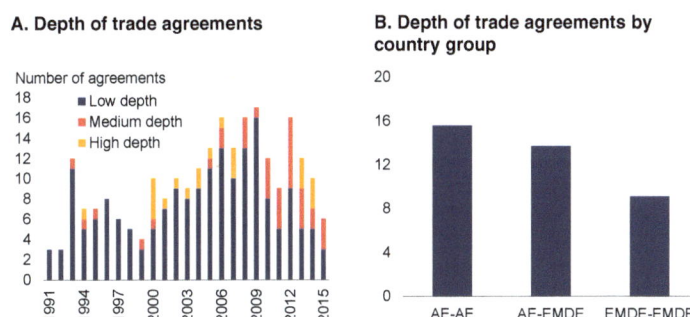

A. Depth of trade agreements

B. Depth of trade agreements by country group

Sources: Hofman, Osnago, and Ruta (2017); World Bank.
A. Includes provisions outside the mandate of the WTO. Low depth refers to free trade agreements (FTAs) with less than 10 provisions. Medium depth refers to FTAs with between 10 and 20 provisions. High depth refers to FTAs with more than 20 provisions.
B. Depth of trade agreements measured by average number of enforceable provisions for FTAs in 1958-2015. "AE" denotes advanced economies.

Policy measures aimed at removing domestic trade bottlenecks and improving the availability of credit for exporters, along with increased trade facilitation efforts, may help counteract the negative effects on EMDEs of trade policy uncertainty. In addition, measures to address the adverse distributional consequences of trade liberalization could counteract rising protectionist sentiments.

The withdrawal from existing trade agreements or unilateral increases in protectionist measures by some major economies could spiral into widespread trade retaliation involving many countries, including EMDEs. This in turn could result in substantial income losses (Ossa 2014; Perroni and Whalley 2000), as well as reverse the gains from the last seven decades of trade liberalization (Figure 1.24). Such protectionist measures would likely hurt countries that rely heavily on trade, including the poorest EMDEs.

In the current environment, a renewed commitment by EMDE policymakers to trade liberalization through bilateral and regional trade agreements, coupled with commitments under the WTO system, could act as a first line of defense against a potential uptick in protectionism (IMF, World Bank, and WTO 2017; Bown et al. 2017). The temptation for governments to resort to unilateral increases in tariffs to improve their

FIGURE 1.25 Poverty and trade

Protectionist measures could hurt EMDEs in general, and low-income countries (LICs) in particular, especially if they emanate from major economies, which are the main destination of their exports. Countries that graduated from low to middle income status generally had a higher degree of trade openness.

A. Destination of EMDE exports

B. Trade-to-GDP ratio in low-income countries, 2000-15

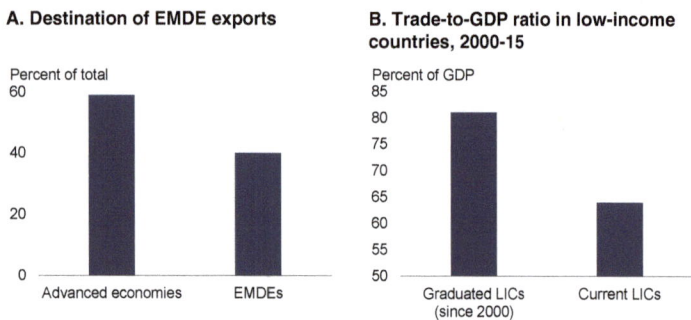

Sources: IMF Direction of Trade Statistics; World Development Indicators, World Bank.
A. Data reflect 2012-16 averages.
B. Simple averages. Graduated LICs include 31 countries. Current LICs include 29 countries.

terms of trade can be reduced by an efficient and rule-based trading system and trade agreements that promote inclusive and sustained growth.

Deep trade agreements—i.e., those that include substantial provisions beyond the mere liberalization of border measures, such as the removal of tariffs—are becoming more common in EMDEs, although they still lag those in advanced economies. They cover an extensive set of provisions, including those that regulate competition and investment policy, consumer protection, worker and environmental standards, and the protection of intellectual property rights. Recent agreements concluded by the European Union and some EMDE trading partners (such as Georgia, Ukraine, and Central America) have a very comprehensive set of provisions—above 30, compared to the average of 20 for advanced economies.

Deep trade agreements are associated with more trade than shallow trade accords. The harmonization or mutual recognition of standards, improved competition policy, and streamlined labor and capital market regulations can boost the regional and global integration of EMDEs (Hofmann, Osnago, and Ruta 2017). Provisions that improve the contractibility of inputs provided by suppliers are associated with increased FDI (Ahcar and Siroën 2014; Osnago, Rocha, and

Ruta 2015). By addressing a number of dimensions that are crucial for well-functioning supply chains—such as investment policy, services, standards, and customs procedures—deep trade agreements have had a positive impact on the formation of global value chains.

Poverty and trade

The poorest EMDEs rely heavily on trade for economic growth. Many are highly dependent on imports of capital goods. In addition, advanced economies are important export destinations for poor EMDEs (Figure 1.25). Protectionist trade policies could impact the most vulnerable populations in EMDEs and would curtail efforts to reduce global poverty.

Greater trade openness has been associated with lower poverty and inequality in EMDEs—with the important proviso that appropriate supporting policies accompany it. Trade expansion appears to have been an important factor in the transition of countries out of low-income status. Declines in tariffs have been estimated to lead, on average, to proportionate increases in incomes of the poor (Dollar and Kraay 2004; Sachs and Warner 1995). Income inequality fell in many EMDEs after the extensive trade liberalization of the 1990s (World Bank 2017i).

Measures that promote trade openness need to be accompanied by other policies to be effective in addressing associated adjustment costs and improving the welfare of the population (Goldberg and Pavcnik 2004; Winters, McCulloch, and McKay 2004). These include measures to encourage savings and investment in human and physical capital, as well as reforms to improve governance and alleviate intra-national frictions associated with market imperfections and transport costs (Bartley Johns et al. 2015). Without these accompanying policies, increased trade openness might have an adverse impact on poverty and inequality (World Bank 2015b; Le Goff and Singh 2013). This suggests the need for a multi-pronged agenda to pair trade liberalization with improved human capital development and institutional reforms to ensure that the gains from increased trade contribute effectively to poverty reduction and the promotion of shared prosperity.

TABLE 1.2 **List of emerging market and developing economies**[1]

Commodity Exporters[2]		Commodity Importers[3]	
Albania*	Madagascar	Afghanistan	Philippines
Algeria*	Malawi	Antigua and Barbuda	Poland
Angola*	Malaysia*	Bahamas, The	Romania
Argentina	Mali	Bangladesh	Samoa
Armenia	Mauritania	Barbados	Serbia
Azerbaijan*	Mongolia	Belarus	Seychelles
Bahrain*	Morocco	Bhutan	Solomon Islands
Belize	Mozambique	Bosnia and Herzegovina	St. Kitts and Nevis
Benin	Myanmar*	Bulgaria	St. Lucia
Bolivia*	Namibia	Cabo Verde	St. Vincent and the Grenadines
Botswana	Nicaragua	Cambodia	Swaziland
Brazil	Niger	China	Thailand
Burkina Faso	Nigeria*	Comoros	Tunisia
Burundi	Oman*	Croatia	Turkey
Cameroon*	Papua New Guinea	Djibouti	Tuvalu
Chad*	Paraguay	Dominica	Vanuatu
Chile	Peru	Dominican Republic	Vietnam
Colombia*	Qatar*	Egypt, Arab Rep.	
Congo, Dem. Rep.	Russia*	El Salvador	
Congo, Rep.*	Rwanda	Eritrea	
Costa Rica	Saudi Arabia*	Fiji	
Côte d'Ivoire	Senegal	Georgia	
Ecuador*	Sierra Leone	Grenada	
Equatorial Guinea*	South Africa	Haiti	
Ethiopia	Sri Lanka	Hungary	
Gabon*	Sudan*	India	
Gambia, The	Suriname	Jamaica	
Ghana*	Tajikistan	Jordan	
Guatemala	Tanzania	Kiribati	
Guinea	Timor-Leste*	Lebanon	
Guinea-Bissau	Togo	Lesotho	
Guyana	Tonga	Macedonia, FYR	
Honduras	Trinidad and Tobago*	Maldives	
Indonesia*	Turkmenistan*	Marshall Islands	
Iran, Islamic Rep.*	Uganda	Mauritius	
Iraq*	Ukraine	Mexico	
Kazakhstan*	United Arab Emirates*	Micronesia, Fed. Sts.	
Kenya	Uruguay	Moldova, Rep.	
Kosovo	Uzbekistan	Montenegro	
Kuwait*	Venezuela, RB*	Nepal	
Kyrgyz Republic	West Bank and Gaza	Pakistan	
Lao PDR	Zambia	Palau	
Liberia	Zimbabwe	Panama	

[1] Emerging Market and Developing Economies (EMDEs) includes all those that are not classified as advanced economies. Advanced economies include Australia; Austria; Belgium; Canada; Cyprus; the Czech Republic; Denmark; Estonia; Finland; France; Germany; Greece; Hong Kong SAR, China; Iceland; Ireland; Israel; Italy; Japan; the Republic of Korea; Latvia; Lithuania; Luxembourg; Malta; Netherlands; New Zealand; Norway; Portugal; Singapore; the Slovak Republic; Slovenia; Spain; Sweden; Switzerland; the United Kingdom; and the United States.

[2] Energy exporters are denoted by an asterisk. An economy is defined as commodity exporter when, on average in 2012-14, either (i) total commodities exports accounted for 30 percent or more of total goods exports or (ii) exports of any single commodity accounted for 20 percent or more of total goods exports. Economies for which these thresholds were met as a result of re-exports were excluded. When data were not available, judgment was used. This taxonomy results in the classification of some well-diversified economies as importers, even if they are exporters of certain commodities (e.g., Mexico).

[3] Commodity importers are all EMDE economies that are not classified as commodity exporters.

References

Adhikari, P. 2013. "Conflict–Induced Displacement, Understanding the Causes of Flight." *American Journal of Political Science* 57 (1): 82–89.

Adrian, T., R. Crump, and E. Moench. 2013. "Pricing the Term Structure with Linear Regressions." *Journal of Financial Economics* 110 (1): 110-138.

Adrian, T., D. Stackman, and E. Vogt. 2016. "Global Price of Risk and Stabilization Policies." Staff Report 786, Federal Reserve Bank of New York.

Ahcar, J., and J. M. Siroën. 2014. "Deep Integration: Free Trade Agreements Heterogeneity and its Impact on Bilateral Trade." IRD Working Paper, Paris Dauphine University.

Alesina, A., J. Harnoss, and H. Rapoport. 2013. "Birthplace Diversity and Economic Prosperity." NBER Working Paper 18699, National Bureau of Economic Research, Cambridge, Massachusetts.

Alexopoulos, M., and J. Cohen, J. 2015. "The Power of Print: Uncertainty Shocks, Markets, and the Economy." *International Review of Economics & Finance* 40 (2015): 8-28.

Andrade, P., J. Breckenfelder, F. De Fiore, P. Karadi, and O. Tristani. 2016. "The ECB's Asset Purchase Programme: An Early Assessment." ECB Working Paper Series 1956, European Central Bank, Frankfurt.

Andrews, D., C. Criscuolo, and P. N. Gal. 2015. "Frontier Firms, Technology Diffusion and Public Policy: Micro Evidence from OECD." Productivity Working Paper 2015-02, Organisation for Economic Co-operation and Development, Paris.

Ariu, A. 2016. "Crisis-Proof Services: Why Trade in Services did not Suffer During the 2008–2009 Collapse." *Journal of International Economics* 98: 138-149.

Arteta, C., M. A. Kose, F. Ohnsorge, and M. Stocker. 2015. "The Coming U.S. Interest Rate Tightening Cycle: Smooth Sailing or Stormy Waters?" Policy Research Note 15/02, World Bank, Washington, DC.

Arteta, C., M. A. Kose, M. Stocker, and T. Taskin. 2016. "Negative Interest Rate Policies: Sources and Implications." CEPR Discussion Paper 11433. Centre for Economic Policy Research, London.

Auerbach, A., and Y. Gorodnichenko. 2012. "Measuring the Output Responses to Fiscal Policy." *American Economic Journal: Economic Policy* 4 (2): 1-27.

Auerbach, A., and D. Holtz-Eakin. 2016. "The Role of Border Adjustments in International Taxation." Research Note, American Action Forum.

Auerbach, A., M. Devereux, M. Keen, and J. Vella. 2017. "Destination-Based Cash Flow Taxation." Working Paper Series 17/1, Oxford University Centre for Business Taxation.

Autor, D., D. Dorn, and G. Hanson. 2016. "The China Shock: Learning from Labor-Market Adjustment to Large Changes in Trade." *Annual Review of Economics* 8: 205-240.

Baba, C., and A. Kokenyne. 2011. "Effectiveness of Capital Controls in Selected Emerging Markets in the 2000s." IMF Working Paper 11/281, International Monetary Fund, Washington, DC.

Baffes, J., M. A. Kose, F. Ohnsorge, and M. Stocker. 2015. "The Great Plunge in Oil Prices: Causes, Consequences, and Policy Responses." Policy Research Note 1, World Bank, Washington, DC.

Baker, D., J. B. De Long, and P. Krugman. 2005. "Asset Returns and Economic Growth." Brookings Papers on Economic Activity, Brookings Institute, Washington, DC.

Baker, S., N. Bloom, and S. Davis. 2015. "Measuring Economic Policy Uncertainty." NBER Working Paper 21633, National Bureau of Economic Research, Cambridge, Massachusetts.

Ball, L. 2014. "The Case for a Long-Run Inflation Target of Four Percent." IMF Working Paper 14/92, International Monetary Fund, Washington, DC.

Ball, L., J. Gagnon, P. Honohan, and S. Krogstrup. 2016. "What Else Can Central Banks Do?" *Geneva Reports on the World Economy* 18 (2). Centre for Economic Policy and Research, London.

Banco Central do Brasil. 2017. "Inflation Report: March 2017." Banco Central do Brasil, Brasília.

Bank for International Settlements. 2016. "Uneasy Calm Gives Way to Turbulence." *BIS Quarterly Review* (March): 1-14.

Bank of Japan. 2016 "Comprehensive Assessment: Developments in Economic Activity and Prices as well as Policy Effects since the Introduction of Quantitative and Qualitative Monetary Easing (QQE)."

Bańkowski, K., M. Ferdinandusse, M. G. Attinasi, C. D. Checherita-Westphal, G. Palaiodimos, and M. M. Campos. 2017. "Euro Area Fiscal Stance." ECB Occasional Paper 182, European Central Bank, Frankfurt.

Bartley Johns, M., P. Brenton, M. Cali, M. Hoppe, and R. Piermartini. 2015. "The Role of Trade in Ending Poverty." World Trade Organization, Geneva.

Bernardini, M., and L. Forni. 2017. "Private and Public Debt: Are Emerging Markets at Risk?" IMF Working Paper 17/61, International Monetary Fund, Washington, DC.

Bivens, J. 2014. "The Short- and Long-Term Impact of Infrastructure Investments on Employment and Economic Activity in the U.S. Economy." EPI Briefing Paper #374, Economic Policy Institute, Washington, DC.

Blanchard, O. J., J. P. L'Huillier, and G. Lorenzoni. 2013. "News, Noise, and Fluctuations: An Empirical Exploration." *American Economic Review* 103 (7): 3045-3070.

Borchert, I., and A. Mattoo. 2009. "The Crisis-Resilience of Services Trade." *The Service Industries Journal* 30 (13): 2115-2136.

Bordo, M. D., J. V. Duca, and C. Koch. 2016. "Economic Policy Uncertainty and the Credit Channel: Aggregate and Bank Level U.S. Evidence over Several Decades." *Journal of Financial Stability* 26 (2016): 90-106.

Borjas, G. 2013. "Immigration and the American Worker: A Review of the Academic Literature." Center for Immigration Studies, April 2013.

Born, B., and J. Pfeifer. 2014. "Policy Risk and the Business Cycle." *Journal of Monetary Economics* 68 (2014): 68-85.

Born, B., A. Peter, and J. Pfeifer. 2013. "Fiscal News and Macroeconomic Volatility." *Journal of Economic Dynamics and Control* 37 (12): 2582-2601.

Bown, C. P., D. Lederman, S. Pienknagura, and R. Robertson. 2017. *Better Neighbors: Toward a Renewal of Economic Integration in Latin America.* Washington, DC: World Bank.

Boz, E., M. Bussière, and C. Marsilli. 2015. "Recent Slowdown in Global Trade: Cyclical or Structural?" In *The Global Trade Slowdown: A New Normal?*, edited by Bernard Hoekman. http://www.VoxEU.org.

Brainard, L. 2017. "Monetary Policy in a Time of Uncertainty." Speech at the Brookings Institution, Washington, DC, January 2017.

Broda, C., N. Limao, and D. E. Weinstein. 2008. "Optimal Tariffs and Market Power: the Evidence." *American Economic Review* 98 (5): 2032-2065.

Brogaard, J., and A. Detzel. 2015. "The Asset-Pricing Implications of Government Economic Policy Uncertainty." *Management Science* 61 (1): 3-18.

Brückner, M., and E. Pappa. 2015. "News Shocks in the Data: Olympic Games and Their

Macroeconomic Effects." *Journal of Money, Credit and Banking* 47 (7): 1339-1367.

Bruno, R., N. F. Campos, and S. Estrin. 2017. "The Benefits from Foreign Direct Investment in a Cross-Country Context: Meta-Analysis." CEPR Discussion Paper 11959, Centre for Economic Policy and Research, London.

Bruno, V., and H. S. Shin. 2015. "Capital Flows and the Risk-Taking Channel of Monetary Policy." *Journal of Monetary Economics* 71: 119-132.

Buera, J., and E. Oberfield. 2016. "The Global Diffusion of Ideas." NBER Working Paper 21844, National Bureau of Economic Research, Cambridge, MA.

Bussière, M., G. Callegari, F. Ghironi, G. Sestieri, and N. Yamano. 2013. "Estimating Trade Elasticities: Demand Composition and the Trade Collapse of 2008–09." *American Economic Journal: Macroeconomics* 5 (3): 118–51.

Cashin, P., K. Mohaddes, and M. Raissi. 2014. "The Differential Effects of Oil Demand and Supply Shocks on the Global Economy." *Energy Economics* 44: 113-134.

Cecchetti, S., and K. Schoenholtz. 2016. "The Bank of Japan at the Policy Frontier." VoxEU.org, December 7. http://voxeu.org/article/bank-japan-policy-frontier.

Cerdeiro, D., and D. Plotnikov. 2017. "Taking Stock: Who Benefited from the Oil Price Shocks?" IMF Working Paper No. 17/104, International Monetary Fund, Washington, DC.

Chen, K., and Y. Wen. Forthcoming 2017. "The Great Housing Boom of China." *American Economic Journal: Macroeconomics.*

Chow, J. T., F. Jaumotte, S. G. Park, and Y. S. Zhang. 2015. "Spillovers from Dollar Appreciation." IMF Policy Discussion Paper 15/2, International Monetary Fund, Washington, DC.

Christiano, L., M. Eichenbaum, and S. Rebelo. 2011. "When is the Government Spending Multiplier Large?" *Journal of Political Economy* 119 (1): 78 -121.

Chui, M., E. Kuruc, and P. Turner. 2016. "A New Dimension to Currency Mismatches in the Emerging Markets: Nonfinancial Companies." BIS Working Papers 550, Bank for International Settlements, Basel, Switzerland.

Ciccarelli, M., C. Osbat, E. Bobeica, C. Jardet, M. Jarocinski, C. Mendicino, A. Notarpietro, S. Santoro, and A. Stevens. 2017. "Low Inflation in the Euro Area: Causes and Consequences." ECB Occasional Paper Series 181, European Central Bank, Frankfurt.

Comin, D., and M. Mestieri. 2013. "Technology Diffusion: Measurement, Causes and Consequences." NBER Working Paper No. 19052, National Bureau of Economic Research, Cambridge, MA.

Copeland, D. 2014. *Economic Interdependence and War.* Princeton University Press: Princeton.

CBO (Congressional Budget Office). 2017. *The Budget and Economic Outlook: 2017 to 2027.* Washington, DC: Congressional Budget Office.

Constantinescu, I. C., A. Mattoo, and M. Ruta. 2017. *Global Trade Watch: Trade Developments in 2015.* Washington, DC: World Bank.

Cordes, T., T. Kinda, P. Muthoora, and A. Weber. 2015. "Expenditure Rules: Effective Tools for Sound Fiscal Policy?" IMF Working Paper 15/29, International Monetary Fund, Washington, DC.

Crowley, M. A., H. Song, and N. Meng. 2016. "Tariff Scares: Trade Policy Uncertainty and Foreign Market Entry by Chinese Firms." CEPR Discussion Paper 11722, Centre for Economic Policy and Research, London.

Dabla-Norris, E., G. Ho, and A. Kyobe. 2016. "Structural Reforms and Productivity Growth in Emerging Market and Developing Economies." IMF Working Paper 16/15, International Monetary Fund, Washington, DC.

Debrun, X., and T. Kinda. Forthcoming. "Strengthening Post-Crisis Fiscal Credibility: Fiscal Councils on the Rise." *Fiscal Studies.*

Decker, R., J. Haltiwanger, R. Jarmin, and J. Miranda. 2017. "Declining Dynamism, Allocative Efficiency, and the Productivity Slowdown." Finance and Economics Discussion Series 2017-019, Federal Reserve Board, Washington, DC.

De Santis, R. 2017. "Sovereign Spreads in the Eurozone on the Rise: Redenomination Risk versus Political Risk." VoxEU.org, March 16. http://voxeu.org/article/sovereign-spreads-eurozone-redenomination-versus-political-risk.

De Long, J. B. 2017. "NAFTA and other Trade Deals Have Not Gutted American Manufacturing—Period." Vox.org, January 24. http://www.vox.com/the-big-idea/2017/1/24/14363148/trade-deals-nafta-wto-china-job-loss-trump.

Diakantoni, A., H. Escaith, M. Roberts, and T. Verbeet. 2017. "Accumulating Trade Costs and Competitiveness in Global Value Chains." WTO Working Paper ERSD-2017-02, World Trade Organization, Geneva, Switzerland.

Dollar, D., and A. Kraay. 2004. "Trade, Growth, and Poverty." *The Economic Journal* 114 (493): F22-F49.

Eichengreen, B., P. Gupta, and O. Masetti. 2017. "Are Capital Flows Fickle? Increasingly? And Does the Answer Still Depend on Type?" Policy Research Paper 7972, World Bank, Washington, DC.

Engemann, K., K. Kliesen, and M. Owyang. 2011. "Do Oil Shocks Drive Business Cycles? Some U.S. and International Evidence." *Macroeconomic Dynamics* 15 (Supplement 3): 498–517.

ECB (European Central Bank). 2016. "Understanding the Weakness in Global Trade. What is the New Normal?" ECB Occasional Paper Series 178, European Central Bank, Frankfurt.

European Commission. 2014. "Cross-Border Spillovers in the Euro Area." *Quarterly Report on the Euro Area* 13 (4). Brussels, Belgium: European Commission.

_____. 2016. *Communication from the Commission to the European Parliament, the Council, the European Economic and Social Committee and the Committee of the Regions: Towards a Positive Fiscal Stance for the Euro Area.* Brussels: European Commission.

_____. 2017. "Winter 2017 Economic Forecast." Directorate-General for Economic and Financial Affairs, European Economy, Institutional Paper 048. European Commission, Brussels.

Evenett, S. J., and J. Fritz. 2016. "Global Trade Plateaus." *Global Trade Alert Report* 19. Centre for Economic Policy and Research, London.

Eyraud, L., V. Gaspar, and T. Poghosyan. 2017. "Fiscal Politics in the Euro Area." IMF Working Paper 17/18, International Monetary Fund, Washington, DC.

FOMC (Federal Open Market Committee). 2017. "Economic Projections of Federal Reserve Board Members and Federal Reserve Bank Presidents Under their Individual Assessments of Projected Appropriate Monetary Policy, March 2017." Board of Governors of the Federal Reserve System, Washington, DC.

Felipe, J., and A. Mehta. 2016. "Deindustrialization? A Global Perspective." *Economics Letters* 149: 148-151.

Fernández-Villaverde, J., P. Guerrón-Quintana, J. F. Rubio-Ramírez, and M. Uribe. 2011. "Risk Matters: the Real Effects of Volatility Shocks." *American Economic Review* 101 (6): 2530-2561.

Freund, C. 2016. "The Global Trade Slowdown and Secular Stagnation." Peterson Institute of International Economics blog. https://piie.com/blogs/trade-investment-policy-watch/global-trade-slowdown-and-secular-stagnation.

Ghodsi, M., S. Jokubauskaite, and R. Stehrer. 2015. "Non-Tariff Measures and the Quality of Imported Products." Mimeo, Vienna Institute for International Economic Studies.

Goldberg, P. K., and N. Pavcnik. 2004. "Trade, Inequality, and Poverty: What Do We Know? Evidence from Recent Trade Liberalization Episodes in Developing Countries." NBER Working Paper 10593, National Bureau of Economic Research, Cambridge, MA.

Gordon, R. 2014. "The Demise of U.S. Economic Growth: Restatement, Rebuttal, and Reflections." NBER Working Paper 19895, National Bureau of Economic Research, Cambridge, MA.

G20. 2015. *G20/OECD Report on G20 Investment Strategies. Vol 2.* Organisation for Economic Co-operation and Development, Paris.

Haltiwanger, J. 2015. "Top Ten Signs of Declining Business Dynamism and Entrepreneurship in the U.S." Manuscript, University of Maryland, August.

Hamilton, J. 2011. "Nonlinearities and the Macroeconomic Effects of Oil Prices." *Macroeconomic Dynamics* 15 (Suppl. 3): 364–78.

_____. 2017. "Measuring the Economic Effects of Uncertainty." Econbrowser blog, January 15. http://econbrowser.com/archives/2017/01/measuring-the-economic-effects-of-uncertainty.

Hofmann, C., A. Osnago, and M. Ruta. 2017. "Horizontal Depth: A New Database on the Content of Preferential Trade Agreements." Policy Research Working Paper 7981, World Bank, Washington, DC.

Hong, G. H., J. Lee, W. Liao, D. Seneviratne. 2016. "China and Asia in Global Trade Slowdown." IMF Working Paper 16/105, International Monetary Fund, Washington, DC.

Huidrom, R., M. A. Kose, and F. Ohnsorge. 2017. "How Important are Spillovers from Major Emerging Markets?" Discussion Paper No. 12022, Center for Economic and Policy Research, Washington, DC.

IMF (International Monetary Fund). 2014a. *Global Financial Stability Report: Risk Taking, Liquidity, and Shadow Banking.* Washington, DC: International Monetary Fund.

_____. 2014b. "The Liberalization and Management of Capital Flows: An Institutional View." International Monetary Fund, Washington, DC.

_____. 2015. *World Economic Outlook: Uneven Growth: Short and Long-Term Factors.* Washington, DC: International Monetary Fund.

_____. 2016a. "Macroeconomic Developments and Prospects in Low-Income Developing Countries—2016." Policy Paper, International Monetary Fund, Washington, DC.

_____. 2016b. *Global Financial Stability Report: Potent Policies for a Successful Normalization.* Washington, DC: International Monetary Fund.

_____. 2016c. "People's Republic of China 2015 Article IV Consultation—Staff Report." International Monetary Fund, Washington, DC.

_____. 2017a. "Global Prospects and Policy Challenges. G-20 Finance Ministers and Central Bank Governors' Meetings." International Monetary Fund, March 17-18.

_____. 2017b. "West African Economic and Monetary Union: Staff Report on Common Policies of Member Countries." Country Report No. 17/99, International Monetary Fund, Washington, DC.

_____. 2017c. Global Prospects and Policy Challenges. G-20 Finance Ministers and Central Bank Governors' Meetings. International Monetary Fund. March 17-18.

IMF (International Monetary Fund), World Bank, and WTO (World Trade Organization). 2017. "Making Trade an Engine of Growth for All the Case for Trade and for Policies to Facilitate Adjustment." Policy Paper, IMF, World Bank, and WTO, Washington, DC.

Jaumotte, F., K. Koloskova, and S. C. Saxena. 2016. *Impact of Migration on Income Levels in Advanced Economies.* Washington, DC: International Monetary Fund.

Jo, S. 2014. "The Effects of Oil Price Uncertainty on Global Real Economic Activity." *Journal of Money, Credit and Banking* 46 (6): 1113–35.

Jurado, K., S. C. Ludvigson, and S. Ng. 2015. "Measuring Uncertainty." *American Economic Review* 105 (3): 1177-1216.

Karnizova, L., and J. C. Li. 2014. "Economic Policy Uncertainty, Financial Markets and Probability of U.S. Recessions." *Economics Letters* 125 (2): 261-265.

Kawamoto, T., T. Ozaki, N. Kato, and K. Maehashi. 2017. "Methodology for Estimating Output Gap and Potential Growth Rate: An Update." Bank of Japan Research Paper.

Kiley, M., and J. Roberts. 2017. "Monetary Policy in a Low Interest Rate World." Brookings Paper on Economic Activity, Brookings Institute, Washington, DC.

Kose, M. A., C. Lakatos, F. Ohnsorge, and M. Stocker. 2017a. "The Global Role of the U.S. Economy: Linkages, Policies and Spillovers." Policy Research Working Paper 7962, World Bank, Washington, DC.

Kose, M. A., F. Ohnsorge, L. Ye, and E. Islamaj. 2017b. "Weakness in Investment Growth: Causes, Implications and Policy Responses." CAMA Working Papers 2017-19, Centre for Applied Macroeconomic Analysis, Crawford School of Public Policy, The Australian National University.

Lanz, R., and A. Maurer. 2015. "Services and Global Value Chains: Some Evidence on Servicification of Manufacturing and Services Networks." ERSD-2015-03, WTO Staff Working Paper, Geneva, Switzerland.

Lardy, N. R., and Z. Huang. 2017. "Chinese Private Investment Growth Decelerates Sharply in 2016." Peterson Institute of International

Economics blog. https://piie.com/blogs/china-economic-watch/chinese-private-investment-growth-decelerates-sharply-2016.

Le Goff, M., and R. J. Singh. 2013. "Can Trade Reduce Poverty in Africa?" Economic Premise 114, World Bank, Washington, DC.

Mattoo, A., A. Mulabdic, and M. Ruta. 2017. "Trade Creation and Trade Diversion in Deep Agreements." Mimeo, World Bank, Washington, DC.

Mojon, B. 2017. "Decoupling Eurozone and U.S. Interest Rates Using Unconventional Monetary Policy." VoxEU.org, March 4. http://voxeu.org/article/us-elections-interest-rates-and-europe-s-monetary-sovereignty.

Mokyr, J. 2014. "The Next Age of Invention: Technology's Future is Brighter than Pessimists Allow." *City Journal* (Winter).

Mulas-Granados, C., J. T. Jalles., M. Schena., and S. Gupta. 2017. "Governments and Promised Fiscal Consolidations: Do They Mean What They Say?" IMF Working Paper 17/39, International Monetary Fund, Washington, DC.

OECD (Organisation for Economic Co-operation and Development) and World Bank. 2017. "Policy Options to Foster More Inclusive Growth." G20 Framework Working Group, Varanasi, India.

Osada, M., M. Ojima, Y. Kurachi, K. Miura, and T. Kawamoto. 2016. "Economic Impact of the Tokyo 2020 Olympic Games." Bank of Japan Reports & Research Papers.

Osnago, A., N. Rocha, and M. Ruta. 2015. "Deep Trade Agreements and Vertical FDI: the Devil is in the Details." Policy Research Working Paper 7464, World Bank, Washington, DC.

Ossa, R. 2014. "Trade Wars and Trade Talks with Data." *American Economic Review* 104 (12): 4104-4146.

Page, B. 2017. "The Macroeconomic Effects of Taxes." TPC Federal Budget and Economy Brief, Tax Policy Center, Washington, DC.

Pastor, L., and P. Veronesi. 2013. "Political Uncertainty and Risk Premia." *Journal of Financial Economics* 110 (3): 520-545.

Peri, G. 2012. "The Effect of Immigration on Productivity: Evidence from U.S. States." *Review of Economics and Statistics* 94 (1): 348-358.

Perroni, C., and J. Whalley. 2000. "The New Regionalism: Trade Liberalization or Insurance?" *Canadian Journal of Economics* 33 (1): 1–24.

Rachel, L., and T. Smith. 2015. "Secular Drivers of the Global Real Interest Rate." Staff Working Paper 571, Bank of England, London.

Rouzet, D., and S. Miroudot. 2013. "The Cumulative Impact of Trade Barriers Along The Value Chain: An Empirical Assessment Using the OECD Inter-Country Input-Output Model." Paper prepared for the 16th Annual Conference on Global Economic Analysis, Shanghai, China.

Sachs, J. D., and A. M. Warner. 1995. "Natural Resource Abundance and Economic Growth." NBER Working Paper 5398, National Bureau of Economic Research, Cambridge, MA.

Shintani, K., Y. Kurachi, S. Nishioka, and T. Okamoto. 2016. "Administered Prices in Japan: Institutional Comparisons with Europe and the United States." Bank of Japan Review 16-E-9, Bank of Japan.

Sims, C. 2016. "Fiscal Policy, Monetary Policy and Central Bank Independence." Paper prepared for the 2016 Economic Symposium, Jackson Hole, Wyoming.

Tabakis, C., and M. Zanardi. 2016. "Antidumping Echoing." *Economic Inquiry* 55 (2): 655-681.

UNIDO (United Nations Industrial Development Organization). 2011. *Africa Investor Report: Towards Evidence-Based Investment Promotion Strategies.* December 2011. Vienna: United Nations.

Werner, A. M., G. Adler, and N. E. Magud. 2017. "Terms-of-Trade Cycles and External Adjustment." IMF Working Paper 17/29, International Monetary Fund, Washington, DC.

Whalen, C., and F. Reichling. 2015. "The Fiscal Multiplier and Economic Policy Analysis in the United States." Working Paper Series 2015/02, Congressional Budget Office, Washington, DC.

Winters, L. A., N. McCulloch, and A. McKay. 2004. "Trade Liberalization and Poverty: The Evidence So Far." *Journal of Economic Literature* 42 (1): 72-115.

Wood, A. 2017. "Variation in Structural Change Around the World, 1985-2015: Patterns, Causes, and Implications." WIDER Working Paper 2017/34, World Institute for Development Economic Research, Helsinki, Finland.

World Bank. 2015a. *Global Economic Prospects: Having Fiscal Space and Using It.* January 2015. Washington, DC: World Bank.

_____. 2015b. *Global Monitoring Report 2015/2016: Development Goals in an Era of Demographic Change.* Washington, DC: World Bank.

_____. 2016a. *Global Economic Prospects: Divergences and Risks.* June 2016. Washington, DC: World Bank.

_____. 2016b. *East Asia and Pacific Economic Update: Reducing Vulnerabilities.* October 2016. Washington, DC: World Bank.

_____. 2016c. *Global Economic Prospects: Spillovers amid Weak Growth.* January 2016. Washington, DC: World Bank.

_____. 2017a. *Global Economic Prospects: Weak Investment in Uncertain Times.* January 2017. Washington, DC: World Bank.

_____. 2017b. "East Asia Pacific Economic Update." April. World Bank, Washington, DC.

_____. 2017c. "Commodity Markets Outlook: Investment Weakness in Commodity Exporting Countries." World Bank, Washington, DC.

_____. 2017d. "Russia Monthly Economic Developments." March issue. World Bank, Washington, DC.

_____. 2017e. "Europe and Central Asia Economic Update." May issue. World Bank, Washington, DC.

_____. 2017f. "Africa's Pulse." Volume 15, April 2017, World Bank, Washington, DC.

_____. 2017g. *World Development Report 2017: Governance and the Law.* Washington, DC: World Bank.

_____. 2017h. *Doing Business 2017: Equal Opportunity for All.* Washington, DC: World Bank.

_____. 2017i. *Better Neighbors: Toward a Renewal of Economic Integration in Latin America.* Washington, DC: World Bank.

Yellen, J. 2017. "From Adding Accommodation to Scaling It Back." Speech at the Executives' Club of Chicago, Chicago, Illinois, March 3.

SPECIAL FOCUS 1

Debt Dynamics in Emerging Market and Developing Economies: Time to Act?

Debt Dynamics in Emerging Market and Developing Economies: Time to Act?

Since the global financial crisis, rising private sector debt and deteriorating government debt dynamics have made some emerging market and developing economies (EMDEs) more vulnerable to financing shocks. Specifically, at end-2016, government debt exceeded its 2007 level by more than 10 percentage points of GDP in more than half of EMDEs and the fiscal balance worsened from its 2007 level by more than 5 percentage points of GDP in one-third of EMDEs. Although many EMDEs have strengthened their monetary policy frameworks and accumulated significant reserve buffers over the past two decades, they now need to shore up their fiscal positions to prevent sudden spikes in financing cost from forcing them into fiscal tightening.

Introduction

As growth becomes more durable and inflation rates get closer to central banks' targets, monetary policy in advanced economies is expected to normalize. While this normalization is likely to proceed smoothly, there is a possibility that it could stir financial market volatility with adverse implications for EMDEs (Arteta et al. 2015). In many EMDEs, both public and private sector vulnerability to financing cost spikes has risen since the global financial crisis.

Government debt dynamics in EMDEs have deteriorated since the global financial crisis (Huidrom, Kose, and Ohnsorge 2016; World Bank 2015a). On average across EMDEs, government debt has risen by 12 percentage points of GDP since 2007 to 47 percent of GDP by 2016, and fiscal deficits have widened to about 5 percent of GDP in 2016 from a surplus of roughly 1 percent of GDP in 2007 (Figure SF1.1). At end-2016, government debt exceeded its 2007 level by more than 10 percentage points of GDP in more than half of EMDEs. In addition, the fiscal balance worsened from 2007 levels by more than 5 percentage points of GDP in one-third of EMDEs.

Benign financing conditions have contributed to shifts in the composition of government balance sheets, but not always to strengthen its resilience (Kose et al., forthcoming). In the median EMDE,

FIGURE SF1.1 Evolution of fiscal space in EMDEs

In many EMDEs, both government and private sector debt has risen sharply since the global financial crisis. During periods of severe financial stress, private sector debt can burden public balance sheets.

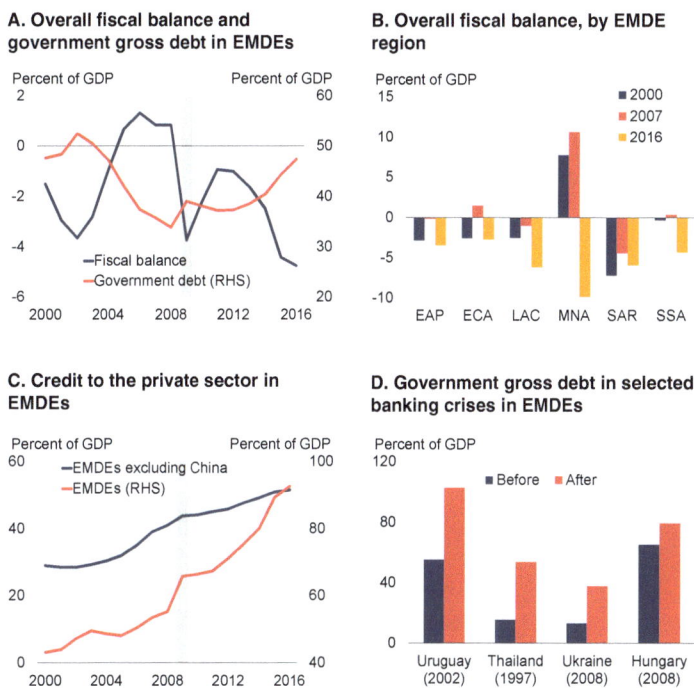

A. Overall fiscal balance and government gross debt in EMDEs

B. Overall fiscal balance, by EMDE region

C. Credit to the private sector in EMDEs

D. Government gross debt in selected banking crises in EMDEs

Sources: International Monetary Fund, World Bank.
A.-C. GDP-weighted averages.
A.C. The year of global recession (2009) is shaded in gray.
B. EAP, ECA, LAC, MNA, SAR, and SSA stand for, respectively, East Asia and Pacific, Europe and Central Asia, Latin America and the Caribbean, Middle East and North Africa, South Asia, and Sub-Saharan Africa.
D. The year of the onset of banking crises is in parentheses. Bars show average general government gross debt-to-GDP ratios in the two years before and the two years after the onset of crises.

for example, the share of short-term components of debt securities held by nonresidents has been smaller since 2007. However, the share of nonresident-held debt itself has risen and the maturity of government debt has been on a

---

Note: This Special Focus was prepared by M. Ayhan Kose, Franziska Ohnsorge, and Naotaka Sugawara.

FIGURE SF1.2 Debt relief under the HIPC and MDRI initiatives

Debt relief from both multilateral and bilateral creditors has helped significantly reduce debt in recipient countries.

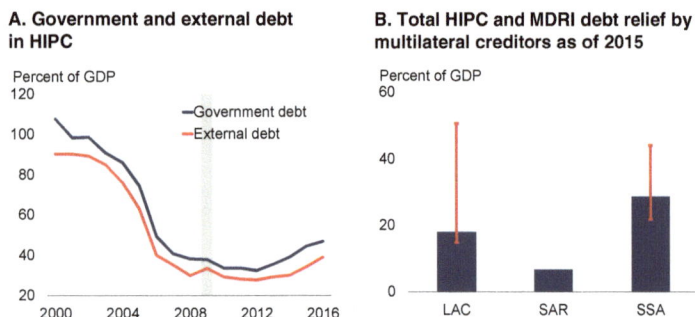

A. Government and external debt in HIPC

B. Total HIPC and MDRI debt relief by multilateral creditors as of 2015

Sources: IMF (2016a), International Monetary Fund, World Bank.
Note: There are a total of 36 Heavily Indebted Poor Countries (HIPC) that have reached completion points as of April 2017: 5 from Latin America and the Caribbean (LAC), 1 from South Asia (SAR), and 30 from Sub-Saharan Africa (SSA).
A. GDP-weighted average general government gross debt and external debt in 36 HIPC. The year of global recession (2009) is shaded in gray.
B. Blue bars refer to median, red lines to interquartile range. Both HIPC assistance committed (under the assumption of full participation of creditors) and MDRI (multilateral debt relief initiative) delivered by multilateral creditors as of end-August 2015 are included. GDP data are for 2015.

declining path. The share of government debt in foreign currency has increased in the median EMDE since the late 2000s.

In addition, private sector debt in EMDEs has risen sharply since 2007, reflecting a combination of financial deepening and credit booms. Since 2007, domestic bank credit to the private sector has risen by 12 percentage points of GDP to 52 percent of GDP in 2016 (excluding China) and by more than 20 percentage points of GDP in one-fifth of EMDEs. Firm-level data also suggest that the corporate sector has become more financially fragile since the global financial crisis as solvency positions weakened (Alfaro et al. 2017). During episodes of severe financial stress, private sector debt may become a contingent liability for the public sector. For example, before 2008, some EMDEs suffered systemic banking crises that required governments to provide substantial financial support. Though typically not fully reflected in deficits, such outlays significantly increased public debt above and beyond increases attributable to an accumulation of fiscal imbalances (Laeven and Valencia 2013). As these experiences show, the fiscal space implicit in low debt levels can shrink rapidly during periods of elevated financial stress.

Long-term government debt dynamics depend on debt and deficits but also on the macroeconomic context, especially the paths of GDP growth and interest rates. This Special Focus examines the evolution of EMDE fiscal positions since the global financial crisis as well as during typical episodes of financial stress. To do so, it combines fiscal indicators and macroeconomic factors into a single measure of government debt dynamics: the fiscal sustainability gap, defined as the difference between the actual fiscal balance and the debt-stabilizing fiscal balance.[1] Specifically, this Special Focus addresses the following questions:

- How have fiscal positions in EMDEs evolved since the global financial crisis?

- How do fiscal positions typically evolve during episodes of financial stress?

Evolution of fiscal positions

Definitions. A simple summary metric of the evolution of government debt dynamics is the fiscal sustainability gap (Blanchard 1993; Buiter 1985; Cottarelli and Escolano 2014; Escolano 2010). The fiscal sustainability gap compares a country's actual fiscal balance with its debt-stabilizing balance. The debt-stabilizing balance captures the long-term, cumulative impact of sustained fiscal deficits on debt stocks under assumed macroeconomic and financial conditions. For example, the debt burden generated by sustained fiscal deficits will be easier to service if interest rates are lower and growth (and, hence, the potential for tax revenue raising) is stronger.

Specifically, the sustainability gap (*pbsusgap*) for country c in year t is defined (in Kose et al., forthcoming) as:

$$pbsusgap_{c,t} = p_{c,t} - \left(\frac{i_c - \gamma_c}{1 + \gamma_c}\right) d_c^*,$$

where p is the primary balance (in percent of GDP), i is the nominal interest rate, γ the

[1] The analysis in this Special Focus is based on a new database on fiscal space, which includes a wide range of indicators of fiscal space for a large number of countries over the period of 1990-2016 (Kose et al., forthcoming).

nominal GDP growth, and d^* the target debt ratio (in percent of GDP) defined as the country-specific historical median ratio. The interest rate and nominal GDP growth are evaluated at their fixed long-term averages.[2] Implicitly, this assumes that future trends will not deviate materially from their long-term averages and that the historical median debt level is an appropriate reference point for future sustainable debt levels. This approach yields similar results to that of a common benchmark: the median debt ratio across all EMDEs over 1990-2016 (about 45 percent of GDP). A positive gap indicates a primary balance that would, over time, diminish government debt below its historical median, if sustained. Conversely, a negative gap shows a primary balance that would increase the stock of debt above its historical median.[3] These sustainability gaps are calculated for 72 EMDEs for 1990-2016.[4]

Evolution. Since 2000, debt sustainability in EMDEs has steadily improved as debt stocks declined and deficits narrowed or turned into surpluses. Among low-income countries, this partly reflected major debt relief initiatives such as the Highly Indebted Poor Countries (HIPC) initiative and the Multilateral Debt Relief Initiative (MDRI). The largest beneficiaries of these initiatives were EMDEs in Sub-Saharan Africa (SSA) and Latin America and the Caribbean (LAC) (Figure SF1.2; IMF 2016a). Between the HIPC decision and completion dates, government debt in recipient countries fell by up to 150 percentage points of GDP.

Following a steady pre-crisis improvement, government debt dynamics have deteriorated sharply since the global financial crisis (Figure

---

[2]This assumption implies that variations over time in the sustainability gap are only attributable to changes in debt and deficits. It also implies that sharp exchange rate swings do not affect the benchmark stock of debt, although they affect fiscal balances through higher interest cost.

[3]Depending on country specifics, some countries may be able to support debt above historical medians (i.e., run negative sustainability gaps) for extended periods of time, whereas financial markets may force others to reduce debt below its historical median (i.e., run positive sustainability gaps).

[4]Sustainability can also be defined as the difference between the level of government debt and the debt limit, defined as the value at which debt becomes unsustainable (Ostry et al. 2010). The existing literature employs different analytical frameworks to examine fiscal sustainability (e.g., Bohn 1998; Kose et al., forthcoming).

FIGURE SF1.3 **Evolution of sustainability gaps**

In EMDEs, fiscal sustainability has deteriorated materially from pre-crisis averages. The deterioration was largest among commodity-exporting EMDEs.

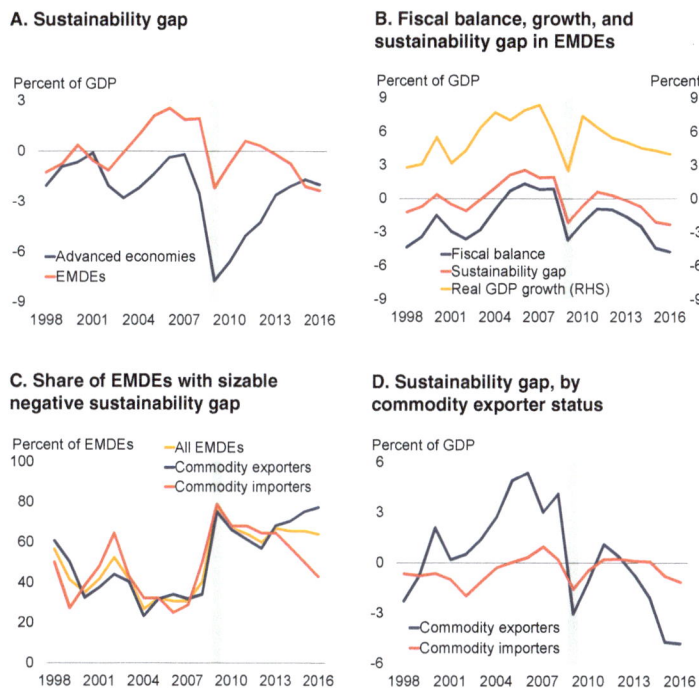

A. Sustainability gap

B. Fiscal balance, growth, and sustainability gap in EMDEs

C. Share of EMDEs with sizable negative sustainability gap

D. Sustainability gap, by commodity exporter status

Sources: International Monetary Fund, World Bank.
Note: A sustainability gap is defined as the difference between the actual fiscal balance and the debt-stabilizing balance. The year of global recession (2009) is shaded in gray.
A.B.D. GDP-weighted averages.
B. Figure shows overall fiscal balance.
C. Share of EMDEs with negative sustainability gaps of 1 percent of GDP or more. Sample includes 72 EMDEs, consisting of 44 commodity-exporting economies and 28 commodity-importing economies.
D. Samples include 44 commodity-exporting EMDEs and 28 commodity-importing EMDEs.

SF1.3). In EMDEs, debt-reducing fiscal positions (i.e., positive sustainability gaps of, on average, almost 2 percent of GDP) in 2007 turned into debt-increasing fiscal positions (i.e., negative gaps of more than 2 percent of GDP, on average) by 2016. In the two-thirds of EMDEs that are commodity-exporting, this deterioration partly reflected the sharp growth slowdown that accompanied the steep post-crisis slide in commodity prices. In commodity-importing EMDEs, fiscal positions remain weak as a result of fiscal stimulus implemented during the global financial crisis, chronic primary deficits, and, in some EMDEs, anemic post-crisis growth.

By 2016, fiscal positions in most EMDEs set government debt on clearly rising trajectories. Negative sustainability gaps exceeded 1 percent of GDP in roughly 80 percent of commodity-

FIGURE SF1.4 Evolution of fiscal space in EMDE regions

Sustainability gaps are particularly wide in MENA, LAC, and SSA, which host a large number of commodity-exporting EMDEs, whereas rapid growth supported sustainability in EAP and SAR.

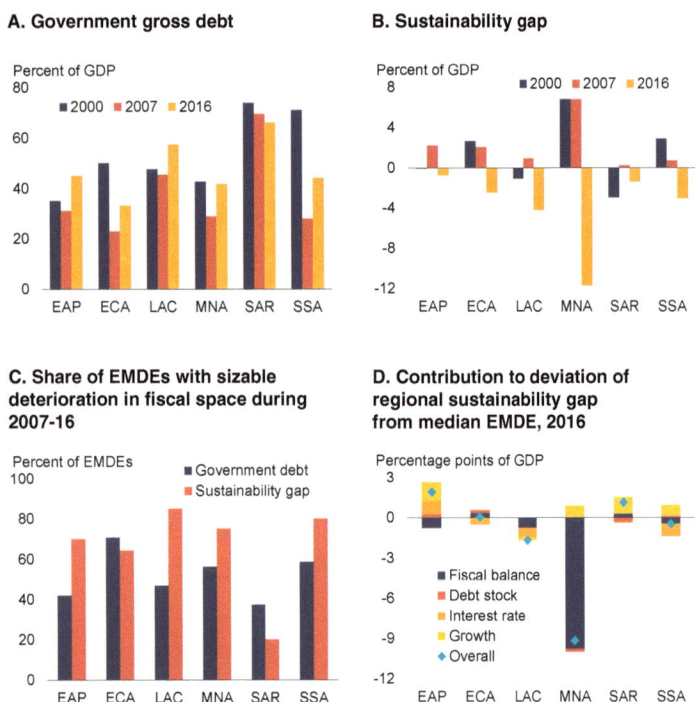

A. Government gross debt

Percent of GDP

■ 2000 ■ 2007 ■ 2016

EAP, ECA, LAC, MNA, SAR, SSA

B. Sustainability gap

Percent of GDP

■ 2000 ■ 2007 ■ 2016

EAP, ECA, LAC, MNA, SAR, SSA

C. Share of EMDEs with sizable deterioration in fiscal space during 2007-16

Percent of EMDEs

■ Government debt
■ Sustainability gap

EAP, ECA, LAC, MNA, SAR, SSA

D. Contribution to deviation of regional sustainability gap from median EMDE, 2016

Percentage points of GDP

■ Fiscal balance
■ Debt stock
■ Interest rate
■ Growth
◆ Overall

EAP, ECA, LAC, MNA, SAR, SSA

Sources: International Monetary Fund, World Bank.

Note: GDP-weighted averages. EAP, ECA, LAC, MNA, SAR, and SSA stand for, respectively, East Asia and Pacific, Europe and Central Asia, Latin America and the Caribbean, Middle East and North Africa, South Asia, and Sub-Saharan Africa.

C. For government debt, a sizable deterioration refers to an increase, between 2007 and 2016, by at least 10 percentage points of GDP in government gross debt (about top quarter of nine-year changes in all the EMDEs since 1990). For sustainability gaps, a sizable deterioration refers to a decline by at least 1 percentage point of GDP over 2007-16.

D. Bars show the contribution of each factor to the deviation of the region's GDP-weighted average sustainability gap from the hypothetical median sustainability gap in 2016 assuming the median primary deficit (1.9 percent of GDP), median stock of debt (45 percent of GDP), median long-term interest rate (9 percent), and median growth (7.4 percent). For example, MNA has, on average, about 9.2 percentage points of GDP wider negative sustainability gaps than the median EMDE, even though growth is higher than and interest rates are the same as in the median EMDE. Of this, about 9.9 percentage points is attributed to wider-than-median fiscal deficits that are only partially offset by faster-than-median growth (by 0.9 percentage points of GDP).

exporting EMDEs and in about 40 percent of commodity-importing EMDEs. In more than 70 percent of EMDEs, debt dynamics had worsened materially (i.e., sustainability gaps had deteriorated by more than 1 percentage point of GDP) from 2007. In principle, temporary negative sustainability gaps that are quickly reversed would be of limited concern; however, sustainability gaps and fiscal deficits in EMDEs have worsened steadily since 2012. That said, in 27 percent of EMDEs, debt dynamics in 2016 were still more favorable than in 2000, when a period of steady improvement began that lasted until the global financial crisis.

Regional dimensions. Pre-crisis improvements and post-crisis deteriorations in government debt dynamics were most pronounced in regions hosting large numbers of commodity-exporting countries (LAC, Middle East and North Africa (MENA), and SSA; Figure SF1.4). In Europe and Central Asia (ECA), falling commodity prices in the eastern part of the region and private sector deleveraging in the western part following the global financial crisis slowed growth from pre-crisis rates. This aggravated the challenges of debt sustainability despite fiscal consolidation efforts that kept fiscal deficits the smallest among EMDE regions. Sustainability gaps have remained positive since the global financial crisis in East Asia and Pacific (EAP) but narrowed to below-zero in 2016. In South Asia (SAR), sizable primary deficits contributed to persistently negative sustainability gaps through most of the 2000s, although deficits and negative sustainability gaps have narrowed since the global financial crisis.

In 2016, the drivers of fiscal sustainability gaps differed across regions. In MENA, EAP, LAC and SSA, above-median fiscal deficits widened sustainability gaps.[5] In EAP, and to a much lesser extent in MENA, this was mitigated by above-median growth and below-median interest rates (in EAP). In LAC and to a lesser extent in SSA, in contrast, weak growth (in LAC) and elevated interest rates (in both) compounded fiscal sustainability concerns. In SAR, strong growth was the main source of above-median sustainability gaps.

Deep fiscal deteriorations have taken place throughout SSA and LAC (IMF 2016b; World Bank 2017a, 2017b). On average, fiscal sustainability gaps widened between 2007 and 2016—by 4 percentage points of GDP (to -3 percent of GDP) in SSA and by 5 percentage points of GDP (to -4 percent of GDP) in LAC. This deterioration reflects both rising debt levels, especially in SSA, and widening fiscal deficits, especially in LAC. The erosion of fiscal sustainability was widespread in both regions: In SSA, the share of EMDEs with sizable

---

[5]For comparison, the median sustainability gap is defined as that implied by the median primary deficit (1.9 percent), median stock of debt (45 percent of GDP), median growth (7.4 percent) and median long-term interest rate (9 percent).

deterioration in sustainability gaps (i.e., worsened by 1 percentage point of GDP or more) over 2007-16 was 80 percent; in LAC, 85 percent of economies in the region experienced sizable deteriorations over the same period. In both regions, improvements in government debt dynamics that occurred in the early 2000s were unwound by 2016.

Weakening government debt dynamics in those regions were also accompanied by a rapid increase in private sector debt, although from modest initial levels, reflecting a combination of financial deepening and credit booms (World Bank 2016). In 2016, private credit by domestic banks averaged 48 percent of GDP in LAC and 29 percent of GDP in SSA. In one-third of EMDEs in SSA and more than one-quarter of EMDEs in LAC, private sector credit rose by more than 10 percentage points of GDP between 2007 and 2016.

Fiscal positions in episodes of financial stress

The deterioration in government debt dynamics since the global financial crisis is considerably more persistent than after previous episodes of financial stress. For EMDE commodity exporters, such episodes of financial stress can also be associated with terms-of-trade shocks. EMDEs typically emerge within two years of such episodes with restored government debt dynamics. After adverse terms-of-trade shocks, a deterioration in government debt dynamics is typically rapidly reversed.

Financial stress episodes. To analyze the evolution of fiscal debt sustainability around financial stress events since 1990, 117 episodes are identified in 94 EMDEs for which data on government debt, fiscal balance, sustainability gaps, and private sector credit are available (Gourinchas and Obstfeld 2012; Laeven and Valencia 2013). Figure SF1.5 presents the evolution of debt sustainability around these stress episodes, including banking, currency and debt crises, and compares these events against recent developments.

FIGURE SF1.5 Debt dynamics around financial stress events and in 2016

Within two years of financial stress episodes in EMDEs, government debt typically returns to a stable path.

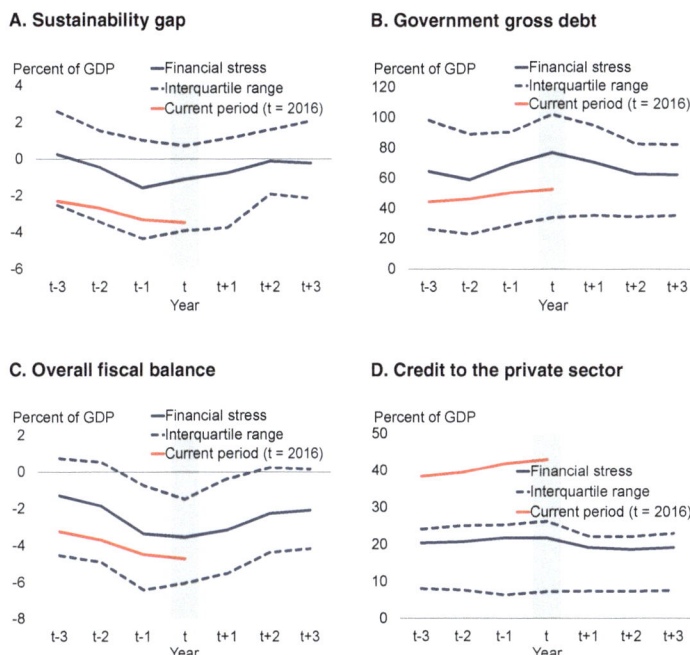

A. Sustainability gap

B. Government gross debt

C. Overall fiscal balance

D. Credit to the private sector

Sources: International Monetary Fund, World Bank.
Note: Year t refers to the year of onset of financial stress episodes. The solid blue lines are simple averages for all episodes, while the dashed blue lines show the interquartile range. The red line is shown for reference and based on all EMDEs, although it is not a stress episode. Financial stress episodes are taken from Gourinchas and Obstfeld (2012) and Laeven and Valencia (2013). When consecutive events are identified within a five-year period in a country, the one associated with the lowest real GDP growth is used.
A.-C. Separately, the statistical significance of restored government debt dynamics in two and three years after financial stress events, from deteriorations during stress events, is confirmed in a linear regression of each fiscal indicator on dummy variables for financial stress events (with up to three lags and leads), with country- and year-fixed effects.
C. Samples are restricted to episodes where data on sustainability gaps are available.

In the run-up to and during these stress episodes, debt dynamics typically deteriorated somewhat as fiscal balances and sustainability gaps weakened, government debt increased, in part because of support to banking systems (Tagkalakis 2013), and (often) exchange rate depreciation raised the local currency value of government debt. However, within two years of financial stress episodes, fiscal debt sustainability improved and debt returned to a stable path. This improvement may have partly reflected debt restructuring and the loss of access to financing that forces governments to rein in spending or raise revenues.

Oil price plunges. Some of the sharpest post-crisis deteriorations in fiscal positions have been among

FIGURE SF1.6 Debt dynamics in EMDE oil exporters around oil price plunges

Oil price plunges are historically accompanied by deteriorating fiscal debt sustainability in oil exporters, reflecting shrinking oil revenues, and weaker growth, but fiscal positions recover quickly after the initial shock.

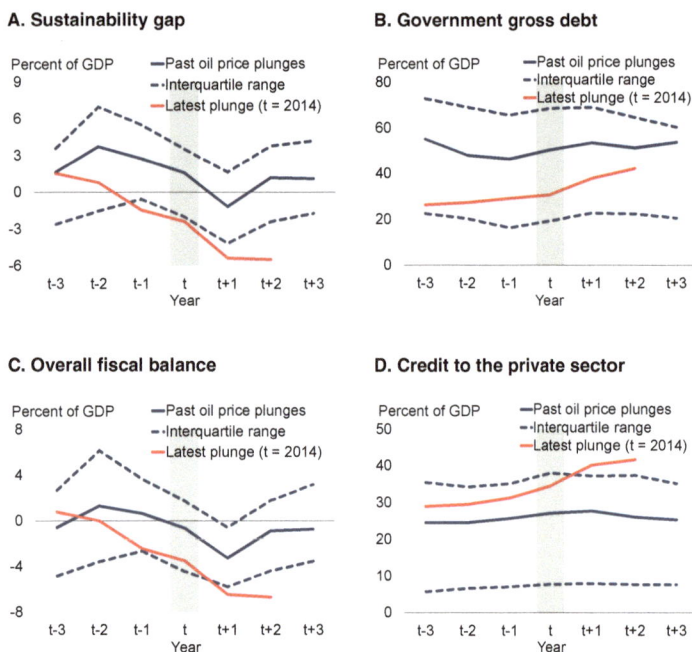

A. Sustainability gap

B. Government gross debt

C. Overall fiscal balance

D. Credit to the private sector

Sources: International Monetary Fund, World Bank.
Note: Year t refers to the year of oil price plunges. Past oil price plunges include collapses in global oil prices in 1991, 1998, 2001, and 2008 (World Bank 2015b). Simple averages of 36 EMDE oil exporters in all episodes. The red lines are for the latest plunge starting in 2014.
C. Samples are restricted to episodes where data on sustainability gaps are available.

energy exporters. Energy-exporting EMDEs rely heavily on fiscal revenues from the resource sector. For example, in 2014, on the eve of the most recent plunge in oil prices, hydrocarbon revenues accounted for more than half of fiscal revenues in Angola, Algeria, Azerbaijan, Iraq, Kuwait, Nigeria, Saudi Arabia, and the United Arab Emirates, and more than one-quarter of revenues in Mexico, the Islamic Republic of Iran, Kazakhstan, and the Russian Federation. The subsequent plunge in oil prices has forced some energy-exporting economies into severe fiscal adjustment and reserve losses (Danforth, Medas, and Salins 2016). Fiscal positions have deteriorated sharply in energy-exporting EMDEs, but less sharply than in earlier episodes of oil price plunges, albeit from a weaker starting position. Figure SF1.6 illustrates fiscal developments in energy-exporting EMDEs during the five major

collapses in global oil prices (in 1991, 1998, 2001, 2008, and 2014), as identified in World Bank (2015b).[6]

Fiscal positions deteriorated sharply during past oil price plunges but subsequently rebounded as a result of a pro-cyclical fiscal tightening. Initially debt-reducing fiscal positions (i.e., positive sustainability gaps of 3 percent of GDP) in the year before the average oil price plunge turned into debt-increasing fiscal positions (i.e., negative sustainability gaps of 1 percent of GDP), on average, in the year following the plunge as resource revenues declined. Within two years after the oil price plunge, however, sustainability gaps and fiscal balances were restored close to their pre-plunge levels. After a steep increase in the wake of the oil price plunge, government debt returned to a stable path. Depending on country circumstances and the depth of the growth slowdown triggered by the oil price plunge, private credit may rise (Miyajima 2017) or decline (Barajas et al. 2010). On average, a small increase in private credit in the year following the oil price plunge is mostly reversed in the subsequent years.

Comparison of current fiscal positions with historical experience. In 2016, despite lower government debt levels on average, government debt dynamics compared unfavorably with those on the eve of typical financial stress episodes and oil price plunges. At -3.5 percent of GDP, sustainability gaps in 2016 were weaker than those prior to the average financial stress episode (although still within the range of such episodes). This mainly reflected the rapid deterioration in fiscal balances in commodity-exporting EMDEs.

Notwithstanding weaker fiscal positions, non-fiscal buffers have strengthened in EMDEs over the 2000s. Monetary policy frameworks have improved. A growing share (more than one-

---

[6]The most recent oil price decline resembles that of 1985-86. The 1985-86 oil price slump was also associated with changing supply conditions, as OPEC reverted to its production target of 30 million barrels per day despite rising unconventional oil supply from the North Sea and Mexico (World Bank 2015b). Prices dropped 60 percent from January to July 1986, ringing in two decades of low oil prices—in contrast with other similarly sharp oil price drops that were quickly reversed.

quarter) of EMDEs with sizable negative sustainability gaps in 2016 anchored monetary policy in inflation-targeting regimes and allowed greater exchange rate flexibility (Figure SF1.7). International reserves in these economies rose from 8 percent of GDP in 2000 to 20 percent of GDP in 2016, on average. Before the oil price collapse of mid-2014, some energy exporters had accumulated sovereign wealth funds with assets amounting to more than one-third of GDP (e.g., Algeria, Azerbaijan, Botswana, Iraq, Kazakhstan, Kuwait, Norway, Saudi Arabia, the United Arab Emirates; World Bank 2015a). Their use helped ease exchange rate and fiscal adjustments to the sharp drop in oil prices since mid-2014.

Conclusion

Weak post-crisis growth and, for commodity exporters, sharp commodity price declines have eroded fiscal positions in many EMDEs. These developments have limited their ability to effectively employ fiscal policy to weather financing shocks (Huidrom et al. 2016). More than 70 percent of EMDEs—and more than four-fifths of those in SSA and LAC—now possess considerably worse government debt dynamics (with a deterioration in sustainability gaps of more than 1 percentage point of GDP) than in 2007.

If fiscal positions are weak on the eve of financial stress episodes or, in the case of commodity exporters, commodity price plunges, a sharp increase in financing costs may force governments into a pro-cyclical fiscal tightening. This—as well as debt restructurings or rapid inflation—may have bolstered fiscal sustainability during typical financial stress episodes in the past; however, in the current environment such pro-cyclical fiscal tightening might further retard the recovery.

Weakening government debt dynamics have been accompanied by mounting private sector debt. While most post-crisis credit booms in EMDEs have subsided, they have left a legacy of elevated debt in some EMDEs (World Bank 2016). By 2016, almost two-thirds of EMDEs with high private sector debt also had sizable negative sustainability gaps; conversely, two-thirds of

FIGURE SF1.7 **Vulnerabilities and buffers in EMDEs**

In several EMDEs, weak fiscal positions coincide with elevated private debt. However, improved external buffers and monetary policy frameworks could help mitigate risks.

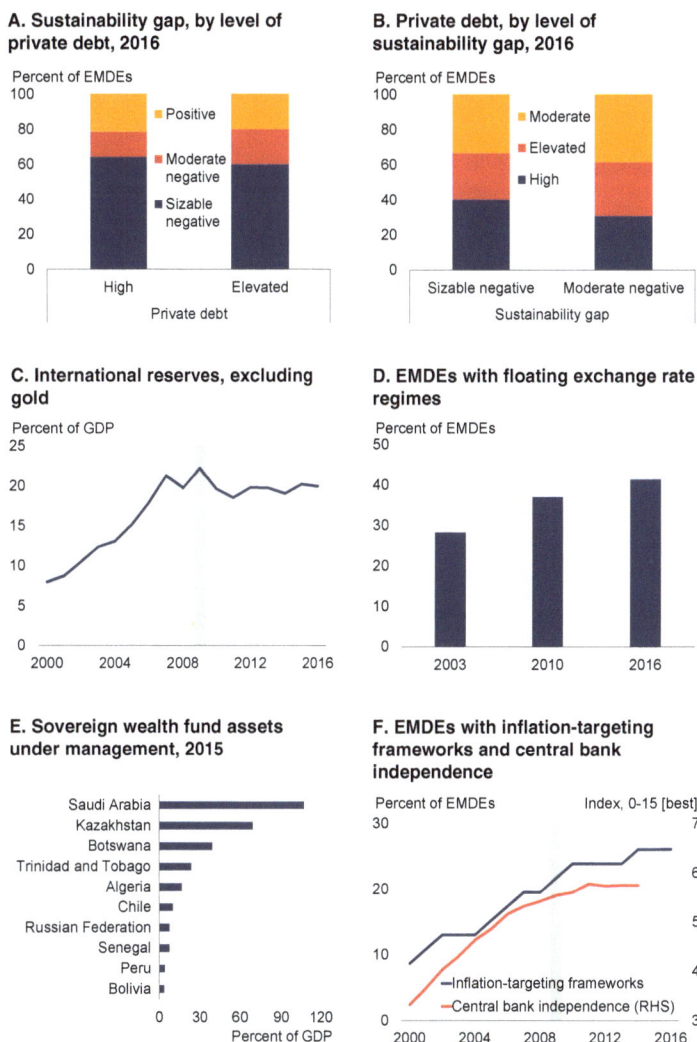

A. Sustainability gap, by level of private debt, 2016

B. Private debt, by level of sustainability gap, 2016

C. International reserves, excluding gold

D. EMDEs with floating exchange rate regimes

E. Sovereign wealth fund assets under management, 2015

F. EMDEs with inflation-targeting frameworks and central bank independence

Sources: Dincer and Eichengreen (2014), Hammond (2012), International Monetary Fund, Sovereign Wealth Fund Institute, World Bank.
A.B. Sample includes 70 EMDEs where data on sustainability gaps and private debt are available in 2016. Sustainability gaps are considered to be "sizable negative" when negative gaps are in excess of 1 percent of GDP and "moderate negative" when negative gaps are below 1 percent of GDP. "High" private debt is defined as private sector credit in the top quartile of the distribution among 70 EMDEs during 2000-16 (53 percent of GDP). "Elevated" private debt is defined as private sector credit in the second highest quartile (32-53 percent of GDP). Charts show the share of EMDEs with respective levels of sustainability gaps out of those with high or elevated private debt (A), and the share of EMDEs with respective levels of private debt out of those with "sizable negative" or "moderate negative" sustainability gaps (B).
C.-F. Sample includes 46 EMDEs with "sizable negative" sustainability gaps (in excess of 1 percent of GDP) in 2016.
C.F. The year of global recession (2009) is shaded in gray.
C. GDP-weighted average.
D. Floating exchange rate regimes are those classified as floating, free floating, or independently floating. Excluding countries with no separate legal tenders, currency boards, conventional fixed pegs, stabilized arrangements, crawling pegs, crawl-like arrangements including crawling bands, pegged exchange rates within horizontal bands, other managed (floating) arrangements (IMF 2016c).
E. For countries with multiple sovereign wealth funds, the sum of all funds' assets is presented. Countries where the size of assets under management in their funds is less than 3 percent of GDP are not shown.
F. Central bank independence is a simple average and measured as an index ranging from 0 to 15, showing the independence and transparency of central banks, based on multiple criteria in central bank objectives, institutions, operations, and policies.

EMDEs with sizable negative sustainability gaps had above-median private debt. In these countries, bouts of financial stress could curtail both private and public sector activity, with weaknesses in both amplifying each other.

While monetary policy normalization in major advanced economies will, in all likelihood, proceed smoothly, there remains a risk of episodes of financial market volatility. These episodes could be accompanied by sharp increases in financing cost for EMDEs. Against this backdrop, the simultaneous weakening of government and private sector balance sheets underscores the need to shore up fiscal positions.

In the short term, while global financial conditions remain benign, measures to strengthen the resilience of government balance sheets can be prioritized. In particular, some EMDE governments with ample market access can take advantage of still-low borrowing costs to lengthen the maturity profile of their debt or shift its currency composition toward domestic currency (World Bank 2015a). Such immediate steps can be complemented with broader public debt management reform measures. Depending on country circumstances, these range from better coordination between debt management, cash management and fiscal policy to legislation and regulation to streamline responsibilities and improved recording and reporting systems (World Bank 2007).

Several measures are also available to shore up fiscal sustainability directly. In many commodity importers, where growth has generally been robust since the global financial crisis, unexpected revenue windfalls can be set aside to reduce fiscal deficits and debt. Across EMDEs, structural reforms can be implemented that support fiscal credibility and generate long-term fiscal gains with limited short-term growth impact (e.g., pension reforms).

Across EMDEs, revenue collection efforts can be enhanced to raise spending envelopes. Such revenue measures could include broadening tax bases to remove loopholes for higher-income households or profitable corporates. In addition, a reallocation of expenditures away from less efficient expenditures (often subsidies) towards more growth-enhancing or better-targeted ones (such as public spending or means-tested income support) can be considered. In low-income countries, strong revenue bases and improvements in spending efficiency are essential to finance investment needed to achieve their development goals (Baum et al. 2017).

In addition to fiscal positions, improved policy frameworks and reserve buffers can mitigate the impact of terms of trade shocks (Adler, Magud, and Werner 2017). A growing number of EMDEs employ inflation targeting and allow greater exchange rate flexibility to absorb shocks. On average, reserve buffers have strengthened significantly and allowed, especially, energy-exporting EMDEs to soften the adjustment to prospects of lower commodity prices.

References

Adler, G., N. E. Magud, and A. Werner. 2017. "Terms-of-Trade Cycles and External Adjustment." Working Paper 17/29, International Monetary Fund, Washington, DC.

Alfaro, L., G. Asis, A. Chari, and U. Panizza. 2017. "Lessons Unlearned? Corporate Debt in Emerging Markets." NBER Working Paper 23407, National Bureau of Economic Research, Cambridge.

Arteta, C., M. A. Kose, F. Ohnsorge, and M. Stocker. 2015. "The Coming U.S. Interest Rate Tightening Cycle: Smooth Sailing or Stormy Waters?" Policy Research Note 2, World Bank, Washington, DC.

Barajas, A., R. Chami, R. Espinoza, and H. Hesse. 2010. "Recent Credit Stagnation in the MENA Region: What to Expect? What can be Done?" IMF Working Paper 10/219, International Monetary Fund, Washington, DC.

Baum, A., A. Hodge, A. Mineshima, M. Moreno Badia, and R. Tapsoba. 2017. "Can They Do It All? Fiscal Space in Low-Income Countries." IMF

Working Paper 17/110, International Monetary Fund, Washington, DC.

Blanchard, O. J. 1993. "Suggestions for a New Set of Fiscal Indicators." In *The Political Economy of Government Debt*, edited by H. A. A. Verbon and F. A. A. M. van Winden, 307–325. New York: North-Holland.

Bohn, H. 1998. "The Behavior of U.S. Public Debt and Deficits." *The Quarterly Journal of Economics* 113 (3): 949–963.

Buiter, W. H. 1985. "A Guide to Public Sector Debt and Deficits." *Economic Policy* 1 (1): 13–79.

Cottarelli, C., and J. Escolano. 2014. "Debt Dynamics and Fiscal Sustainability." In *Post-crisis Fiscal Policy*, edited by C. Cottarelli, P. R. Gerson, and A. S. Senhadji, 31–47. Cambridge: MIT Press.

Danforth, J., P. Medas, and V. Salins. 2016. "Fiscal Policy: How to Adjust to a Large Fall in Commodity Prices." IMF How to Notes 1, International Monetary Fund, Washington, DC.

Dincer, N. N., and B. Eichengreen. 2014. "Central Bank Transparency and Independence: Updates and New Measures." *International Journal of Central Banking* 10 (1): 189–253.

Escolano, J. 2010. "A Practical Guide to Public Debt Dynamics, Fiscal Sustainability, and Cyclical Adjustment of Budgetary Aggregates." IMF Technical Notes and Manuals 10/02, International Monetary Fund, Washington, DC.

Gourinchas, P.-O., and M. Obstfeld. 2012. "Stories of the Twentieth Century for the Twenty-First." *American Economic Journal: Macroeconomics* 4 (1): 226–265.

Hammond, G. 2012. "State of the Art of Inflation Targeting – 2012." Centre for Central Banking Studies Handbook 29, Bank of England, London.

Huidrom, R., M. A. Kose, and F. L. Ohnsorge. 2016. "Challenges of Fiscal Policy in Emerging and Developing Economies." World Bank Policy Research Working Paper 7725, World Bank, Washington, DC.

Huidrom, R., M. A. Kose, J. J. Lim, and F. L. Ohnsorge. 2016. "Do Fiscal Multipliers Depend on Fiscal Positions?" World Bank Policy Research Working Paper 7724, World Bank, Washington, DC.

IMF (International Monetary Fund). 2016a. "Heavily Indebted Poor Countries (HIPC) Initiative and Multilateral Debt Relief Initiative (MDRI)—Statistical Update." A report prepared by IMF and World Bank staff, International Monetary Fund, Washington, DC.

_____. 2016b. *Regional Economic Outlook: Western Hemisphere—Managing Transitions and Risks*. April. Washington, DC: International Monetary Fund.

_____. 2016c. *Annual Report on Exchange Rate Arrangements and Exchange Restrictions 2016*. Washington, DC: International Monetary Fund.

Kose, M. A, S. Kurlat, F. Ohnsorge, and N. Sugawara. Forthcoming. "A Cross-Country Database of Fiscal Space." World Bank Policy Research Working Paper, World Bank, Washington, DC.

Laeven, L., and F. Valencia. 2013. "Systemic Banking Crises Database." *IMF Economic Review* 61 (2): 225–270.

Miyajima, K. 2017. "What Influences Bank Lending in Saudi Arabia?" IMF Working Paper 17/31, International Monetary Fund, Washington, DC.

Ostry, J. D., A. R. Ghosh, J. I. Kim, and M. S. Qureshi. 2010. "Fiscal Space." IMF Staff Position Note 10/11, International Monetary Fund, Washington, DC.

Tagkalakis, A. 2013. "The Effects of Financial Crisis on Fiscal Positions." *European Journal of Political Economy* 29 (March): 197–213.

World Bank. 2007. *Managing Public Debt: From Diagnostics to Reform Implementation.* Washington, DC: World Bank.

_____. 2015a. *Global Economic Prospects: Having Fiscal Space and Using It.* January. Washington, DC: World Bank.

_____. 2015b. *Global Economic Prospects: The Global Economy in Transition.* June. Washington, DC: World Bank.

_____. 2016. *Global Economic Prospects: Divergences and Risks.* June. Washington, DC: World Bank.

_____. 2017a. *Africa's Pulse.* April. Washington, DC: World Bank.

_____. 2017b. *Leaning against the Wind: Fiscal Policy in Latin America and the Caribbean in a Historical Perspective.* April. Washington, DC: World Bank.

SPECIAL FOCUS 2

Arm's-Length Trade: A Source of Post-Crisis Trade Weakness

Arm's-Length Trade:
A Source of Post-Crisis Trade Weakness

Trade growth has slowed sharply since the global financial crisis. Based on U.S. trade data, arm's-length trade—trade between unaffiliated firms—accounts disproportionately for the overall post-crisis trade slowdown. This is partly because arm's-length trade depends more heavily than intra-firm trade on sectors with rapid pre-crisis growth that boosted arm's-length trade pre-crisis but that have languished post-crisis, and on emerging market and developing economies (EMDEs), where output growth has slowed sharply from elevated pre-crisis rates. Unaffiliated firms may also have been hindered more than multinational firms by constrained access to finance during the crisis, a greater sensitivity to adverse income and exchange rate movements, heightened policy uncertainty, and their typical firm-level characteristics.

Introduction

Global trade volume growth reached a post-crisis low of 2.4 percent in 2016—significantly below the pre-crisis average of 7.6 percent. Cyclical factors, such as weak global demand, low commodity prices, and slower growth in China have all contributed to the trade deceleration. In addition, structural factors have lowered trade's responsiveness to global output expansion (World Bank 2015a; Constantinescu, Mattoo, and Ruta 2015).

The maturing of global value chains is a key structural factor contributing to the recent trade slowdown.[1] Global value chains often involve numerous cross-border operations, conducted either "intra-firm," that is, between firms related through ownership or control, or between unaffiliated firms at "arm's-length." A firm's decision between arm's-length and intra-firm transactions has its roots in the underlying motivation for vertical integration (or lack thereof) and foreign direct investment. Firms choose to internalize transactions if the cost of performing these through the market is higher than internal costs (Coase 1937). In particular, contract enforcement imposes costs when contracts are incomplete (Williamson 1985;

Note: This Special Focus was prepared by Csilla Lakatos and Franziska Ohnsorge.

[1]The expansion of global value chains contributed significantly to the rapid rise in trade growth during 1985-2000. However, during 2000-16, growth in value chains has stabilized (Haugh et al. 2016; Constantinescu, Mattoo, and Ruta 2015).

FIGURE SF2.1 Trade growth

Since the global financial crisis, trade growth between unaffiliated companies ("arm's-length") has slowed considerably more steeply, and from more elevated pre-crisis rates, than between related firms ("intra-firm"). The resilience of multinationals was also reflected in the robust value added growth of their foreign affiliates.

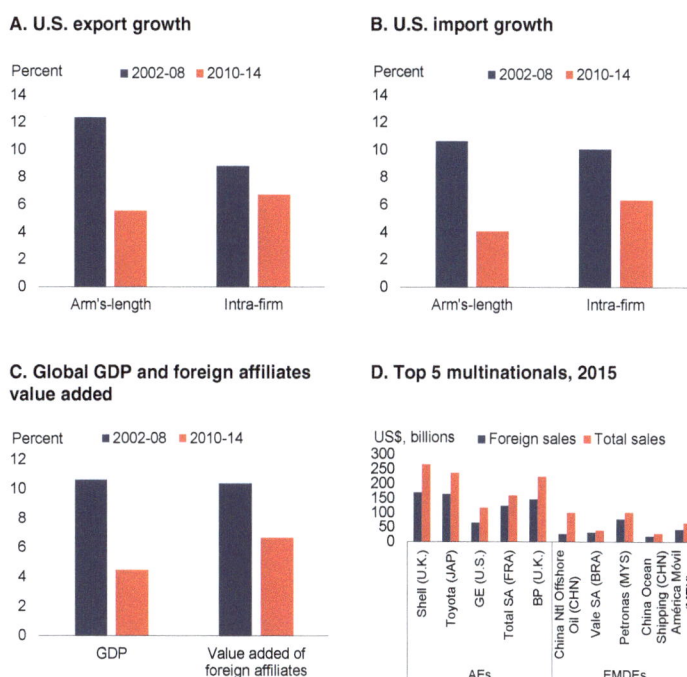

A. U.S. export growth

B. U.S. import growth

C. Global GDP and foreign affiliates value added

D. Top 5 multinationals, 2015

Sources: U.S. Census Bureau, UNCTAD.
A.B. U.S. exports and imports of goods based on data from the U.S. Census Bureau. Global data is not available.
C. Nominal terms. Value added of foreign affiliates is based on estimates from various editions of UNCTAD's *World Investment Report.*
D. Ranked by foreign assets in 2015. Excludes multinational companies in the financial sector. AEs stands for advanced economies. BRA=Brazil, CHN=China, FRA=France, JAP=Japan, MEX=Mexico, MYS=Malaysia.

Grossman and Hart 1986). When contracts are incomplete and their enforcement is costly, firms may prefer vertical integration and internal

FIGURE SF2.2 Role of the United States in trade and foreign direct investment

The United States plays an important role in global trade and foreign direct investment and is deeply integrated into global value chains.

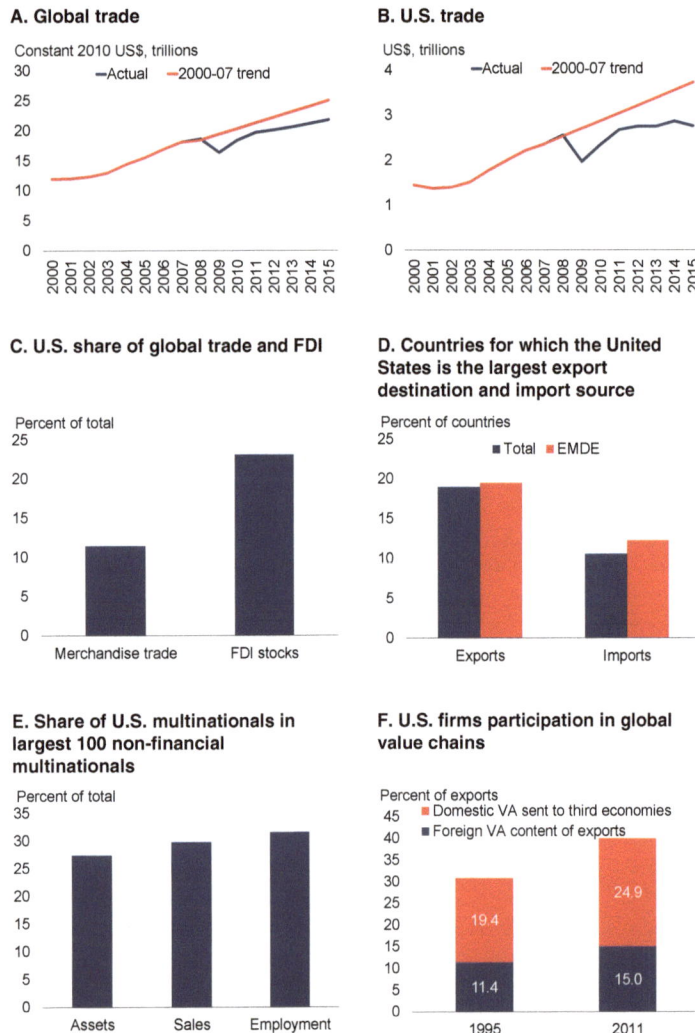

A. Global trade

B. U.S. trade

C. U.S. share of global trade and FDI

D. Countries for which the United States is the largest export destination and import source

E. Share of U.S. multinationals in largest 100 non-financial multinationals

F. U.S. firms participation in global value chains

Sources: UNCTAD, World Bank, WTO.
A.B. Includes merchandise and services imports.
C. Total of merchandise exports and imports and total of inward and outward FDI stocks.
D. The sample includes 190 countries, of which 139 EMDEs, for exports and 189 countries, of which 139 EMDEs, for imports.
F. VA refers to value added.

ownership of assets (Hart and Moore 1990; Antras 2015).[2]

---

[2]Incomplete contracts can result in underinvestment when firms undertake significant relationship-specific investments. Parties to a contract may underinvest in expectation of their counterpart not complying with the terms of a contract. As suppliers often customize their products to fit the needs of a specific buyer and buyers undertake significant investment specific to a particular supplier, such cost could be significant.

In cross-border trade transactions, additional considerations come into play. Firms may favor arm's-length transactions when they seek access to export markets similar to their home markets and when technology, knowledge, or resource transfers are not required (Dunning and Lundan 2008; Lanz and Miroudot 2011). As a result, arm's-length transactions are more prevalent in low-skilled sectors and among less productive firms (Corcos et al. 2013).

In practice, multinationals employ intra-firm and arm's-length transactions to varying degrees. In 2015, intra-firm transactions are estimated to have accounted for about one-third of global exports (UNCTAD 2016). Vertically integrated multinational companies, such as Samsung Electronics, Nokia, and Intel, trade primarily intra-firm. Samsung, the world's biggest communications equipment multinational, has 158 subsidiaries across the world, including 43 subsidiaries in Europe, 32 in China and 30 in North and South America (Samsung 2014). Other multinationals, such as Apple, Motorola, and Nike, rely mainly on outsourcing, and hence on arm's-length trade with non-affiliated suppliers (Lanz and Miroudot 2011).

Multinational companies and their affiliates accounted for one-tenth of global GDP and their sales amounted to about half of global GDP in 2015 (UNCTAD 2016; Figure SF2.1). The world's largest multinationals (Shell, Toyota, and General Electric in advanced economies; China National Offshore Oil, Vale SA, and Petronas in EMDEs) are systemically important in both their home and host economies. Post-crisis, foreign affiliates of multinational companies have fared better than their domestic counterparts and contributed more significantly to the recovery of global GDP. For example, during 2010-14, the value added of multinationals grew faster-than-average, at 6.6 percent—well above global GDP growth of 4.4 percent.

Unfortunately, data on global intra-firm trade are not available. However, a unique dataset on bilateral U.S. exports and imports can provide an indication of developments in intra-firm trade growth. The United States plays an important role in global trade (Figure SF2.2): it accounts for about 11 percent of global goods trade and 23 percent of global foreign direct investment (FDI) stocks. It is the largest export destination for one-fifth of the world's countries and the largest import source for one-tenth. U.S. multinationals account for about 30 percent of the employment and sales of the world's largest 100 non-financial multinational companies.

Most of the post-crisis slowdown in U.S. trade growth can be attributed to the sharp slowdown in arm's-length rather than intra-firm trade. By 2014, intra-firm trade growth had returned to near pre-crisis rates while arm's-length trade growth has lagged significantly below elevated pre-crisis rates.

This Special Focus addresses the following questions:

- What are the characteristics of intra-firm and arm's-length trade?

- How have intra-firm and arm's-length trade evolved since the crisis?

- What accounts for the sharp post-crisis slowdown in arm's-length trade?

Characteristics of intra-firm and arm's-length trade

Data. There is only one publicly available dataset on international intra-firm trade with a comprehensive set of partner economies. This unique U.S. trade dataset from the U.S. Census Bureau uses customs declarations to distinguish arm's-length trade from intra-firm transactions.[3] At the most detailed level, the data contain exports and imports at the 6-digit North American Industry Classification System (NAICS) level as well as information on countries of origin and destination, covering annual bilateral trade flows with 234 partner economies for 2002-14. Similar data

---

[3]The U.S. Bureau of Economic Analysis collects similar data with a confidential dataset on intra-firm trade data based on firm surveys. The Organisation for Economic Co-Operation and Development (OECD) database on the Activities of Multinational Enterprises covers trade between OECD countries.

FIGURE SF2.3 Characteristics of U.S. intra-firm and arm's-length trade

Just over half of total U.S. trade is conducted at arm's-length. Arm's-length transactions account for a larger share of U.S. trade with EMDEs than with advanced countries and are more common in final goods trade. U.S. trade with EMDEs has slightly shifted towards intra-firm transactions since the global financial crisis.

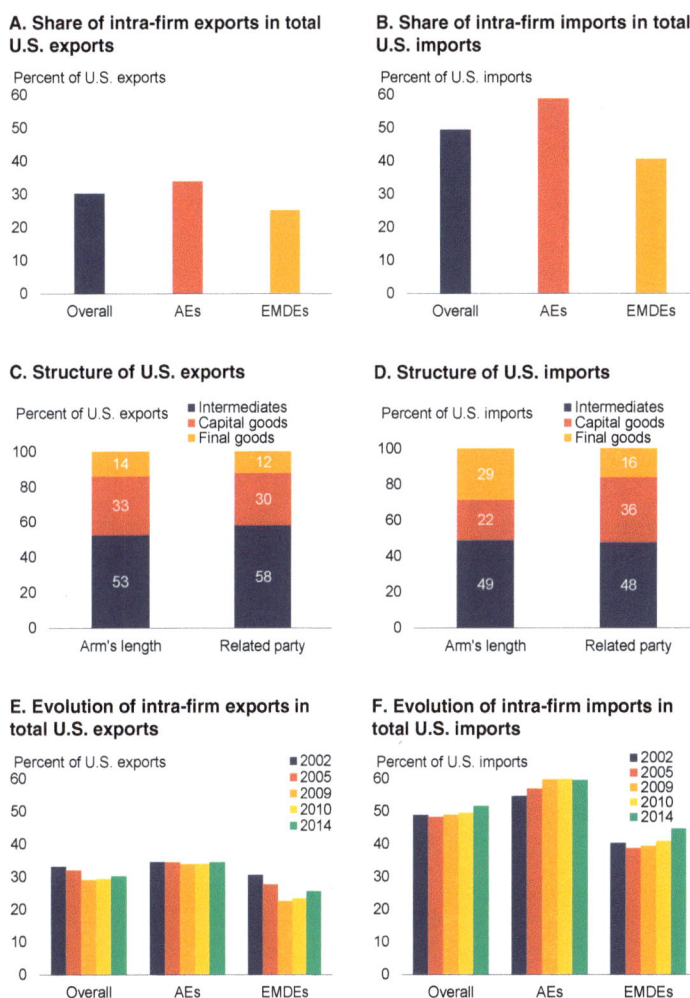

A. Share of intra-firm exports in total U.S. exports

B. Share of intra-firm imports in total U.S. imports

C. Structure of U.S. exports

D. Structure of U.S. imports

E. Evolution of intra-firm exports in total U.S. exports

F. Evolution of intra-firm imports in total U.S. imports

Source: U.S. Census Bureau.
Note: AE stands for advanced economies.
A.B.E.F. U.S. exports and imports of goods, average for 2002-14. The residual to 100 percent is the share of arm's-length trade in total U.S. goods exports or imports with the world, advanced economies (AEs) or EMDEs. The shares are broadly stable over the period.
C.D. 2014 averages. The classification into intermediates, capital, and final goods is according to the Broad Economic Categories (BEC) rev.4 classification of goods according to their use. Category 51—passenger motor cars—has been excluded.

are unavailable at the global level; hence, the analysis here relies on this U.S. trade dataset.

Definition of arm's-length and intra-firm trade. Intra-firm trade consists of cross-border transactions between firms linked by a degree of control and ownership whereas arm's-length trade is defined as cross-border transactions

FIGURE SF2.4 Regional decomposition of U.S. intra-firm and arm's-length trade

Canada is the largest destination of U.S. intra-firm exports and the largest source of U.S. intra-firm imports, followed by Mexico. China is more important as a source of U.S. arm's-length imports. In general, intra-firm trade is more prevalent with higher-income trading partners.

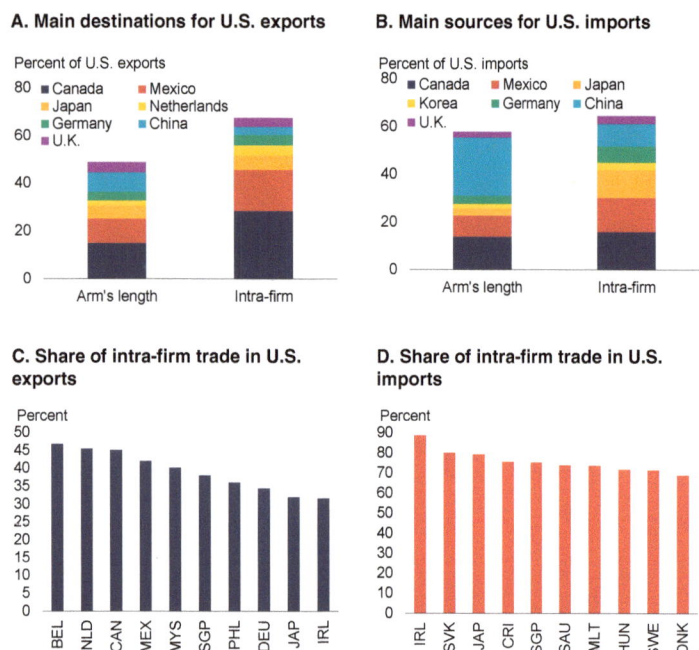

A. Main destinations for U.S. exports

B. Main sources for U.S. imports

C. Share of intra-firm trade in U.S. exports

D. Share of intra-firm trade in U.S. imports

Source: U.S. Census Bureau.
Note: Top 10 trading partners, averages for 2002-14.
A.B. Residual to 100 percent is the share of all other countries in total U.S. arm's-length or intra-firm exports (A) or imports (B).
C.D. Residual to 100 percent is the share of arm's-length transactions in bilateral U.S. exports (C) or imports (D) with each trading partner. BEL=Belgium, NLD=Netherlands, CAN=Canada, MEX=Mexico, MYS=Malaysia, SGP=Singapore, PHL=Philippines, DEU=Germany, JAP=Japan, IRL=Ireland, SVK=Slovak Republic, CRI=Costa Rica, SAU=Saudi Arabia, MLT=Malta, HUN=Hungary, SWE=Sweden, DNK=Denmark.

between unrelated firms. The U.S. Census Bureau records transactions between related-parties. Related-party imports are defined as shipments between "any person directly or indirectly, owning, controlling or holding power to vote 6 percent of the outstanding voting stock or shares of any organization." The ownership threshold for related-party exports is set at 10 percent (U.S. Cen -sus Bureau 2014). For notational convenience, related-party and intra-firm trade are hereinafter interchangeably referred to as intra-firm trade.[4]

Quantitative importance of arm's-length and intra-firm trade. Just over half (about 57 percent) of total U.S. trade is conducted at arm's-length

between unrelated firms. The share of arm's-length trade is much lower for U.S. imports (50 percent) than exports (70 percent), for U.S. trade in capital goods (50 percent) than final goods (60 percent), and for U.S. trade with advanced economies (51 percent) than with EMDEs (64 percent). In general, a higher per capita income of a trading partner is associated with a lower share of arm's-length trade. The share of intra-firm trade of total U.S. trade has remained broadly stable from 2002 until the global financial crisis but subsequently increased, especially for U.S. trade with EMDEs (Figure SF2.3).

Country composition of arm's-length and intra-firm U.S. trade. Geographical proximity and the North American Free Trade Agreement (NAFTA) favor intra-firm transactions with two of the United States' largest trading partners, Mexico and Canada. About half of all U.S. exports to, and more than half of all U.S. imports from, Canada and Mexico are intra-firm transactions. Canada is the single largest destination of U.S. intra-firm exports (almost one-third of total U.S. intra-firm exports) and imports, followed by Mexico (about one-fifth of total U.S. intra-firm exports; Figure SF2.4). More than half of U.S. *imports* from its main non-NAFTA trading partners (with the exception of China and Italy) are also intra-firm transactions. In contrast, U.S. *exports* to its main non-NAFTA trading partners are predominantly arm's-length—53-65 percent of U.S. exports to large European Union and Asian countries (France, Germany, Japan, Korea, Netherlands, and United Kingdom; Figure SF2.4) fit this description.

Evolution of intra-firm and arm's-length trade since the crisis

Global trade growth has slowed sharply since the global financial crisis, from an average of 7.6 percent during 2002-08 to an average of 4.3 percent during 2010-14. During the 2007-09 global financial crisis, global trade volumes contracted by 11 percent, as domestic demand dropped and trade finance was curtailed (Levchenko, Lewis, and Tesar 2010; Chor and

---

[4]Technically, the two terms imply different ownership shares. Intra-firm trade is defined as trade between firms with control and ownership shares of at least 50 percent.

Manova 2012). The contribution of global value chains to propagating the negative effects of the global financial crisis remains unsettled.[5]

The U.S. trade data highlight that arm's-length trade accounted disproportionately for the overall post-crisis trade slowdown. This reflected a higher pre-crisis average and a weaker post-crisis rebound in arm's-length trade growth compared with intra-firm trade. During the crisis itself, the U.S. data suggest a broad-based trade collapse in which intra-firm and arm's-length trade contracted to similar degrees.

By 2014, intra-firm trade growth had returned close to its pre-crisis average (4.3 percent of exports and 5.0 percent for imports). In contrast, arm's-length trade growth remained significantly below its high pre-crisis average: its growth slowed to a post-crisis annual average of 4.7 percent compared to 11.3 percent during 2002-08 (Figure SF2.1).

Factors contributing to the sharp post-crisis slowdown in arm's-length trade

On average, arm's-length U.S. trade growth exceeded U.S. intra-firm trade growth by 1.6 percentage point pre-crisis (2002-08), but fell short of U.S. intra-firm trade growth by 1.7 percentage point post-crisis (2010-14). This sharp slowdown in arm's-length trade reflected in part compositional effects in response to global macroeconomic trends. In addition, several other factors may have disadvantaged firms trading at arm's-length, raised the cost of arm's-length transactions, and hence discouraged arm's-length trade.

Compositional effects. First, a greater share of arm's-length exports than intra-firm exports is shipped to EMDEs, especially BRICS economies. Just as the rapid pre-crisis growth in EMDEs lifted

---

[5]Global production chains may have facilitated the transmission of output contractions across the global economy through intra-firm contagion (Bems, Johnson, and Yi 2009). Conversely, they may have strengthened the resilience of trade by facilitating better access to finance or due to the stability of long-established contractual relationships in supply chains (Altomonte and Ottaviano 2009; Bernard et al. 2009).

FIGURE SF2.5 Sectoral decomposition of U.S. intra-firm and arm's-length trade

Intra-firm trade is concentrated in sectors such as transportation equipment, electronics, and chemicals, while arm's-length transactions are more common in textiles, apparel and leather products, and food and beverages.

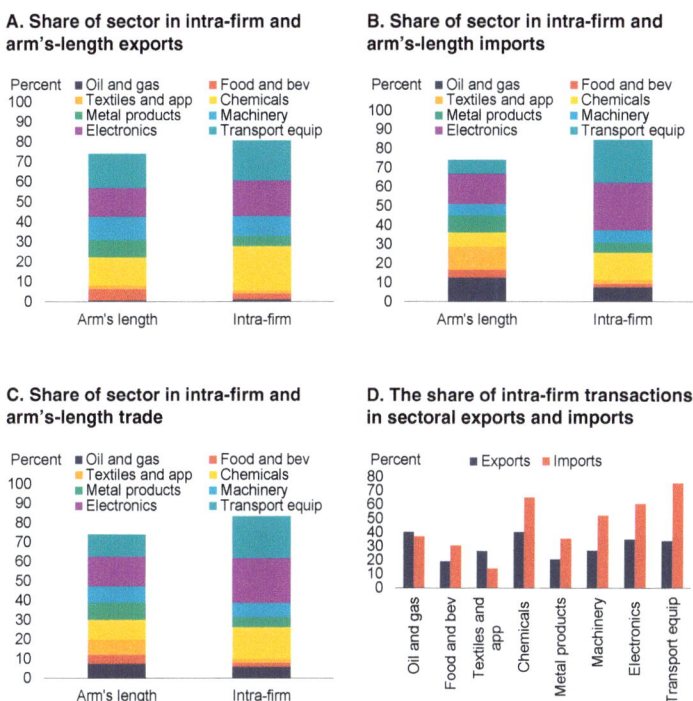

A. Share of sector in intra-firm and arm's-length exports

B. Share of sector in intra-firm and arm's-length imports

C. Share of sector in intra-firm and arm's-length trade

D. The share of intra-firm transactions in sectoral exports and imports

Source: U.S. Census Bureau.
Note: U.S. exports and imports of goods, averages for 2002-14. Agricultural products, paper products, printing, non-metallic minerals, furniture, and miscellaneous manufactures have been omitted as they each account for less than 2 percent of total trade. Food and bev includes food and beverages. Textiles and app include textiles and apparel. Chemicals include chemicals and plastics. Electronics includes electronics and electrical equipment.
A.-C. Residual to 100 percent is the share of all other sectors in exports (A), imports (B), and trade (C).
D. Residual to 100 percent is the share of arm's-length transactions in U.S. exports and imports in each sector.

arm's-length export growth, their sharp post-crisis growth slowdown dampened it (Figure SF2.6; Didier et al. 2016). Second, arm's-length exports and imports include a greater share of sectors that grew rapidly pre-crisis but have struggled post-crisis (textiles and apparel and machinery) or sectors that benefited from the pre-crisis commodity price boom (mining, metals, and energy; Figure SF2.5). The collapse in metals and energy prices from their peak in the first quarter of 2011 has weighed on trade (World Bank 2015a and 2015b; Baffes et al. 2015). These compositional differences are the main reason behind the steeper-than-average slowdown in arm's-length trade growth. Had the composition

FIGURE SF2.6 Pre- and post-crisis growth in U.S. trade

Pre-crisis, a higher share of fast-growing sectors and export markets supported arm's-length export growth. Post-crisis, this effect unwound as EMDE growth and some of the fastest growing sectors slowed. Such compositional effects are the main reason for the steeper-than-average slowdown in arm's-length trade growth.

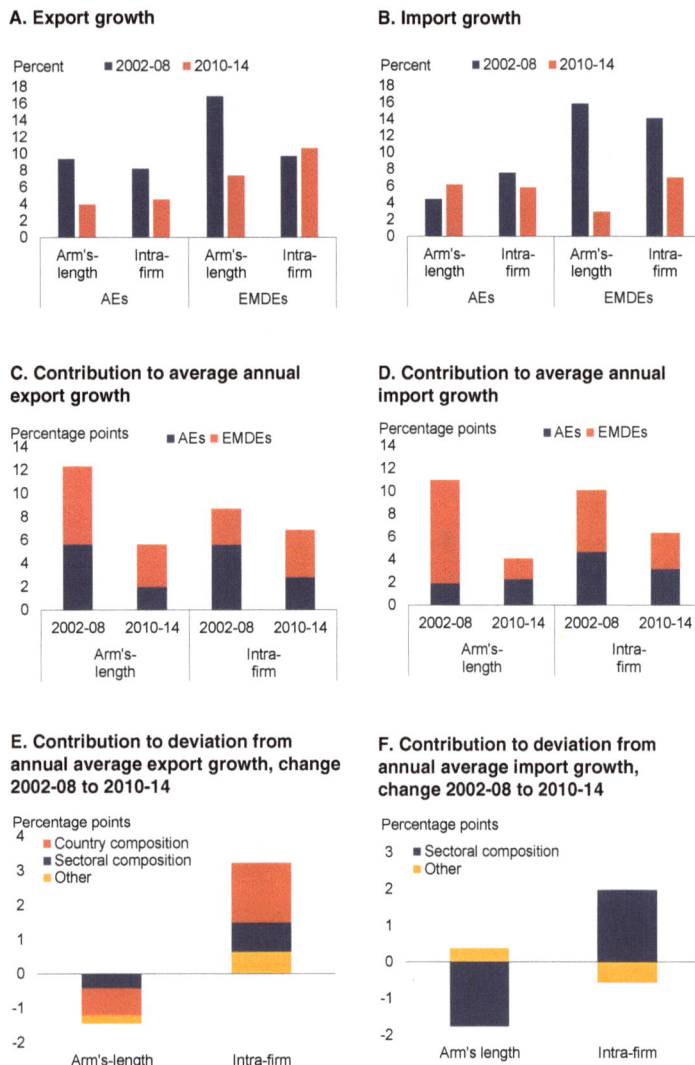

A. Export growth

B. Import growth

C. Contribution to average annual export growth

D. Contribution to average annual import growth

E. Contribution to deviation from annual average export growth, change 2002-08 to 2010-14

F. Contribution to deviation from annual average import growth, change 2002-08 to 2010-14

Source: U.S. Census Bureau.
Note: AE stands for advanced economies.
C.D. Average annual contribution of export (C) and import (D) transactions with EMDEs and AEs to total U.S. merchandize exports (C) or imports (D).
E. "Country composition" measures the extent to which growth in arm's-length or intra-firm exports exceeded that of total exports due to a higher initial share of fast-growing countries. It is defined as the difference between hypothetical arm's-length (intra-firm) export growth, had arm's-length (intra-firm) exports to each country grown at the same rate as total exports to each country, and actual total export growth. "Sector composition" measures the extent to which growth in arm's-length or intra-firm exports exceeded that of total exports because of a higher initial share of fast-growing sectors. It is defined as the difference between hypothetical arm's-length (intra-firm) export growth, had arm's-length (intra-firm) sectoral exports grown at the same rate as total sectoral exports, and actual total export growth. "Other" is the residual. The figure shows the change in these contributions between the 2002-08 average and the 2010-14 average.
F. The definitions are as in E. Country composition is omitted since the destination country of all imports is the United States.

of arm's-length trade matched that of average exports and imports, arm's-length export and import growth would have slowed by 1.2 and 1.8 percentage points less, respectively, between the pre-crisis and post-crisis periods (Figure SF2.6).[6]

Other contributing factors. Other factors may have further contributed to the post-crisis weakness in arm's-length trade.[7]

- **Reduced access to finance for unaffiliated firms.** Tightening lending conditions during and after the global financial crisis restricted access to trade credit and other forms of financing (Chor and Manova 2012). This may have disproportionately affected transactions between non-affiliated parties (Desai, Foley, and Hines 2004; Alvarez and Görg 2012).

- **Disadvantages due to size and productivity.** Vertically integrated firms tend to be larger, more productive, and more skill- and capital-intensive (Corcos et al. 2013). More efficient management of stocks also helps vertically integrated firms adjust to large demand shocks, such as the global financial crisis (Altomonte et al. 2011). Such factors may account for the smaller likelihood of exit from foreign markets for firms exporting on an intra-firm basis, especially since the global financial crisis. The number of U.S. firms exporting intra-firm fell by 8.5 percent during 2009, whereas the number of firms exporting at arm's-length fell by 12.5 percent (Carballo 2015).

- **Shock amplification in complex supply chains.** The demand for complex goods, such as automobiles, reacts more strongly to income shocks than the demand for basic goods (Ferrantino and Taglioni 2014). As a negative

---

[6]The results are robust to using manufacturing trade only.

[7]Trade policy may have favored intra-firm trade. However, in the post-crisis period under consideration here (2010-14) there were no major changes in U.S. trade policy. Apart from three bilateral U.S. FTAs that are slowly being phased in since 2012 (Korea, Panama, Colombia), applied tariffs imposed by the United States on its imports and faced by the United States on its exports did not change significantly.

demand shock spreads through the supply chain, participating firms observe greater swings in demand the further up they are on the supply chain (the "bullwhip effect"). Although intra-firm trade in intermediate goods fell more significantly at the beginning of the crisis, it also benefitted from a stronger recovery thereafter (Alessandria 2011).

- *U.S. dollar appreciation.* Trade conducted through global value chains generally shows less sensitivity to real exchange rates. That's because competitiveness gains from real depreciations are partly offset by rising input costs (Ahmed, Appendino, and Ruta 2015; Mattoo, Mishra, and Subramaniam 2012; Amiti, Itskhoki, and Konings 2014). To the extent that intra-firm trade is more strongly associated with global value chains than arm's-length trade, intra-firm U.S. exports may have benefited less from the pre-crisis U.S. dollar depreciation and been dampened to a lesser degree by the post-crisis appreciation than arm's-length exports. In addition, firms integrated vertically may have a wider range of tools available to them to hedge against exchange rate movements.

- *Uncertainty.* Uncertainty influences whether firms outsource or integrate vertically (Antras and Helpman 2004). Although uncertainty discourages cross-border vertical integration, once established, vertically integrated U.S. firms tend to be less sensitive to uncertainty in their trade decisions (Carballo 2015; Bernard et al. 2010). Heightened economic and trade policy uncertainty during and after the global financial crisis, may therefore have encouraged a post-crisis preference for intra-firm transactions over arm's-length ones.

Conclusion

The United States plays an important role in global trade. It accounts for about 11 percent of global goods trade and is the largest export destination for one-fifth of the world's countries. U.S. multinationals account for about 30 percent of the employment and sales of the world's largest 100 non-financial multinational companies.

U.S. arm's-length trade growth has slowed steeply relative to intra-firm trade in the aftermath of the global financial crisis, from high pre-crisis rates. During the 2010-14 recovery, trade between non-affiliated firms grew at about half the pre-crisis rate. Intra-firm trade growth also slowed but to a considerably lesser degree.

The sharp slowdown in arm's-length trade growth stems from a number of factors. A high share of arm's-length exports is conducted with EMDEs, where growth has slowed sharply from elevated pre-crisis rates. In addition, firms trading at arm's-length are more concentrated in sectors that grew particularly rapidly pre-crisis and sectors that benefited from the pre-crisis commodity price boom, which boosted pre-crisis trade but have languished since the crisis. Such compositional effects simply reflect cyclical trends in the global economy. For the United States, these effects account for a significant part of the post-crisis growth gap between arm's-length and intra-firm trade.

Other factors have also been at play. Among these, the characteristics that make firms engaged in arm's-length trade less resilient to the severe demand and financing shocks of the global financial crisis contributed to the post-crisis weakness of arm's-length trade. Firms engaged in outsourcing tend to be smaller, less productive, less efficient in inventory management, and have more restricted access to finance than firms integrated vertically. Such factors may have accelerated the exit of firms trading at arm's-length during the global financial crisis and its aftermath. In addition, the macroeconomic environment has been less favorable to arm's-length trade than to intra-firm trade in the post-crisis period. The post-crisis U.S. dollar appreciation has weighed more heavily on U.S. exports from non-affiliated firms. Heightened financial risks and policy uncertainty may also have discouraged arm's-length transactions.

While the post-crisis environment has favored multinationals that focus on intra-firm transactions, their activities can also raise policy challenges. For example, multinationals may have an incentive to adjust their transfer pricing—the prices assigned to intra-firm transactions—to raise the value of goods and services produced in countries with low corporate income taxes and reduce the value of those produced in countries with higher taxes. Policies to promote FDI and trade therefore have to be carefully calibrated to protect fiscal revenues. A number of global initiatives have been introduced since the global financial crisis to make global tax practices more transparent (IMF/OECD/UN/World Bank 2011, 2016). In addition, large and internationally active firms also tend to be better able to absorb the significant fixed costs of exporting. Measures to reduce asymmetries of information and help small and medium-sized companies overcome regulatory burdens can help level the playing field (World Bank 2016).

References

Ahmed, S., M. Appendino, and M. Ruta. 2015. "Depreciations Without Exports. Global Value Chains and the Exchange Rate Elasticity of Exports." Policy Research Working Paper 7390, World Bank, Washington, D.C.

Alessandria, G., J. P. Kaboski, and V. Midrigan. 2011. "US Trade and Inventory Dynamics." *American Economic Review* 101 (3) 303-07.

Altomonte, C., and G. I. Ottaviano. 2009. "Resilient to the Crisis? Global Supply Chains and Trade Flows," in *The Great Trade Collapse: Causes, Consequences and Prospects*, edited by R. E. Baldwin. Center for Economic and Policy Research, Geneva.

Altomonte, C., F. Di Mauro, G. Ottaviano, A. Rungi, and V. Vicard. 2011. "Global Value Chains During the Great Trade Collapse: A Bullwhip Effect?" Working Paper Series 1412, European Central Bank.

Álvarez, R., and H. Görg. 2012. "Multinationals as Stabilisers? Economic Crisis, Access to Finance, and Employment Growth." *Journal of Development Studies* 48 (7): 847-863.

Antras, P., and E. Helpman. 2004. "Global Sourcing." *Journal of Political Economy* 112 (3): 552-580.

Antras, P. 2015. *Global Production: Firms, Contracts, and Trade Structure.* Princeton: Princeton University Press.

Amiti, M., O. Itskhoki, and J. Konings. 2014. "Importers, Exporters, and Exchange Rate Disconnect." *American Economic Review* 104 (7): 1942-78.

Baffes, J., M. A. Kose, F. Ohnsorge, and M. Stocker. 2015. "The Great Plunge in Oil Prices: Causes, Consequences, and Policy Responses." Policy Research Note 15/01, World Bank, Washington, DC.

Bems, R., R. C. Johnson, and K. M. Yi. 2009. "The Collapse of Global Trade: Update On the Role of Vertical Linkages." in *The Great Trade Collapse: Causes, Consequences and Prospects*, edited by R. E. Baldwin. Center for Economic and Policy Research, Geneva.

Bernard, A. B., B. J. Jensen, S. J. Redding, and P. K. Schott. 2009. "The Margins of US Trade." *American Economic Review* 99 (2): 487-93.

Bernard, A. B., B. J. Jensen, S. J. Redding, and P. K. Schott. 2010. "Intrafirm Trade and Product Contractibility." *American Economic Review* 100 (2): 444.

Carballo, J. R. 2015. Essays in Trade and Uncertainty. PhD Dissertation. University of Maryland, College Park.

Chor, D., and K. Manova. 2012. "Off The Cliff and Back? Credit Conditions and International Trade During the Global Financial Crisis." *Journal of International Economics* 87 (1): 117-133.

Coase, R. 1937. "The Nature of the Firm." *Economica* 4 (16): 386-405.

Constantinescu, C., A. Mattoo, and M. Ruta. 2015. "The Global Trade Slowdown: Cyclical or Structural?" Policy Research Working Paper 7158, World Bank, Washington, D.C.

Corcos, G., D. M. Irac, G. Mion, and T. Verdier. 2013. "The Determinants of Intrafirm Trade: Evidence from French Firms." *Review of Economics and Statistics* 95 (3): 825-838.

Desai, M. A., C. F. Foley, and J. R. Hines. 2004. "A Multinational Perspective on Capital Structure Choice and Internal Capital Markets." *The Journal of Finance* 59 (6): 2451-2487.

Didier T., M. A. Kose, F. Ohnsorge, and L. S. Ye. 2016. "Slowdown in Emerging Markets: Rough Patch or Prolonged Weakness?" Policy Research Note 4, World Bank, Washington, D.C.

Dunning, J., and S. Lundan. 2008. *Multinational Enterprises and the Global Economy.* Cheltenham, UK: Edward Elgar.

Ferrantino, M. J., and D. Taglioni. 2014. "Global Value Chains in the Current Trade Slowdown." World Bank Economic Premise 137, Washington DC.

Grossman, S. J., and O. Hart. 1986. "The Costs and Benefits of Ownership: A Theory of Vertical and Lateral Integration." *Journal of Political Economy* 94 (4): 691–719.

Hart, O. D., and J. Moore. 1990. "Property Rights and the Nature of the Firm." *Journal of Political Economy* 98 (6): 1119–58.

Haugh, D., A. Kopoin, E. Rusticelli, D. Turner, and R. Dutu. 2016. "Cardiac Arrest or Dizzy Spell: Why is World Trade So Weak and What Can Policy Do about It?" OECD Economic Policy Papers 18, OECD, Paris.

IMF/OECD/UN/World Bank. 2011. "Supporting the Development of More Effective Tax Systems." Report to the G-20 Development Working Group.

_____. 2016. "The Platform for Collaboration on Tax." Inter-agency Task Force on Finan -cing for Development. Concept Note.

Lanz, R., and S. Miroudot. 2011. "Intra-Firm Trade: Patterns, Determinants and Policy Implications." OECD Trade Policy Papers 114, OECD Publishing, Paris.

Levchenko, A. A., L. T. Lewis, and L. L. Tesar. 2010. "The Collapse of International Trade during the 2008–09 Crisis: In Search Of the Smoking Gun." *IMF Economic Review* 58 (2): 214-253.

Mattoo, A., P. Mishra, and A. Subramanian. 2012. "Spillover Effects of Exchange Rates: A Study of the Renminbi," Policy Research Working Paper Series 5989, World Bank, Washington, DC.

Samsung. 2014. "Samsung Electronics Annual Report 2014." Samsung, Seoul, South Korea.

UNCTAD. 2016. "World Investment Report 2016 Investor Nationality: Policy Challenges." United Nations, Geneva.

U.S. Census Bureau. 2014. "U.S. Goods Trade: Imports & Exports by Related-Parties 2014." U.S. Department of Commerce, Washington, DC.

Williamson, O. E. 1975. *Markets, Hierarchies: Analysis. Antitrust Implications.* New York: The Free Press.

World Bank. 2015a. *Global Economic Prospects: Having Fiscal Space and Using It.* January. Washington, DC: World Bank.

_____. 2015b. *Global Economic Prospects: Global Economy in Transition.* June. Washington, DC: World Bank.

_____. 2016. *Global Economic Prospects: Spillovers Amid Weak Growth.* January. Washington, DC: World Bank.

CHAPTER 2

REGIONAL OUTLOOKS

EAST ASIA and PACIFIC

The East Asia and Pacific region is projected to grow at 6.2 percent in 2017, and at a slightly lower 6.1 percent on average in 2018-19, in line with previous forecasts. A gradual slowdown in China is offsetting a continued modest pickup in the rest of the region, led by a rebound in commodity exporters and a gradual recovery in Thailand. Growth in commodity importers excluding China is projected to remain robust, as stronger exports will offset the negative effects of eventual policy tightening on domestic demand. Downside risks are mainly external. They include heightened policy uncertainty and increased protectionism in key advanced economies, and the risk of an abrupt tightening of global financing conditions. A sharp slowdown in China is a low-probability risk, but it would have major negative consequences for the region.

Recent developments

Regional growth continued to be robust, and in line with expectations, in the first half of 2017. Solid domestic demand growth reflected accommodative macroeconomic policies and tight labor markets (World Bank 2017a). Export volumes firmed across the region, reflecting gradually strengthening global activity. Purchasing managers' indexes and consumer sentiment indicators point to solid activity across the region in the second quarter of the year. Regional inflation is trending up, reflecting positive inflation in Thailand and increased price pressures in the rest of the region, particularly in Malaysia. Producer prices have recovered, particularly in China and commodity exporting economies, reflecting the stabilization of commodity prices and a rebound in economic activity. Regional financial markets stabilized after a period of volatility in late 2016, net capital outflows declined, and regional currencies and asset prices firmed (Figure 2.1.1).

In China, following strong growth in 2016Q4 (6.8 percent y/y), GDP expanded by 6.9 percent y/y in 2017Q1, helped by robust consumption

and a recovery of exports. Rebalancing from investment to consumption resumed as state-driven investment growth slowed and private sector investment growth recovered from a mid-2016 dip, but remained weak (Figure 2.1.2). House price growth declined in major cities and credit growth slowed (but remained above nominal GDP growth and credit to the household sector accelerated) on tighter regulations and less accommodative monetary policy (Campanaro and Masic 2017). Consumer price inflation has remained below target. Producer price inflation has moderated somewhat from its peak in February, reflecting higher commodity prices and reduced overcapacity in heavy industry. Export growth accelerated on stronger external demand. The pace of foreign reserve drawdowns slowed following a tightening of capital controls on capital outflows and measures to encourage foreign direct investment.

Growth continues to strengthen in *commodity-exporting economies* (Table 2.1.1). Domestic demand and imports are firming, reflecting improved confidence, higher corporate profits, and diminishing drag from macroeconomic adjustment. In Indonesia, investment climate reforms and recovering commodity prices have supported a private investment recovery (World Bank 2017b). In Malaysia, stabilizing commodity prices have lifted business sentiment and invest-

---

Note: This section was prepared by Ekaterine Vashakmadze. Research assistance was provided by Liwei Liu.

FIGURE 2.1.1 **EAP: Recent developments**

Activity remained robust in the first half of 2017, on solid domestic demand and firming exports. Regional financial markets have recently stabilized and regional equity prices have generally recovered their earlier losses. Inflation across the region picked up, but remained below central banks' targets in China and Thailand. Real credit growth generally moderated on tighter regulations and higher inflation, but remained high in China and Vietnam, and accelerated in the Philippines.

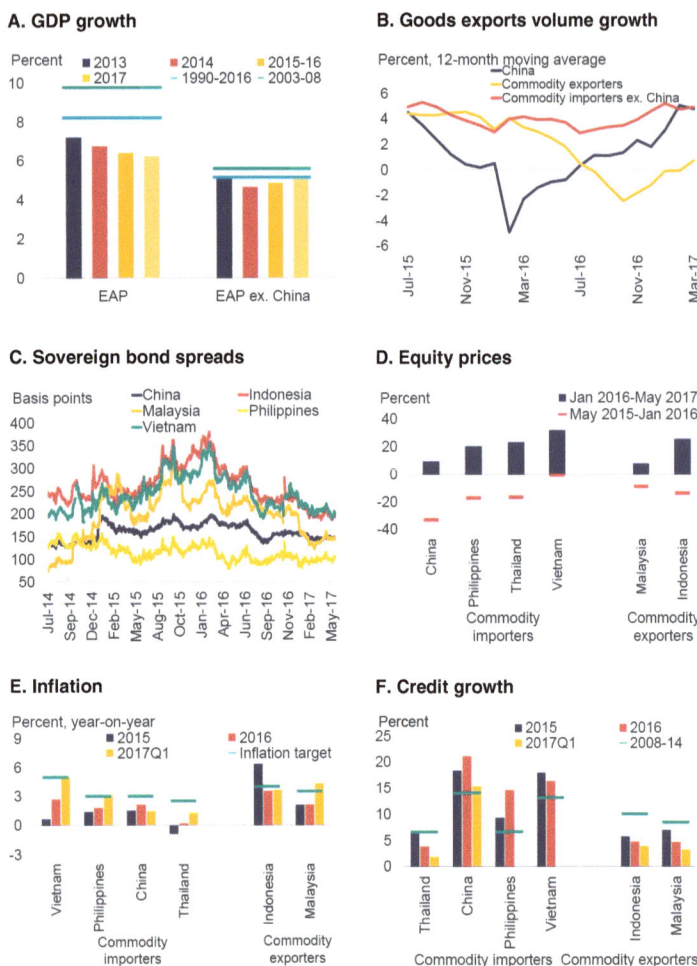

A. GDP growth

B. Goods exports volume growth

C. Sovereign bond spreads

D. Equity prices

E. Inflation

F. Credit growth

Sources: Central Bank News, Haver Analytics, International Monetary Fund, World Bank.
Note: EAP stands for East Asia and Pacific. Commodity importers ex. China include Cambodia, Philippines, Solomon Islands, Thailand, Vietnam, and Vanuatu. Commodity exporters include Indonesia, Lao PDR, Mongolia, and Malaysia. GDP-weighted averages.
B. Last observation is March 2017.
C. Measures the average spread of a country's sovereign debt (as measured by J.P. Morgan's Emerging Markets Bond Index) over their equivalent maturity U.S. Treasury bond. Lat observation is May 24, 2017.
D. Last observation is May 24, 2017.
E. Average year-on-year growth. Inflation targets for 2017 are 3 percent in China and 5 percent in Vietnam. The figure shows the mid-points of targeted ranges in Indonesia (3-5 percent), Philippines (2-4 percent), and Thailand (1-4 percent). For Malaysia, the mid-point of Bank Negara's 2017 forecast of 3-4 percent is used.
F. Real private sector credit growth. Average year-on-year growth. Data for Vietnam in 2016 are through October.

ment. In Indonesia, export volumes, which had contracted through mid-2016, rebounded strongly in 2016Q4, and export values continued to accelerate in the first two months of 2017 on

strong demand from China. In Malaysia, export growth (especially in electrical and electronics goods) is being bolstered by a global pickup in manufacturing and trade and a modest recovery of oil and gas shipments.

Growth in *commodity-importing economies* remains robust, as accommodative policies continue to support solid growth of domestic demand. In the Philippines, expansionary fiscal policy has boosted capital formation, while robust remittances, credit growth, and low inflation have supported private consumption. In Thailand, domestic demand is gradually recovering from several years of subdued performance, but policy uncertainty continues to weigh on growth. Overall, exports in commodity-importing economies are generally benefitting from strengthening global demand, although performance remains mixed.

After a period of financial market volatility in late 2016—which contributed to capital outflows from the region and put pressure on regional exchange rates and equity prices—global financing conditions have improved in 2017 (World Bank 2017a). Sovereign bond spreads have narrowed, most notably in commodity exporters (e.g., Indonesia and Malaysia) and Vietnam. Capital inflows to EAP bond and equity mutual funds have resumed (including in Malaysia and Thailand, which had experienced substantial outflows) and have been broadly stable in 2017. Most regional currencies have strengthened against the U.S. dollar. Regional equity prices have generally recovered their earlier losses, reflecting improved confidence and a stabilization of global bond yields.

Authorities are gradually moving to a less accommodative policy stance, with some exceptions. China raised its short-term interest rates in the first quarter of 2017 and continued to tighten macro-prudential regulations to address financial stability risks. Malaysia made some progress in renewing medium-term fiscal consolidation efforts. Indonesia is not planning to extend expenditure cuts into 2017 and has signaled a more accommodative stance for the medium term. Policies in the Philippines remain accommodative, despite rapid credit growth, accelerated inflation, widening fiscal deficits, and falling current account surpluses.

Outlook

The regional growth outlook for 2017-19 remains solid (World Bank 2017a). Growth is projected to reach 6.2 percent in 2017—a touch below the 6.3 percent pace in 2016 (Figure 2.1.3). This reflects a gradual slowdown in China, which offsets a pickup of activity in the rest of the region led by a rebound in commodity exporters (Table 2.1.2). The outlook is predicated on a modest recovery of commodity prices and stronger external demand. A rebound in global trade is expected to offset the negative effects on activity of a gradual tightening of global financing conditions.

Growth in China is projected to slow from a projected 6.5 percent in 2017 to 6.3 percent on average in 2018-19. Fiscal support will continue to offset monetary tightening. Policies will continue to support growth and contain financial risks and encourage rebalancing (World Bank and Development Research Center of China's State Council 2014). A moderate recovery in Chinese imports reflects robust domestic demand. Improving global demand supports export, but rising cost pressures will limit export growth. The baseline forecast assumes no material change in trade or political relations between China and the United States, notwithstanding policy efforts to reduce China's trade surplus with the United States.

Growth in the rest of the region is projected to pick up from an estimated 5.1 percent in 2017 to 5.2 percent on average in 2018-19, reflecting a continued recovery in commodity exporters and Thailand. Growth in *commodity exporters* will continue to accelerate, from an estimated 5.1 percent in 2017 to its long-term average of 5.3 percent in 2019. This assumes that the adjustment to low commodity prices runs its course over the forecast horizon, exports rebound, and investment growth stabilizes around its long-term trend.

In Indonesia, growth is projected to firm from an estimated 5.2 percent in 2017 to 5.4 percent in

FIGURE 2.1.2 China

Growth in China continues to slow gradually. The rebalancing from investment to consumption resumed in 2017Q1. Fixed asset investment by state-owned enterprises and enterprises with state participation eased as support from policy-led investment spending gradually dissipated. Private investment growth recovered, but remained weak. Tighter regulations contributed to further moderation of credit growth, especially to the non-financial corporate sector. Credit to the household sector accelerated. House price growth in Tier 1 and 2 cities has decelerated since mid-2016 on tightening regulations and less accommodative monetary policy.

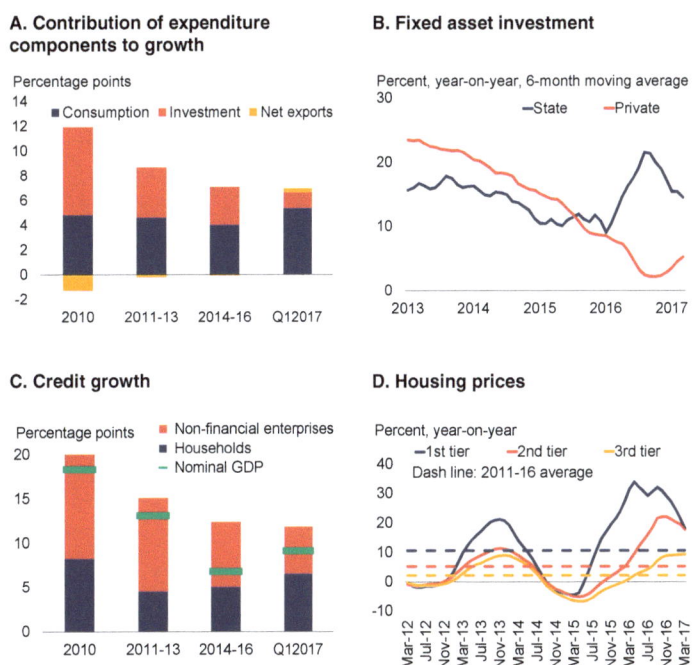

A. Contribution of expenditure components to growth

B. Fixed asset investment

C. Credit growth

D. Housing prices

Sources: Haver Analytics, World Bank.
B. 2017YTD is March 2017 data.
D. The National Bureau of Statistics of China surveys house prices in 70 cities and divides them into three tiers. The first tier includes Shanghai, Beijing, Guangzhou, and Shenzhen. The second tier includes 31 provincial capital and sub-provincial capital cities. The third tier includes 35 other cities. Last observation is March 2017.

2019 (World Bank 2017b). The impact of fiscal consolidation is expected to gradually dissipate. Private activity will pick up, helped by modestly rising commodity prices, improving external demand, and increased confidence bolstered by reform measures and recent upgrades of Indonesia's sovereign ratings by major credit rating agencies. These include streamlining business regulations, liberalizing the foreign direct investment (FDI) regime, and a stable rupiah (IMF 2017a; World Bank 2017b). In Malaysia, income support measures, higher infrastructure spending, and improved exports are forecast to raise growth (World Bank 2016a). In Mongolia, growth is projected to stagnate in 2017, partly reflecting efforts to reduce public debt to

FIGURE 2.1.3 EAP: Outlook and risks

Regional growth is projected to reach 6.2 percent in 2017, a touch below 2016 growth of 6.3 percent. This reflects a gradual slowdown in China, which offsets a pickup of activity in the rest of the region led by a rebound in commodity exporters and a recovery in Thailand. Risks remain tilted to the downside and are mainly external. In addition, a steeper-than-expected slowdown in China would have sizable regional spillovers. Elevated domestic debt (e.g., China, Malaysia, Thailand) and sizeable external financing needs (e.g., Indonesia, Mongolia) would amplify the impact of external shocks.

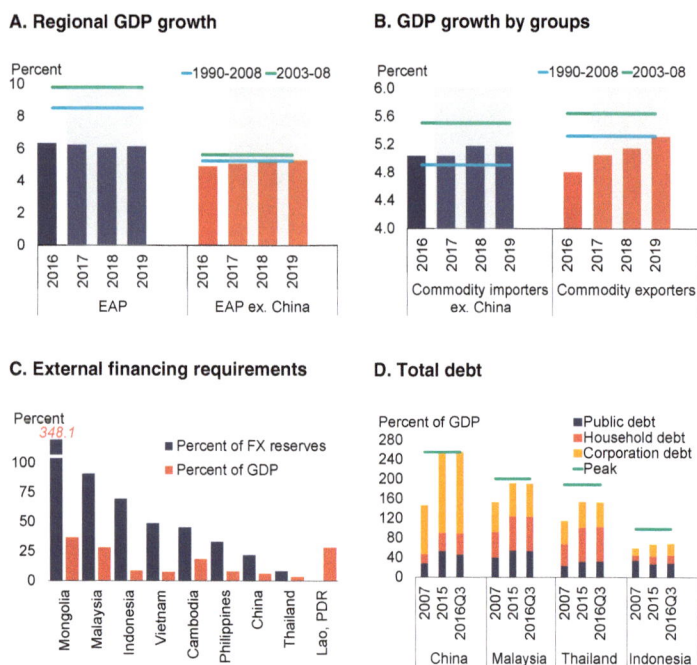

A. Regional GDP growth

B. GDP growth by groups

C. External financing requirements

D. Total debt

Sources: Bank of International Settlements, Haver Analytics, International Monetary Fund, World Bank, Quarterly External Debt Statistics.
Note: EAP stands for East Asia and Pacific.
A. B. Commodity importers ex. China include Cambodia, Philippines, Solomon Islands, Thailand, Vietnam, and Vanuatu. Commodity exporters include Indonesia, Lao PDR, Mongolia, and Malaysia.
C. Data are from 2016. For Malaysia, Vietnam, and Lao PDR, the data are from 2015. External financing requirements are defined as total debt obligations (sum of short-term external debt and long-term debt obligations) minus the current account balance.
D. The highest debt-to-GDP ratio since 1995Q1. The peak is identified to have occurred in 1997Q4 in Thailand, 1998Q4 in Malaysia, 2001Q4 in Indonesia, and 2016Q3 in China.

sustainable levels, before staging a modest recovery in 2018. A solid rebound is expected starting in 2019, reflecting macroeconomic stabilization, structural reforms, large new investments into coal and gold mines, and a rebound of production in the Oyu Tolgoi copper mine (World Bank 2017a).

Growth in *commodity importers* is projected to accelerate from 5.0 percent in 2017 to 5.2 percent on average in 2018-19, slightly above the long-term average of 4.8 percent. In the Philippines, growth, led by accelerated public and private investment, is expected to remain at just under 7

percent in 2017-19—significantly higher than the long-term average of 4.3 percent (World Bank 2017c). Accelerated public investment spending and recovering private consumption are expected to support slightly stronger growth in Thailand in 2018-19 (IMF 2016a; World Bank 2016b). Nevertheless, growth in Thailand will remain below the long-term trend of 4.5 percent, as policy uncertainty and slowing productivity growth dampen private investment. In Vietnam, growth is projected to remain solid, at slightly below 6.5 percent throughout the forecast period, helped by strong exports (World Bank and Ministry of Planning and Investment of Vietnam 2016). The outlook for Pacific Island countries is benign, reflecting favorable conditions for fisheries, tourism, and migration, conditional on proper domestic policies.

Risks

Risks to the outlook remain tilted to the downside and are mainly external. They include heightened policy uncertainty in the United States and Europe, increased protectionism, and the risk of an abrupt tightening of financing conditions. In addition, a steeper-than-expected slowdown in China would have sizable regional spillovers (World Bank 2016c).

Global economic policy uncertainty has been particularly elevated since the start of 2017. Sources of economic policy uncertainty are extensive. In the United States, the new administration has suggested major shifts in fiscal, trade, and immigration policies. In Europe, the rising influence of populist parties could re-orient policies and affect economic integration in the European Union. Negotiations around the exit of the United Kingdom from the European Union also carry risks. If the uncertainty persists, it could weigh on investor confidence and derail the ongoing recovery in growth (World Bank 2017a).

Rising protectionist sentiments in advanced economies are creating uncertainty about the future of established trading relationships (Chapter 1). The new U.S. administration has started reassessing a number of existing trade agreements. Some recent related actions, including the withdrawal of the United States from the Trans-Pacific Partnership (TPP), are already in effect. These could remove significant opportunities from Vietnam, and, to a lesser extent, Malaysia (World Bank 2016c). Changing trade policies would disproportionately affect the more open economies in the EAP region, especially those with sizable exports to advanced economies (e.g., Cambodia, China, Malaysia, Thailand, Vietnam). Significant disruption to China's exports would undermine its growth, with large spillovers on the region (IMF 2016b-e; World Bank 2016c). Furthermore, trade-restricting measures in the United States could trigger retaliatory measures.

A faster-than-expected tightening of global financing conditions could set back regional growth and exacerbate existing financial vulnerabilities.

The shock would transmit to the region through reduced capital flows, high volatility, pressure on nominal exchange rates and asset prices, and increased risk premiums. This could result in increased debt-service burdens and rollover risks, especially for unhedged short-term, foreign-currency-denominated debt (e.g., Malaysia, Mongolia) (IMF 2016f; World Bank 2016d and 2017a).

Domestic vulnerabilities, related to elevated domestic debt (e.g., China, Malaysia, Thailand) and large external financing needs in some countries (Indonesia, Malaysia, Mongolia), would amplify the impact of external shocks (BIS 2017; Figure 2.1.3). Shallow policy buffers are a concern in smaller countries (e.g., Mongolia, Papua New Guinea, especially, and to some extent in Lao PDR and Vietnam).

TABLE 2.1.1 East Asia and Pacific forecast summary

(Real GDP growth at market prices in percent, unless indicated otherwise)

	2014	2015	2016	2017	2018	2019	2016	2017	2018	2019
			Estimates	Projections			(percentage point difference from January 2017 projections)			
EMDE EAP, GDP[a]	6.8	6.5	6.3	6.2	6.1	6.1	0.0	0.0	0.0	0.0
(Average including countries with full national accounts and balance of payments data only)[b]										
EMDE EAP, GDP[b]	6.8	6.5	6.3	6.2	6.1	6.1	0.0	0.0	0.0	0.0
GDP per capita (U.S. dollars)	6.0	5.8	5.6	5.6	5.4	5.6	-0.1	0.1	-0.1	0.1
PPP GDP	6.6	6.4	6.3	6.2	6.0	6.1	0.0	0.1	-0.1	0.0
Private consumption	7.3	7.2	7.0	7.1	7.1	7.1	0.1	0.1	0.1	0.1
Public consumption	4.0	8.5	9.1	7.5	6.9	6.8	3.0	1.6	1.1	1.0
Fixed investment	6.5	6.7	6.5	6.4	6.0	6.1	0.1	0.2	0.3	0.4
Exports, GNFS[c]	7.6	0.9	2.2	3.3	3.6	4.1	-1.1	-1.0	-1.2	-0.7
Imports, GNFS[c]	6.8	1.3	3.8	4.9	5.0	5.2	-0.1	0.2	-0.4	-0.2
Net exports, contribution to growth	0.4	-0.1	-0.4	-0.4	-0.3	-0.2	-0.3	-0.4	-0.2	-0.1
Memo items: GDP										
East Asia excluding China	4.7	4.8	4.9	5.1	5.2	5.3	0.1	0.1	0.0	0.1
China	7.3	6.9	6.7	6.5	6.3	6.3	0.0	0.0	0.0	0.0
Indonesia	5.0	4.9	5.0	5.2	5.3	5.4	-0.1	-0.1	-0.2	-0.1
Thailand	0.9	2.9	3.2	3.2	3.3	3.4	0.1	0.0	0.0	0.0

Source: World Bank.

World Bank forecasts are frequently updated based on new information and changing (global) circumstances. Consequently, projections presented here may differ from those contained in other Bank documents, even if basic assessments of countries' prospects do not differ at any given moment in time.

a. EMDE refers to emerging market and developing economy. GDP at market prices and expenditure components are measured in constant 2010 U.S. dollars. Excludes American Samoa and Democratic People's Republic of Korea.

b. Sub-region aggregate excludes American Samoa, the Democratic People's Republic of Korea, Fiji, Kiribati, the Marshall Islands, the Federated States of Micronesia, Myanmar, Palau, Papua New Guinea, Samoa, Timor-Leste, Tonga, and Tuvalu, for which data limitations prevent the forecasting of GDP components.

c. Exports and imports of goods and non-factor services (GNFS).

For additional information, please see www.worldbank.org/gep.

TABLE 2.1.2 East Asia and Pacific country forecasts^a

(Real GDP growth at market prices in percent, unless indicated otherwise)

	2014	2015	2016	2017	2018	2019	2016	2017	2018	2019
			Estimates	Projections			(percentage point difference from January 2017 projections)			
Cambodia	7.1	7.0	6.9	6.9	6.9	6.7	-0.1	0.0	0.0	-0.1
China	7.3	6.9	6.7	6.5	6.3	6.3	0.0	0.0	0.0	0.0
Fiji	5.6	3.6	2.0	3.7	3.5	3.3	-0.4	-0.2	-0.2	-0.2
Indonesia	5.0	4.9	5.0	5.2	5.3	5.4	-0.1	-0.1	-0.2	-0.1
Lao PDR	7.5	7.4	7.0	7.0	6.8	7.2	0.0	0.0	0.0	0.0
Malaysia	6.0	5.0	4.2	4.9	4.9	5.0	0.0	0.6	0.4	0.5
Mongolia	6.9	2.2	1.0	-0.2	1.9	8.0	0.9	-2.2	-1.6	4.3
Myanmar	8.0	7.3	6.5	6.9	7.2	7.3	0.0	0.0	0.0	0.0
Papua New Guinea	7.4	6.8	2.4	3.0	3.2	3.4	0.0	0.0	0.0	0.4
Philippines	6.1	6.1	6.9	6.9	6.9	6.8	0.1	0.0	-0.1	0.1
Solomon Islands	2.0	3.3	3.0	3.3	3.0	3.0	0.0	0.0	0.0	0.0
Thailand	0.9	2.9	3.2	3.2	3.3	3.4	0.1	0.0	0.0	0.0
Timor-Leste^b	5.9	4.3	5.1	4.0	5.0	6.0	0.1	-1.5	-1.0	0.5
Vietnam	6.0	6.7	6.2	6.3	6.4	6.4	0.2	0.0	0.1	0.2

Source: World Bank.

World Bank forecasts are frequently updated based on new information and changing (global) circumstances. Consequently, projections presented here may differ from those contained in other Bank documents, even if basic assessments of countries' prospects do not significantly differ at any given moment in time.
a. GDP at market prices and expenditure components are measured in constant 2010 U.S. dollars. Excludes American Samoa and the Democratic People's Republic of Korea.
b. Non-oil GDP. Timor-Leste's total GDP, including the oil economy, is roughly four times the non-oil economy, and highly volatile, sensitive to changes in global oil prices and local production levels.
For additional information, please see www.worldbank.org/gep.

EUROPE and CENTRAL ASIA

The pickup in regional growth at the end of 2016 has persisted in 2017, with both commodity exporters and importers signaling recovery. The region is benefiting from rising oil prices, benign global financing conditions, robust growth in the Euro Area, and generally supportive policies. The 2017 growth forecast of 2.5 percent remains in line with January projections. Growth in the region is expected to edge up to an average of 2.8 percent in 2018-19, as activity in the Russian Federation and other commodity exporters firms, and growth in Turkey recovers. The main downside risks include renewed declines in oil and other commodity prices, policy uncertainty, and geopolitical risks, as well as international financial market disruptions. Domestic banking system weaknesses are vulnerabilities, and could become amplifiers of the effects of internal and external shocks.

Recent developments

The diverging growth paths in the region reversed in 2016 (Box 2.2.1) and growth momentum strengthened further in early 2017 in both commodity exporters and importers (Figure 2.2.1). Activity and trade in the Europe and Central Asia (ECA) region is benefiting from rising oil prices, benign global financing conditions, and robust growth in the Euro Area. Policies in several large ECA countries have also been supportive.

Commodity exporters have continued on the path of recovery, although with a few stumbles. Strengthening activity indicators for Russia suggest continued expansion in the first quarter of 2017. Modest monetary policy easing, as inflation approached the target of 4 percent at end-March, will support Russian growth in the near term. Early 2017 data indicate some signs of recovery in Azerbaijan, including in the non-oil sector, and a continued recovery in Kazakhstan, assisted by fiscal stimulus (World Bank 2017d). In contrast, renewed conflict in Ukraine is already taking a toll, and is manifested in weak industrial production data. Inflation in commodity exporters is slowing, reflecting easing depreciation pressures.

Recovery is also gaining momentum in commodity importers. Robust construction activity in Central Europe (e.g., Hungary, Poland) points towards firming investment, supported by EU structural funds. Early 2017 data suggest a continued recovery in Turkey despite elevated policy uncertainty. Turkey has remained in a state of emergency even after the approval of the government-proposed constitutional referendum that created a powerful executive presidency. The recession in Belarus shows some signs of abating, amid tailwinds from the Russian recovery. Growth momentum in Croatia, Moldova, and Serbia is steady, around potential growth. Inflation in commodity importers has been consistently undershooting lower monetary policy bounds, but has started gathering speed, with both core and non-core components accelerating.

Outlook

A broad-based acceleration in growth to 2.5 percent is expected in 2017, in line with January forecasts, but with some heterogeneity within the region. A forecast upgrade for Turkey due to the faster-than-anticipated recovery after the failed coup attempt is offset by a downward revision in Russia due to the extension of economic sanctions. Growth is expected to strengthen further in 2018-19, supported by a continuing recovery in commodity exporters in line with firming commodity prices, and the unwinding of

Note: The section was prepared by Yoki Okawa. Research assistance was provided by Shituo Sun.

BOX 2.2.1 Reversal in 2016 of diverging growth paths

Following a sharp slowdown in 2014-15 in the wake of the oil price collapse, regional growth started recovering in 2016. The growth rebound in large commodity exporters (e.g., Kazakhstan, Russia, Ukraine) in late 2016 was partly offset by a growth deceleration in large commodity importers (e.g., Hungary, Poland, Turkey), bringing the 2016 regional average to 1.5 percent, up from 1 percent in 2015.

The Russian economy, hit hard by the oil price plunge and economic sanctions, emerged from recession in the last quarter of 2016 (World Bank 2016f). Annual GDP remained virtually flat, in a notable improvement over the 2.8 percent contraction of 2015. The recovery was supported by rising oil prices and facilitated by exchange rate flexibility (World Bank 2017e). A strengthening oil sector and supportive policies, including fiscal stimulus in infrastructure and monetary policy easing, also contributed to the recovery in Kazakhstan in the second half of 2016, with growth stabilizing at 1 percent. In Ukraine, government stabilization efforts, supported by international financial institutions and a bumper agricultural crop, led to a sharp rebound in growth to 2.3 percent, following a

cumulative 15.8 percent contraction in 2014-15 in the wake of geopolitical tensions with Russia. In contrast, growth in Azerbaijan declined precipitously from 1.1 percent in 2015 to negative 3.8 percent in 2016 amid contraction in the non-oil sector. This, in part, reflected credit constraints as currency devaluations in 2015 strained the solvency of banks in Azerbaijan's highly dollarized banking system.

The pace of expansion in large commodity importers slowed. Despite strong recovery in the fourth quarter, growth in Turkey halved, to 2.9 percent—the lowest rate since the global financial crisis. The sharp deceleration reflected deteriorating business conditions in the wake of the failed coup attempt and sanctions imposed by Russia. In Poland and Hungary, slow disbursement of EU structural funds contributed to a contraction in investment, which weighed on growth. In contrast, an incipient recovery in Russia and Ukraine reduced adverse spillovers from these two large economies to neighboring economies in the eastern part of the region (e.g., Belarus, Moldova), although the economy of Belarus continued to contract.

geopolitical risks and domestic policy uncertainty in major economies in the region (Figure 2.2.2).

Growth in commodity exporters is projected to accelerate in 2017, driven by private consumption and investment amid strengthening commodity prices, although economic performance is expected to vary widely. In Russia, the 1.3 percent expansion this year, after a two-year recession, will be driven by consumption, as easing inflation will contribute to growth in real incomes. Strengthening oil prices and output and an accommodative macroeconomic policy stance will support Kazakhstan's growth recovery to 2.4 percent. Growth in Ukraine is projected to edge down to 2 percent. In contrast, output will continue contracting in Azerbaijan, although at a slower pace than in 2016 as weaknesses in the banking system as well as tight monetary and fiscal policies continue weighing on growth.

Growth in commodity importers is also expected to gather momentum in 2017, albeit only

modestly and to varying degrees. Output in Turkey is set to expand by 3.5 percent, supported by accommodative fiscal policy. Countries in Central Europe will benefit from EU infrastructure financing, with an acceleration of growth to 3.4 percent. Countries in the eastern part of the region will benefit from the continued recovery in Russia, though growth in Belarus is being held back by continued fiscal tightening needed to finance public debt repayment. While fiscal relaxation will contribute less to growth in Romania, it will put pressure on public and external deficits.

Growth in the region is expected to edge up to an average of 2.8 percent in 2018-19, as activity in Russia and other commodity exporters firms, and growth in Turkey recovers. Russia is expected to continue growing at a modest 1.4 percent, as low oil prices, demographic pressures, and slow implementation of structural reforms weigh on potential growth. In contrast, growth in Turkey is expected to accelerate to 4 percent as policy uncertainty abates, tourism recovers, and corporate balance sheets mend. Structural reforms, including in the banking sector, will help lift growth throughout the forecast horizon in Azerbaijan, Belarus, and Kazakhstan.

Risks

The projected upturn is fragile. Heightened policy uncertainties and geopolitical risks, within and outside the region, could set back growth in ECA. Other major risks include renewed decline in commodity prices and international financial market disruptions. Domestic banking system weaknesses are vulnerabilities, and could become amplifiers of the effects of internal and external shocks.

Subdued growth and growing anti-immigration sentiment have fueled populist opposition to European integration. An unwinding of integration in Europe would have implications for ECA given its close trade, financial, and remittances ties with advanced economies in the region (Figure 2.2.2; EBRD 2015; World Bank 2016c). Even in the absence of concrete anti-integration steps, uncertainty about policies can weigh on growth by discouraging investment, employment, foreign firm entry, and FDI (Crowley, Song, and Meng 2016; Kose et al. 2017a).

Geopolitical tensions may also suppress growth. A re-escalation of violence in Syria could undermine investor and consumer confidence, thereby putting a strain on growth. Within the region, geopolitical risks have been highlighted by the first major terrorist attack in Russia since 2012, a cargo blockade on eastern region in Ukraine in March, a renewed territorial dispute between Armenia and Azerbaijan since early 2016, reemerging political tension among Western Balkan countries, and domestic policy uncertainties in Belarus, Russia, and Turkey. In contrast, strengthening relations between Central Asian countries, including a provisional agreement on the demarcation between the Kyrgyz Republic and Uzbekistan, and restoration of direct flights between Tajikistan and Uzbekistan, could help boosting regional integration.

FIGURE 2.2.1 ECA: Recent developments

Growth momentum strengthened further in early 2017 for a majority of countries. Inflation in commodity exporters is slowing as depreciation pressures have eased, while inflation in commodity importers gathered speed.

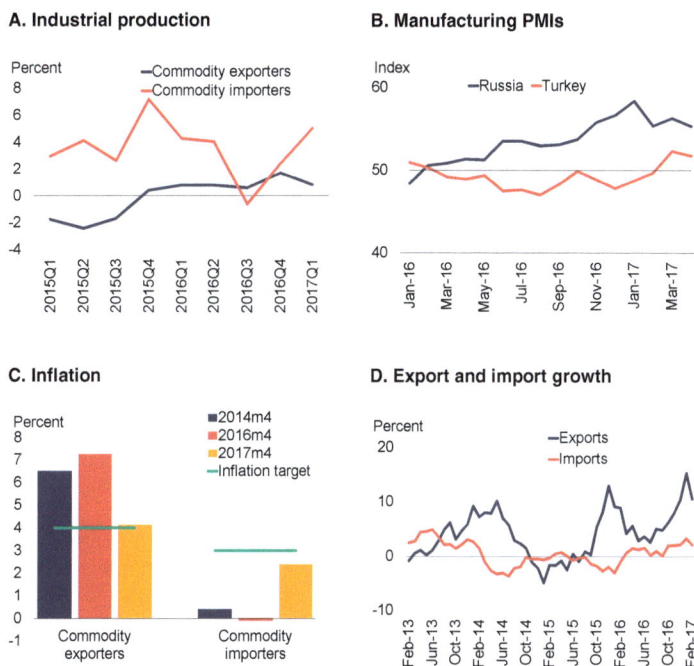

A. Industrial production

B. Manufacturing PMIs

C. Inflation

D. Export and import growth

Sources: Haver Analytics, World Bank.
Note: ECA stands for Europe and Central Asia.
A. Values are GDP weighted-average year-on-year growth. Commodity exporters include Armenia, Azerbaijan, Kazakhstan, Kyrgyz Republic, Russia, and Ukraine. Commodity importers include Belarus; Bosnia and Herzegovina; Bulgaria; Croatia; Hungary; Macedonia, FYR; Moldova; Montenegro; Poland; Romania; Serbia; and Turkey. Last observation is 2017Q1.
B. Purchasing managers' indexes for manufacturing. Values above 50 indicate expansion. Last observation is April 2017.
C. Inflation is median in each sub-grouping. Commodity exporters include Albania, Armenia, Azerbaijan, Kazakhstan, Kyrgyz Republic, Russia, and Ukraine. Commodity importers include Belarus; Bosnia and Herzegovina; Bulgaria; Croatia; Georgia; Hungary; Kosovo; Macedonia, FYR; Moldova; Poland; Romania; Serbia; and Turkey. Last observation is March 2017.
D. GDP weighted-average volume of exports and imports for Armenia, Hungary, Kazakhstan, Poland, Russia, Turkey, and Ukraine. Last observation is February 2017.

A renewed decline in commodity prices could negatively affect investment and consumption among ECA commodity exporters. The resulting slower growth could have spillovers to neighboring countries (World Bank 2016c). In addition, a disorderly tightening of global financing conditions may put pressure on currencies, raise borrowing costs, and lead to an outflow of capital from ECA region.

Domestic vulnerabilities may exacerbate the impact of external and internal shocks. Banking and corporate sector balance sheets with high degrees of dollarization (e.g., Azerbaijan, Armenia, Belarus, Georgia, Kazakhstan, Kyrgyz Republic,

FIGURE 2.2.2 **ECA: Outlook and risks**

A broad-based acceleration in activity, supported by consumption and investment, is expected in 2017-19. However, growth outcomes are projected to vary widely, especially in commodity exporters. Growth is expected to edge up further in 2018-19. Heightened policy uncertainties and geopolitical risks in Europe could inflict damage on growth in the ECA region. Domestic banking system weaknesses are vulnerabilities, and could become amplifiers of the effects of internal and external shocks.

A. Distribution of growth

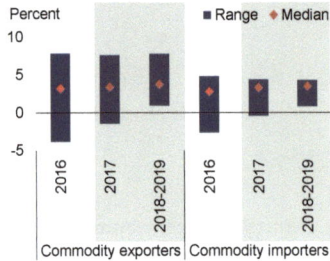

B. Country decomposition of growth

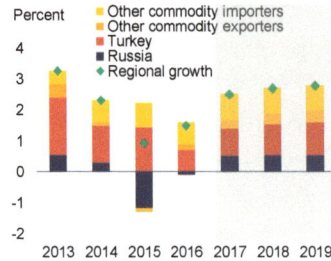

C. GDP decomposition of commodity exporters

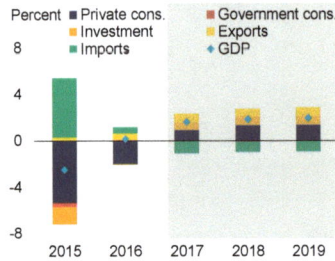

D. GDP decomposition of commodity importers

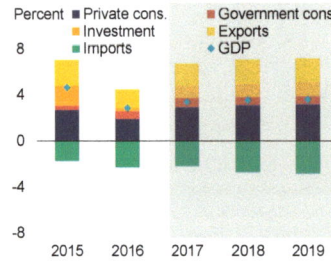

E. Trade and financial exposure

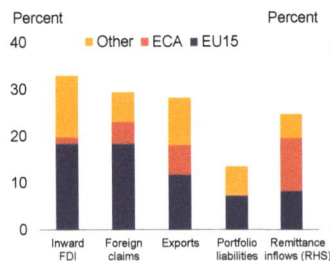

F. Non-performing loans

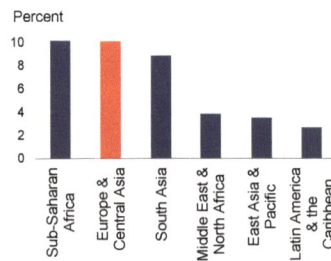

Sources: BIS, Bloomberg, Haver Analytics, World Bank.
Note: ECA stands for Europe and Central Asia.
A. Median and range among each sub-grouping. Commodity exporters include Albania, Armenia, Azerbaijan, Kazakhstan, Kosovo, Kyrgyz Republic, Russia, Tajikistan, Turkmenistan, Ukraine, and Uzbekistan. Commodity importers include Belarus; Bulgaria; Bosnia and Herzegovina; Croatia; Georgia; Hungary; Macedonia, FYR; Moldova; Montenegro; Poland; Romania; Serbia; and Turkey.
B. GDP-weighted growth. Commodity exporters include Albania, Armenia, Azerbaijan, Kazakhstan, Kyrgyz Republic, Ukraine, and Uzbekistan. Commodity importers include Belarus; Bulgaria; Croatia; Georgia; Hungary; Macedonia, FYR; Moldova; Poland; Romania and Uzbekistan.
C. Commodity exporters include Albania, Armenia, Azerbaijan, Kazakhstan, Kyrgyz Republic, Russia, Ukraine, and Uzbekistan. Cons. = consumption.
D. Commodity importers include Belarus; Bulgaria; Croatia; Georgia; Hungary; Macedonia, FYR; Moldova; Poland; Romania; and Turkey. Cons. = consumption.
E. Foreign claims refer to stock of total claims of BIS-reporting banks on foreign banks and non-banks. Trade refers to goods exports and imports. Data are average of 2010-15. Exports to the United States/Euro Area, remittances from the United States/Euro Area, and FDI from the United States/Euro Area (all in percent of GDP). FDI is stock of total FDI. ECA refers to EMDE ECA countries. EU15 includes Austria, Belgium, Denmark, Finland, France, Germany, Greece, Ireland, Italy, Luxembourg, Netherlands, Portugal, Spain, Sweden, and United Kingdom.
F. Share of non-performing loans to gross loans. Simple average of each sub-grouping of countries.

Tajikistan), low asset quality (e.g., Azerbaijan, Bosnia and Herzegovina, Croatia, Russia, Kazakhstan, Tajikistan, Serbia), and reliance on external funding (e.g., Belarus, Croatia, Georgia, Tajikistan, Turkey) are weak spots. While reforms aimed at strengthening financial systems are ongoing in many countries, including Azerbaijan, Belarus, Kazakhstan, Turkey, and Russia, the process of restoring banking sector health may be protracted (Reinhart and Rogoff 2014). Fiscal deficits in several ECA countries (e.g., Kyrgyz Republic, Tajikistan, Turkey, Romania) widened in 2016. Further deterioration in fiscal positions could exacerbate vulnerabilities.

TABLE 2.2.1 Europe and Central Asia forecast summary

(Real GDP growth at market prices in percent, unless indicated otherwise)

	2014	2015	2016	2017	2018	2019	2016	2017	2018	2019
			Estimates	Projections			(percentage point difference from January 2017 projections)			
EMDE ECA, GDP[a]	**2.3**	**1.0**	**1.5**	**2.5**	**2.7**	**2.8**	**0.3**	**0.1**	**-0.1**	**-0.1**
EMDE ECA, GDP excl. Russia	3.4	3.6	2.7	3.3	3.5	3.7	0.3	0.3	0.1	0.1
(Average including countries with full national accounts and balance of payments data only)[b]										
EMDE ECA, GDP[b]	2.3	0.9	1.5	2.5	2.7	2.8	0.3	0.1	0.0	-0.1
GDP per capita (U.S. dollars)	1.9	0.5	1.2	2.3	2.5	2.6	0.3	0.2	-0.1	-0.1
PPP GDP	2.2	0.7	1.5	2.5	2.7	2.8	0.4	0.1	-0.1	-0.1
Private consumption	2.0	-2.5	-0.1	3.4	3.9	4.0	-2.1	0.8	0.9	1.0
Public consumption	0.9	0.0	2.4	2.3	1.9	2.1	1.7	1.1	0.5	0.7
Fixed investment	2.3	0.4	0.4	3.8	4.2	4.3	0.1	-0.9	-2.6	-1.1
Exports, GNFS[c]	3.3	3.7	3.2	3.7	3.9	3.8	0.9	0.6	0.5	0.2
Imports, GNFS[c]	-0.5	-5.8	3.1	5.4	5.9	6.0	-0.2	0.7	-0.3	1.0
Net exports, contribution to growth	1.3	3.1	0.2	-0.3	-0.4	-0.5	0.4	0.0	0.3	-0.2
Memo items: GDP										
Commodity exporters[d]	0.8	-2.4	0.2	1.7	1.9	2.0	0.3	-0.1	-0.3	-0.3
Commodity importers[e]	4.0	4.6	2.8	3.4	3.5	3.6	0.2	0.4	0.2	0.2
Central Europe[f]	3.0	3.7	3.1	3.5	3.3	3.2	0.2	0.3	0.0	0.0
Western Balkans[g]	0.4	2.2	2.9	3.2	3.5	3.7	0.2	0.0	-0.1	0.0
Eastern Europe[h]	-3.8	-7.7	0.8	1.4	2.6	3.2	0.9	0.1	0.1	0.6
South Caucasus[i]	2.7	1.7	-2.1	0.1	1.6	2.2	-0.9	-2.0	-1.4	-0.7
Central Asia[j]	5.4	3.1	3.0	3.9	4.1	4.5	0.2	0.1	-0.7	-0.6
Russia	0.7	-2.8	-0.2	1.3	1.4	1.4	0.4	-0.2	-0.3	-0.4
Turkey	5.2	6.1	2.9	3.5	3.9	4.1	0.4	0.5	0.4	0.4
Poland	3.3	3.9	2.8	3.3	3.2	3.2	0.3	0.2	-0.1	-0.2

Source: World Bank.

World Bank forecasts are frequently updated based on new information and changing (global) circumstances. Consequently, projections presented here may differ from those contained in other Bank documents, even if basic assessments of countries' prospects do not differ at any given moment in time.

a. EMDE refers to emerging market and developing economy. GDP at market prices and expenditure components are measured in constant 2010 U.S. dollars.

b. Sub-region aggregate excludes Bosnia and Herzegovina, Kosovo, Montenegro, Serbia, Tajikistan, and Turkmenistan, for which data limitations prevent the forecasting of GDP components.

c. Exports and imports of goods and non-factor services (GNFS).

d. Includes Albania, Armenia, Azerbaijan, Kazakhstan, Kyrgyz Republic, Kosovo, Russia, Tajikistan, Turkmenistan, Ukraine, and Uzbekistan.

e. Includes Belarus; Bosnia and Herzegovina; Bulgaria; Croatia; Georgia; Hungary; Macedonia, FYR; Moldova; Montenegro; Poland; Romania; Serbia; and Turkey.

f. Includes Bulgaria, Croatia, Hungary, Poland, and Romania.

g. Includes Albania; Bosnia and Herzegovina; Kosovo; Macedonia, FYR; Montenegro; and Serbia.

h. Includes Belarus, Moldova, and Ukraine.

i. Includes Armenia, Azerbaijan, and Georgia.

j. Includes Kazakhstan, Kyrgyz Republic, Tajikistan, Turkmenistan, and Uzbekistan.

For additional information, please see www.worldbank.org/gep.

TABLE 2.2.2 Europe and Central Asia country forecasts[a]

(Real GDP growth at market prices in percent, unless indicated otherwise)

	2014	2015	2016	2017	2018	2019	2016	2017	2018	2019
			Estimates	Projections			(percentage point difference from January 2017 projections)			
Albania	1.8	2.6	3.2	3.5	3.5	3.8	0.0	0.0	0.0	0.1
Armenia	3.6	3.0	0.2	2.7	3.1	3.4	-2.2	0.0	0.1	0.2
Azerbaijan	2.0	1.1	-3.8	-1.4	0.6	1.3	-0.8	-2.6	-1.7	-1.0
Belarus	1.7	-3.9	-2.6	-0.4	0.5	1.2	-0.1	0.1	-0.8	-0.2
Bosnia and Herzegovina	1.1	3.0	2.8	3.2	3.7	4.0	0.0	0.0	0.0	0.1
Bulgaria	1.3	3.6	3.4	3.0	3.2	3.3	-0.1	-0.2	0.1	0.2
Croatia	-0.4	1.6	2.9	2.9	2.5	2.6	0.2	0.4	0.0	0.0
Georgia	4.6	2.9	2.7	3.5	4.0	4.5	-0.7	-1.7	-1.3	-0.5
Hungary	4.0	3.1	2.0	3.7	3.7	3.0	-0.1	0.6	0.3	0.0
Kazakhstan	4.2	1.2	1.0	2.4	2.6	2.9	0.1	0.2	-1.1	-1.1
Kosovo	1.2	4.1	3.6	3.9	4.2	4.4	0.0	0.0	0.5	0.8
Kyrgyz Republic	4.0	3.9	3.8	3.4	4.0	4.8	1.6	0.4	0.3	-0.1
Macedonia, FYR	3.6	3.8	2.4	2.8	3.3	3.8	0.4	-0.5	-0.4	-0.2
Moldova	4.8	-0.5	4.1	4.0	3.7	3.5	1.9	1.2	0.4	-0.2
Montenegro	1.8	3.4	2.5	3.3	3.0	2.0	-0.7	-0.3	0.0	-1.0
Poland	3.3	3.9	2.8	3.3	3.2	3.2	0.3	0.2	-0.1	-0.2
Romania	3.1	3.9	4.8	4.4	3.7	3.5	0.1	0.7	0.3	0.3
Russia	0.7	-2.8	-0.2	1.3	1.4	1.4	0.4	-0.2	-0.3	-0.4
Serbia	-1.8	0.8	2.8	3.0	3.5	3.5	0.3	0.2	0.0	0.0
Tajikistan	6.7	6.0	6.9	5.5	5.9	6.1	0.9	1.0	0.7	1.6
Turkey	5.2	6.1	2.9	3.5	3.9	4.1	0.4	0.5	0.4	0.4
Turkmenistan	10.3	6.5	6.2	6.3	6.5	6.5	0.0	-0.2	-0.3	-0.5
Ukraine	-6.6	-9.8	2.3	2.0	3.5	4.0	1.3	0.0	0.5	1.0
Uzbekistan	8.1	8.0	7.8	7.6	7.7	7.8	0.5	0.2	0.3	0.4

Source: World Bank.

World Bank forecasts are frequently updated based on new information and changing (global) circumstances. Consequently, projections presented here may differ from those contained in other Bank documents, even if basic assessments of countries' prospects do not significantly differ at any given moment in time.

a. GDP at market prices and expenditure components are measured in constant 2010 U.S. dollars.

For additional information, please see www.worldbank.org/gep.

LATIN AMERICA and THE CARIBBEAN

The regional economy appears to be stabilizing in 2017, but the recovery is uneven. Growth is expected to be 0.8 percent in 2017 as private consumption strengthens and the contraction in investment eases. Growth is projected to increase to 2.1 percent in 2018 as the recovery in Brazil and other commodity exporters gains traction. Risks to the outlook remain tilted to the downside and stem from domestic political and policy uncertainty, uncertainty about policy changes in the United States, and potential financial market disruptions that could hinder external financing.

Recent developments

Recent data for the largest economies in Latin American and the Caribbean are lackluster, yet broadly improving. Real activity data (for example, industrial production and PMI) have improved somewhat from the lows of 2016, while confidence has stabilized after falling in the three years to early 2016 (Figure 2.3.1, Box 2.3.1). The recent recovery in global trade is also evident in Latin America, where export volumes have picked up since mid-2016.

The recovery is uneven, however. While Argentina and Brazil appear to be pulling out of recessions, growth in Colombia slowed in 2017Q1, in part due to a value-added tax (VAT) hike. First quarter activity in Chile and Peru was held back by natural disasters and mining sector strikes.

Disinflation is underway in most large economies in the region, underpinned by exchange rate appreciation, monetary policy actions over the past year, and, especially in Brazil, falling food prices (Figure 2.3.2). Mexico is an exception, where inflation is increasing due to a still weak peso (reflecting the uncertain policy path in the United States) and rising fuel prices. Hyperinflation continues in República Bolivariana de Venezuela.

International bond issuance in Latin America accelerated in the first quarter of 2017 amid low market volatility and robust investor appetite for emerging market assets. Private sector debt issuance rose notably as energy firms sought to extend debt maturities or lower interest costs.

Early 2017 was marked by fiscal reforms in several countries. Mexico took steps to liberalize fuel prices in January. Colombia enacted a structural tax reform that includes adjustments to the VAT, simplification of the corporate and personal tax regimes, the imposition of some excise and subnational taxes, and measures to reduce tax evasion. Argentina initiated a quarterly path for fiscal targets. In Brazil, the pension reform plan being negotiated in the National Congress is expected to be finalized later this year, following the adoption in late 2016 of a constitutional amendment introducing a ceiling on federal primary expenditures for the next 20 years.

Nearly all countries in the region have fiscal deficits, and more than one-quarter have deficits of greater than 5 percent of GDP, in part reflecting the lingering effects of low commodity prices on government revenues. There was some correction in 2016, however, with nearly half of the countries in the region managing to improve their budget positions. The largest improvements occurred in small economies, including Grenada (stronger adherence to fiscal rules and improved tax administration and compliance), Belize (rising

Note: This section was prepared by Dana Vorisek. Research assistance was provided by Shituo Sun.

BOX 2.3.1 Continued growth divergence within Latin America and the Caribbean

Latin America and the Caribbean experienced a second year of contraction in 2016—the continent's first multi-year recession since the 1980s—with output contracting 1.4 percent. Performance in the subregions varied substantially, however. While growth eased to a moderate 2.5 percent in Mexico and Central America, and in the Caribbean, the contraction in South America deepened, to 2.9 percent. Growth for the region as a whole was nevertheless in line with expectations in January 2017.

Within South America, output contracted in four countries in 2016—Argentina, Brazil, Ecuador, and República Bolivariana de Venezuela—while the majority of other South American countries saw a slowdown in growth. Adjustment to subdued commodity prices continued to dampen activity in South America. In Brazil, rising unemployment, tightening financial conditions, and continued political tensions extended deep declines in private consumption and investment. In Argentina, the short-term rise in inflation that resulted from the removal of public service subsidies contributed to a contraction in private consumption and investment. Peru was a notable exception to the trend in South America, as growth was lifted by booming copper production as a large new mine began operating. Conditions in the two largest economies of

South America (Brazil and Argentina) improved somewhat in the second half of the year, however. Argentina saw the start of a recovery in the third quarter of 2016. Although Brazil experienced its eighth quarterly contraction in Q4, the decline moderated on a year-on-year basis.

The slight growth deceleration in Mexico and Central America in 2016 mainly reflects easing growth in Mexico, where investment and net exports were less supportive of growth in the context of subdued capital inflows and global trade. Growth in Central America also eased, mainly reflecting slowing growth in Guatemala on heightened political uncertainty and contracting public spending. Guatemala and other Central American countries did, however, experience robust growth in remittances in 2016 as the U.S. labor market recovered, and in anticipation of changes in U.S. immigration policy (World Bank 2017f).

In the Caribbean, the deceleration in 2016 reflected a modest slowdown in the Dominican Republic, the largest economy in the region, on the completion of construction projects and weakening manufacturing growth. Contraction in several commodity-exporting countries (Belize, Suriname, Trinidad and Tobago) also contributed to the deceleration.

revenue, including from fuel tax hikes), and Suriname (reduced procurement spending). The median deficit in commodity-exporting countries is on track to recede in 2017 as recovering commodity prices bolster government revenues and budget reform programs progress.

Outlook

Growth in Latin America and the Caribbean is projected to strengthen to 0.8 percent in 2017, as Argentina and Brazil emerge from recessions (Figure 2.3.3, Table 2.3.1). A growth recovery in commodity exporters in the region will be offset to some extent by easing growth in Mexico. The pace of the regional recovery is projected to be slower than forecasted in the January *Global Economic Prospects* as a result of a more protracted adjustment to previous commodity price declines and continued policy uncertainty.

After dropping sharply in response to falling commodity prices and domestic political uncertainty, investment appears set to return to positive growth in 2017 in some countries (e.g., Argentina, Colombia). In Argentina, investment will be supported by an improved business climate following reforms by the Macri administration and a strong increase in public investment, albeit projected within the planned fiscal consolidation path. In Colombia, a rebound in infrastructure investment will be supported by a large national road project. Nonetheless, for the region as whole, the investment contribution to growth will continue to be slightly negative in 2017. Private consumption and net exports are expected to provide a boost to growth as activity in commodity exporters recovers.

A rising forecast for metals prices should favor metals and minerals producers. However, the metal-exporting economies in the region face diverging growth paths, due to idiosyncratic factors. Copper production in Chile, which was deeply disrupted early in the year by a strike at the largest mine, should recover sufficiently for growth to accelerate modestly, to 1.8 percent. Growth in Peru is projected to decelerate in 2017, reflecting the adverse impacts of major floods early in the year and softening copper production and exports.

Growth in energy exporters is projected to be mixed this year. In Colombia, stable growth reflects rebounding investment and exports and an uptick in imports, while the higher VAT is expected to keep private consumption growth flat. Growth in Ecuador is projected to continue contracting, though less deeply than in 2016, reflecting slowing momentum in fiscal consolidation.

Growth in Mexico is projected to slow to 1.8 percent, from 2.3 percent in 2016, mainly on an expected contraction of investment, in turn reflecting uncertainty about U.S. economic policy. In the remainder of Central America, growth is expected to be stable. Strengthening tourism demand underlies an expected acceleration in growth to 3.3 percent in the Caribbean.

The regional recovery is expected to gather pace in 2018 and 2019 as growth picks up in the largest economy, Brazil, and in energy exporters. In Argentina and Brazil, reforms implemented over the past two years to stabilize government finances are expected to begin to yield dividends, as will efforts in Argentina to improve the business climate. The medium-term outlook for Brazil is constrained, however, by the need for private and public sector deleveraging, following a rapid increase in debt prior to the 2015–16 recession, and the medium-term forecast for Argentina is subject to significant uncertainty. For Mexico, the negative impacts from potential U.S. policy changes will weigh on investment and growth prospects. More generally, long-term growth in the region is constrained by infrastructure bottle-necks, highlighting the trade-off with short-term fiscal consolidation needs, and by expected sub-dued long-term commodity price growth following the end of the latest commodity supercycle.

FIGURE 2.3.1 LAC: Recent developments

Early 2017 data for the largest economies in the region are lackluster, yet broadly improving. Exports from the region have picked up since mid-2016. Disinflation is underway in most large Latin American economies, reflecting strengthening currencies. In Mexico, however, currency depreciation has pushed inflation above the central bank target range. Despite bouts of market volatility in late 2016, external financing conditions remain accommodative.

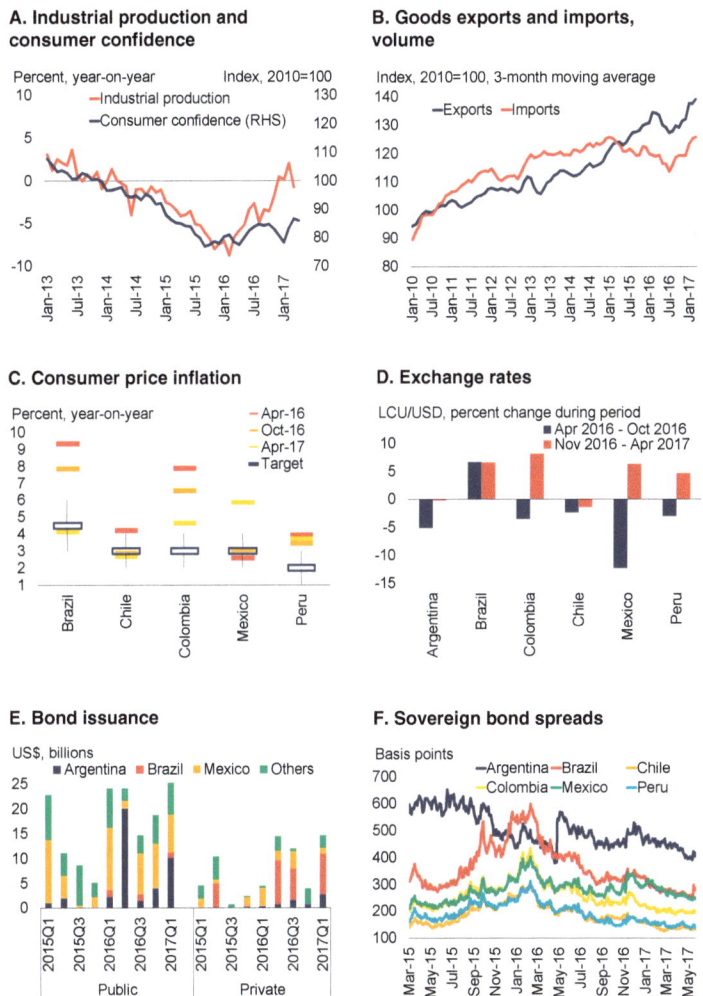

A. Industrial production and consumer confidence

B. Goods exports and imports, volume

C. Consumer price inflation

D. Exchange rates

E. Bond issuance

F. Sovereign bond spreads

Sources: CPB Netherlands Bureau for Economic Policy Analysis, Dealogic, Haver Analytics, World Bank.
Note: LAC stands for Latin America and the Caribbean.
A. GDP-weighted averages using seasonally-adjusted data for Brazil and Mexico. Last observation is March 2017 for industrial production and April 2017 for consumer confidence.
B. Lines show aggregate volumes for Argentina, Bolivia, Brazil, Chile, Colombia, Costa Rica, the Dominican Republic, Ecuador, Guatemala, Mexico, Paraguay, Peru, and Uruguay. Last observation is March 2017.
C. Blue boxes show central inflation targets; vertical lines show target bands.
D. LCU is local currency unit.
F. Measures the average spread of a country's sovereign debt (as measured by J.P. Morgan's Emerging Markets Bond Index) over the equivalent maturity U.S. Treasury bond. Last observation is May 24, 2017.

FIGURE 2.3.2 LAC: Outlook and risks

The two-year contraction in growth in Latin America and the Caribbean is expected to end in 2017. Net exports are projected to support growth in 2017–19, in part due to firming commodity prices. But the recovery will be largely driven by accelerating private consumption and investment. Strong trade and financial linkages with the United States mean that U.S. policy changes could impact regional activity. Fiscal imbalances, particularly in South America, make the region vulnerable to global financing shocks. The rising impact of natural disasters in the region stands to derail growth in some countries.

A. Contribution to GDP growth

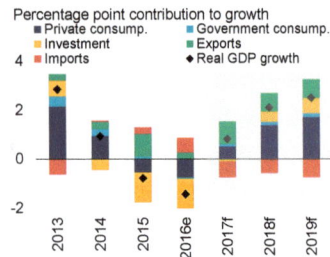

B. Commodity prices

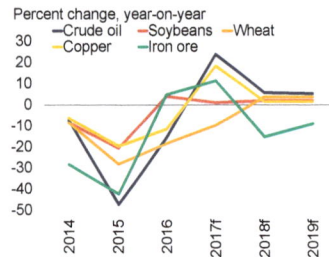

C. Exports to the United States and China, 2015–16

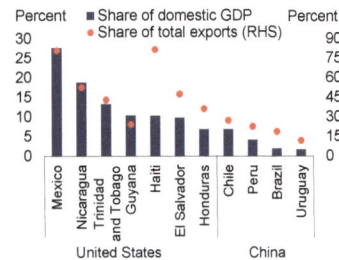

D. Remittance inflows, 2015

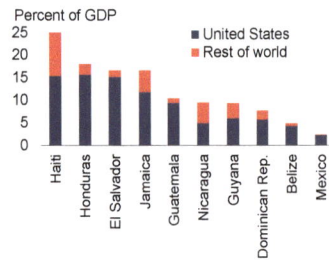

E. Fiscal balances

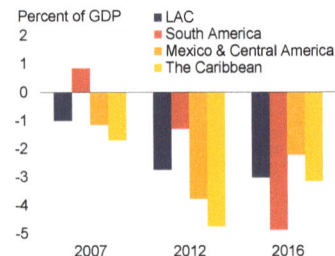

F. Natural disasters

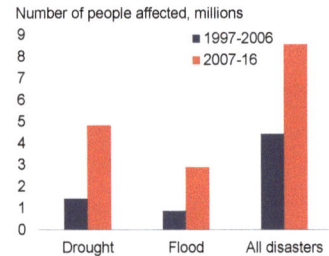

Sources: Centre for Research on the Epidemiology of Disasters, Haver Analytics, International Monetary Fund, national sources, World Bank.
Note: LAC stands for Latin America and the Caribbean.
A. GDP-weighted averages. Countries covered are Antigua and Barbuda, Argentina, The Bahamas, Barbados, Belize, Bolivia, Brazil, Chile, Colombia, Costa Rica, Dominica, the Dominican Republic, Ecuador, El Salvador, Guatemala, Guyana, Haiti, Honduras, Jamaica, Mexico, Nicaragua, Panama, Paraguay, Peru, St. Lucia, St. Vincent and the Grenadines, Trinidad and Tobago, Uruguay, and República Bolivariana de Venezuela. e = estimate. f = forecast.
B. Percent change of average annual prices. f = forecast.
C. 2015–16 average for share of GDP and share of goods exports.
E. Median for each country group.
F. Annual average for year spans indicated. "All disasters" include droughts, floods, storms, landslides, and wildfires. Countries covered are Antigua and Barbuda, Argentina, The Bahamas, Barbados, Belize, Bolivia, Brazil, Chile, Colombia, Costa Rica, Cuba, Dominica, the Dominican Republic, Ecuador, El Salvador, Grenada, Guatemala, Guyana, Haiti, Honduras, Jamaica, Mexico, Nicaragua, Panama, Paraguay, Peru, St. Kitts and Nevis, St. Lucia, St. Vincent and the Grenadines, Suriname, Trinidad and Tobago, Uruguay, and República Bolivariana de Venezuela. The population of these countries averaged 533 million in 1997-2006 and 605 million in 2007-16.

Risks

Risks to the growth outlook for Latin America and the Caribbean remain tilted to the downside. They stem most prominently from domestic political and policy uncertainty, possible policy changes in major advanced economies (in particular, the United States), a sharp or disorderly tightening of global financing conditions, lower-than-expected commodity prices, and the increasingly severe impact of natural disasters.

In a number of countries in the region, persistent domestic political uncertainty could hinder growth in the short and medium term by reducing confidence. In addition, the region faces an elevated level of policy uncertainty related to election cycles. Four major countries in the region (Brazil, Chile, Colombia, Mexico) are scheduled to hold legislative and presidential elections between November 2017 and October 2018.

Although expansionary U.S. fiscal policy stands to have positive spillovers for exports from the region, a more protectionist trade policy stance in the United States would be detrimental to Mexico and many Central American and Caribbean economies (IADB 2017). For Mexico, a renegotiation of the North American Free Trade Agreement (NAFTA) could have repercussions not only for exports, but also for investment, which was boosted by the agreement. NAFTA has also been found to have boosted total factor productivity in Mexico (Shiff and Wang 2002) and accelerated economic convergence in North America (Easterly, Fiess, and Lederman 2003). Central America would suffer from rising U.S. trade protectionism through its strong trade linkages to both the United States and Mexico. For commodity producers in South America, a shift in the composition of GDP in China toward services could also hinder growth through a reduction in exports.

More restrictive U.S. immigration policy may reduce remittance flows to the region, with a follow-on drop in private consumption and investment. Central America and some Caribbean countries, where remittances are an important source of household income are particularly vulnerable. In the medium term, the adverse effects on growth of tighter U.S. immigration policy may be mitigated, at least to some degree, by expanding labor forces as returning migrants begin to be reabsorbed by the domestic labor markets.

Faster-than-expected U.S. interest rate hikes or U.S. dollar appreciation could make it more difficult and costlier to secure financing in some countries in the region—in particular, those with elevated dollar-denominated debt or high government financing needs (Argentina, Chile, some Caribbean economies). Despite the recent pursuit of countercyclical fiscal policies in some countries, the lack of fiscal buffers remains a vulnerability in the region (World Bank 2017g; IMF 2017b).

The path of commodity prices also stands to impact growth in the region. In particular, a less-robust-than-expected recovery of global oil and natural gas prices in 2017 would undermine the expected pace of growth in Bolivia, Colombia, Ecuador, and Trinidad and Tobago, all of which are heavily reliant on energy exports.

Finally, changing environmental patterns pose growing risks (World Bank 2014). The average number of people per year in the region affected by natural disasters, especially droughts and floods, doubled in 2007–16 compared to the previous decade. Drought impacted approximately 4.3 million people in the region in 2016.

TABLE 2.3.1 Latin America and the Caribbean forecast summary

(Real GDP growth at market prices in percent, unless indicated otherwise)

	2014	2015	2016	2017	2018	2019	2016	2017	2018	2019
			Estimates	Projections			(percentage point difference from January 2017 projections)			
EMDE LAC, GDP[a]	0.9	-0.8	-1.4	0.8	2.1	2.5	0.0	-0.4	-0.2	-0.1
(Average including countries with full national accounts and balance of payments data only)[b]										
EMDE LAC, GDP[b]	0.9	-0.8	-1.4	0.8	2.1	2.5	0.0	-0.4	-0.2	-0.1
GDP per capita (U.S. dollars)	-0.2	-1.9	-2.5	-0.2	1.1	1.5	0.0	-0.3	-0.1	-0.1
PPP GDP	1.1	-0.2	-0.9	1.1	2.2	2.6	0.0	-0.3	-0.2	0.0
Private consumption	1.5	-0.8	-1.2	0.8	2.1	2.7	0.3	-0.1	-0.1	0.3
Public consumption	1.9	0.6	-0.3	0.5	0.9	0.9	0.9	1.7	0.4	0.0
Fixed investment	-2.0	-5.8	-6.4	-0.6	2.3	3.3	-1.5	-1.0	0.0	-0.1
Exports, GNFS[c]	1.5	4.5	1.2	4.2	3.2	3.2	-0.3	0.9	-0.1	-0.3
Imports, GNFS[c]	-0.2	-1.2	-2.7	2.9	2.6	3.4	-0.3	2.7	0.5	0.6
Net exports, contribution to growth	0.3	1.2	0.9	0.3	0.2	0.0	0.1	-0.4	-0.1	-0.2
Memo items: GDP										
South America[d]	0.3	-2.1	-2.9	0.3	1.9	2.3	-0.1	-0.5	-0.2	-0.1
Mexico and Central America[e]	2.5	2.9	2.5	2.1	2.4	2.7	0.2	0.0	-0.3	-0.2
Caribbean[f]	3.9	3.4	2.5	3.3	3.8	3.7	-0.7	0.2	0.4	0.4
Brazil	0.5	-3.8	-3.6	0.3	1.8	2.1	-0.2	-0.2	0.0	-0.1
Mexico	2.3	2.6	2.3	1.8	2.2	2.5	0.3	0.0	-0.3	-0.3
Argentina	-2.5	2.6	-2.3	2.7	3.2	3.2	0.0	0.0	0.0	0.0

Source: World Bank.
World Bank forecasts are frequently updated based on new information and changing (global) circumstances. Consequently, projections presented here may differ from those contained in other Bank documents, even if basic assessments of countries' prospects do not differ at any given moment in time.
a. EMDE refers to emerging market and developing economy. GDP at market prices and expenditure components are measured in constant 2010 U.S. dollars. Excludes Cuba.
b. Aggregate includes all countries in notes d, e, and f except Grenada, St. Kitts and Nevis, and Suriname, for which data limitations prevent the forecasting of GDP components.
c. Exports and imports of goods and non-factor services (GNFS).
d. Includes Argentina, Bolivia, Brazil, Chile, Colombia, Ecuador, Paraguay, Peru, Uruguay, and República Bolivariana de Venezuela.
e. Includes Costa Rica, El Salvador, Guatemala, Honduras, Mexico, Nicaragua, and Panama.
f. Includes Antigua and Barbuda, The Bahamas, Barbados, Belize, Dominica, the Dominican Republic, Grenada, Guyana, Haiti, Jamaica, St. Kitts and Nevis, St. Lucia, St. Vincent and the Grenadines, Suriname, and Trinidad and Tobago.
For additional information, please see www.worldbank.org/gep.

TABLE 2.3.2 Latin America and the Caribbean country forecasts[a]

(Real GDP growth at market prices in percent, unless indicated otherwise)

	2014	2015	2016	2017	2018	2019	2016	2017	2018	2019
			Estimates	Projections			(percentage point difference from January 2017 projections)			
Argentina	-2.5	2.6	-2.3	2.7	3.2	3.2	0.0	0.0	0.0	0.0
Belize	4.1	1.0	-1.5	2.1	2.0	2.0	-0.5	0.6	0.0	-0.5
Bolivia	5.5	4.9	4.3	3.7	3.7	3.4	0.6	0.2	0.3	0.0
Brazil	0.5	-3.8	-3.6	0.3	1.8	2.1	-0.2	-0.2	0.0	-0.1
Chile	1.9	2.3	1.6	1.8	2.0	2.3	0.0	-0.2	-0.3	-0.2
Colombia	4.4	3.1	2.0	2.0	3.1	3.4	0.3	-0.5	0.1	0.1
Costa Rica	3.7	4.7	4.3	3.8	3.6	3.5	0.0	-0.1	-0.1	-0.2
Dominica	3.9	2.2	0.6	3.0	2.1	2.1	-0.7	0.2	-0.6	-0.6
Dominican Republic	7.6	7.0	6.6	5.3	5.0	4.8	-0.2	0.8	0.8	0.8
Ecuador	4.0	0.2	-1.5	-1.3	-0.4	0.3	0.8	1.6	0.2	-0.7
El Salvador	1.4	2.3	2.4	2.0	1.8	1.7	0.2	0.1	-0.2	-0.3
Guatemala	4.2	4.1	3.1	3.5	3.5	3.6	0.2	0.3	0.1	0.2
Guyana	3.8	3.1	3.3	3.5	3.6	3.7	0.7	-0.3	-0.3	-0.4
Haiti[b]	2.8	1.2	1.4	0.5	1.7	2.3	0.2	1.1	0.2	0.3
Honduras	3.1	3.6	3.6	3.4	3.3	3.3	-0.1	-0.1	-0.1	0.1
Jamaica	0.7	1.0	1.4	2.0	2.1	2.3	-0.2	0.0	-0.2	-0.2
Mexico	2.3	2.6	2.3	1.8	2.2	2.5	0.3	0.0	-0.3	-0.3
Nicaragua	4.8	4.9	4.7	4.3	4.2	4.2	0.2	0.3	0.3	0.4
Panama	6.1	5.8	4.9	5.2	5.4	5.8	-0.5	-0.2	-0.1	0.3
Paraguay	4.7	3.0	4.1	3.6	3.8	3.8	0.3	0.0	0.5	0.5
Peru	2.4	3.3	3.9	2.8	3.8	3.6	-0.1	-1.4	0.0	0.0
St. Lucia	0.5	1.6	0.8	0.5	0.7	0.7	-0.2	-1.3	-1.5	-1.8
St. Vincent and the Grenadines	-0.5	2.1	1.8	2.5	2.8	2.9	-0.2	0.3	0.4	0.5
Suriname	0.4	-2.7	-10.4	0.9	2.2	1.2	-3.4	0.4	1.1	-0.1
Trinidad and Tobago	-0.6	-0.6	-5.1	0.3	3.4	3.3	-2.3	-2.0	-0.2	0.1
Uruguay	3.2	0.4	1.5	1.6	2.4	3.4	0.8	0.0	-0.1	-0.3
Venezuela, RB	-3.9	-8.2	-12.0	-7.7	-1.2	0.7	-0.4	-3.4	-1.7	-0.3

Source: World Bank.
World Bank forecasts are frequently updated based on new information and changing (global) circumstances. Consequently, projections presented here may differ from those contained in other Bank documents, even if basic assessments of countries' prospects do not significantly differ at any given moment in time.
a. GDP at market prices and expenditure components are measured in constant 2010 U.S. dollars.
b. GDP is based on fiscal year, which runs from October to September of next year.
For additional information, please see www.worldbank.org/gep.

MIDDLE EAST and NORTH AFRICA

Growth in the Middle East and North Africa region is projected to fall from 3.2 percent in 2016 to 2.1 percent in 2017. The adverse impact of OPEC-led oil production cuts in oil exporters is expected to more than offset the modestly improving growth in oil importers. Regional growth is forecast to pick up gradually, reaching 3.1 percent by 2019, despite continued fiscal consolidation in both oil exporters and importers. The key risks to the outlook include continued geopolitical tensions and conflicts, a lower-than-expected rise in oil prices for oil exporters, and challenges that may delay implementation of key structural reforms.

Recent developments

Growth in the Middle East and North Africa (MENA) region remained subdued at 3.2 percent in 2016, due in part to the impact of low oil prices on the region's key oil exporters (Figure 2.4.1).[1] Growth in Gulf Cooperation Council (GCC) economies was held back by low oil prices and fiscal consolidation. Lower transfers from oil funds to general budgets were accompanied by tightened liquidity in the banking sector, which is reliant on public sector deposits, and has weighed on non-oil activity. Offsetting the slower growth in GCC oil exporters was stronger-than-expected growth in non-GCC oil exporters, due to rising oil production in the Islamic Republic of Iran following the lifting of sanctions, as well as improved security in Iraq.

In 2017, growth in the MENA region continues to be held back by oil production cuts, fiscal

consolidation, and regional conflicts. Production in the oil sector has declined in the first four months of 2017 as a result of the November 2016 OPEC production cut agreement.[2] Among the top five oil producers in the region (Iraq, Islamic Republic of Iran, Kuwait, Saudi Arabia, and the United Arab Emirates), oil production cuts in the first quarter of 2017 amounted to more than one million barrels a day relative to October 2016 levels. The largest cuts were implemented by Saudi Arabia, but compliance with OPEC mandates has been higher than expected across most oil exporters.

Oil importers have been gradually gaining momentum since 2016, during which poor harvests (e.g., severe drought in Morocco) as well as geopolitical conflicts (e.g., terrorist attacks in the Arab Republic of Egypt and Jordan, repercussions from closure of export routes from Jordan to the Syrian Arab Republic) constrained growth. Egypt, the largest oil importer, has been adjusting to a flexible exchange rate regime since November 2016, contributing to improving exports and industrial production in the beginning of 2017. Egypt and other large importers are also beginning to undertake reforms to their business environments, such as the launch of Morocco's

---

Note: This section was prepared by Lei Sandy Ye, with contributions from Ergys Islamaj. Research assistance was provided by Liwei Liu.

[1] The World Bank's Middle East and North Africa aggregate includes 16 economies, and is grouped into three subregions. Bahrain, Kuwait, Oman, Qatar, Saudi Arabia, and the United Arab Emirates comprise the Gulf Cooperation Council (GCC); all are oil exporters. Other oil exporters in the region are Algeria, the Islamic Republic of Iran, and Iraq. Oil importers in the region are Djibouti, the Arab Republic of Egypt, Jordan, Lebanon, Morocco, Tunisia, and West Bank and Gaza. The Syrian Arab Republic, the Republic of Yemen, and Libya are excluded from regional growth aggregates due to data limitations.

[2] The OPEC production cut agreement attempts to contain the increase in global oil stocks and rebalance global oil markets. These cuts were initially scheduled to last until June 2017 and have subsequently been extended to March 2018.

FIGURE 2.4.1 MENA: Recent developments

Growth in MENA is softening in 2017. The adverse impact of OPEC-led production cuts in oil exporters more than offsets stronger growth in other regional economies. Inflation has picked up sharply in several countries. The peg to the dollar has contained inflation, but has led to real exchange rate appreciations in Saudi Arabia and the United Arab Emirates.

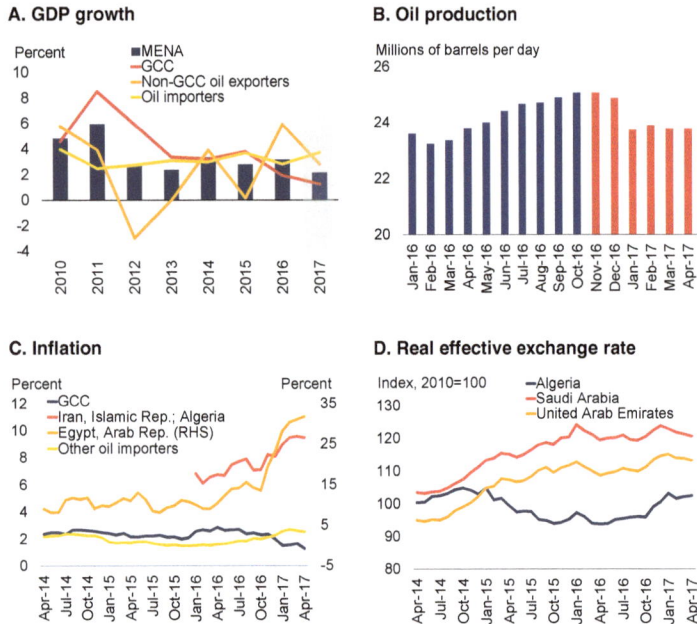

A. GDP growth

B. Oil production

C. Inflation

D. Real effective exchange rate

Sources: Bank for International Settlements, Haver Analytics, International Energy Agency, World Bank.
Note: MENA stands for Middle East and North Africa.
A. Weighted average growth of real GDP.
B. Sum of daily crude oil productions of Iraq, Islamic Republic of Iran, Kuwait, Saudi Arabia, and the United Arab Emirates. Red columns denote period since November 2016 OPEC production cut agreement. Last observation is April 2017.
C. Unweighted averages. GCC includes Bahrain, Kuwait, Oman, Saudi Arabia, Qatar, and the United Arab Emirates. Other oil importers include Morocco, Tunisia, Lebanon, and Jordan. Year-on-year growth rates. Last observation is April 2017.
D. Broad indexes of weights comprising 61 economies. Last observation is April 2017.

Islamic banking services in January, to relieve structural bottlenecks and improve private sector activity.

Inflation has picked up in several large economies. Egypt's core and overall inflation rate exceeded 30 percent (y/y) in March 2017 due to currency depreciation and rising food prices. As a result of higher oil prices, inflation in most oil importers outside of Egypt has also begun to edge up this year. Food price pressures have further contributed to rising inflation in Algeria and the Islamic Republic of Iran, climbing back to double digits (y/y) in March 2017 in the latter (although still on a declining trend from an annual rate of about 35 percent in 2013). In contrast, exchange

rates largely pegged to the U.S. dollar and subdued oil prices helped keep inflation below 3 percent among GCC economies. The peg to the U.S. dollar has, however, implied appreciations of the real effective exchange rate in Saudi Arabia and the United Arab Emirates, which may hinder their adjustment to low oil prices.

Fiscal consolidation programs continue against the backdrop of sizable current account and fiscal deficits in the region. These programs feature expenditure cuts, new or increased value-added and excise taxes, and energy subsidy reforms. In several economies (e.g., GCC), some of these programs are part of longer-term policies to promote diversification beyond the energy sector. These include Saudi Arabia's National Transformation Plan and Vision 2030; and a GCC-wide value-added tax of 5 percent, effective in 2018. While consolidation programs have already contributed to estimated fiscal improvements by the start of 2017 in a few economies (e.g., Morocco, Jordan), most others registered weaker external and fiscal accounts from 2015 to 2016.

Supported by benign global financing conditions, renewed investor risk appetite since the start of 2017, and driven by the need to finance fiscal deficits, international bond issuances in the region have been resilient, amounting to more than $45 billion in early 2017. GCC economies have also embarked on efforts to promote equity investor confidence, including in the context of the impending initial public offering of Saudi Aramco, the state oil company, under what is expected to be the largest valuation on record. In Saudi Arabia and the United Arab Emirates, higher composite purchasing managers' indexes (PMIs) over the past five months suggest that business confidence is improving.

Outlook

Regional growth is projected to fall from 3.2 percent in 2016 to 2.1 percent in 2017. The adverse impact of OPEC-led oil production cuts in oil exporters more than offsets the modestly improving growth in oil importers. Growth is expected to recover to an average of 3.0 percent in 2018-19. While the deceleration in 2017 is driven by oil exporters, the modest recovery in the longer-term outlook is broad-based. This forecast assumes a moderation of geopolitical tensions, as well as an increase in oil prices, which are expected to average $53 per barrel (bbl) in 2017 and $56 per bbl in 2018—a slight downgrade from January projections. Given the considerable uncertainty associated with oil prices in 2017, fiscal consolidation is expected to continue, as the fiscal break-even prices for most oil exporters in the region remain above projected oil prices (Figure 2.4.2). Oil importers are expected to see higher growth starting in 2017, aided by improved competitiveness, reforms, and a recovery in agricultural conditions.

The forecast assumes that OPEC-mandated production cuts constrain GCC growth in 2017. Growth in Saudi Arabia, the largest economy in the region, and Iraq will slow as a result of continued production cuts. In the Islamic Republic of Iran, the second-largest economy in the region, limited spare capacity in oil production and difficulty in accessing finance are weighing on the country's growth. Offsetting factors include solid current account and fiscal positions, which are expected to support a steady growth outlook of about 4 percent over 2017-19.

The non-oil sectors in most oil exporters are expected to modestly recover in 2017 from the weakness in 2016, as improved revenues from higher oil prices provide space for more expansionary fiscal policy, and as rising deposits increase the funding capacity for bank lending (Miyajima 2017). However, the real economy's ability to leverage improving conditions may be limited by weaknesses in private sector participation as well as in the governance framework for investors and corporations (EBRD et al. 2016; Schiffbauer et al. 2015). Over 2018-19, growth in oil exporters is expected to modestly improve as oil prices recover, fiscal consolidation eases, and several economies implement planned public investment (e.g., for Dubai's World Expo 2020; Qatar's World Cup 2022) and diversification programs, the benefits of which will be enhanced by ongoing business climate reforms (Callen et al. 2014).

FIGURE 2.4.2 MENA: Outlook and risks

In GCC oil exporters, gradually improving PMIs suggest recovery in the non-oil sectors. A weak governance environment for investors and corporations in MENA may limit potential benefits from more supportive conditions. Current account and fiscal balances are expected to improve over the medium term amid ongoing fiscal consolidation, as reflected in declining fiscal break-even prices, and depreciated exchange rates in economies not pegged to the U.S. dollar. Heightened geopolitical tensions may deter tourism and incur particularly high business costs outside of the GCC. A lower-than-expected rise in oil prices, potentially from higher production outside of the region, may constrain fiscal space.

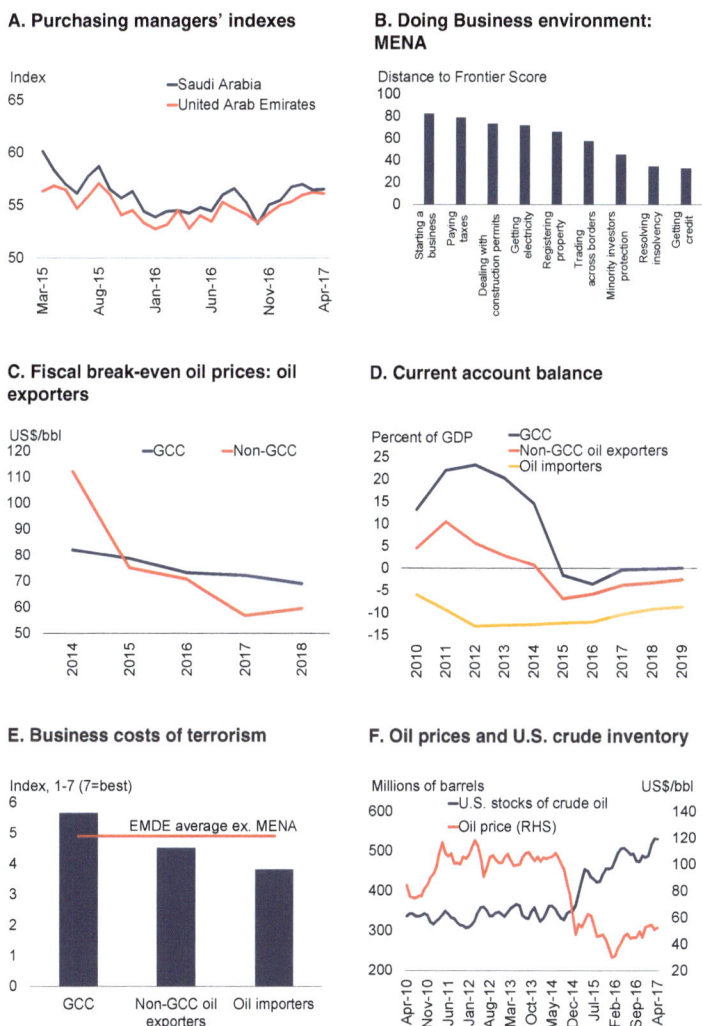

A. Purchasing managers' indexes

B. Doing Business environment: MENA

C. Fiscal break-even oil prices: oil exporters

D. Current account balance

E. Business costs of terrorism

F. Oil prices and U.S. crude inventory

Sources: Haver Analytics, International Monetary Fund, U.S. Energy Information Administration, World Bank, World Economic Forum.
Note: MENA stands for Middle East and North Africa.
A. Composite PMI for total economy (50+ indicates expansion). Last observation is April 2017.
B. Distance to frontier score, where best practice equals 100. Includes 15 economies. Unweighted averages. Data based on 2016/2017 edition.
C. GCC includes Bahrain, Kuwait, Oman, Qatar, Saudi Arabia, and the United Arab Emirates. Non-GCC includes Algeria, Islamic Republic of Iran, and Iraq. Unweighted averages. 2017 and 2018 data are projections.
D. Data for 2017-19 are projections. Includes 6 GCC economies, 3 non-GCC oil exporters, and 6 oil importers. Unweighted averages.
E. Based on survey response to "To what extent does the threat of terrorism impose costs on businesses in your country? (1 = to a great extent, imposes huge costs; 7 = no costs at all)." Unweighted averages. Includes 6 GCC economies, 2 non-GCC oil exporters, and 5 oil importers. Data based on the World Economic Forum's Global Competitiveness Index, 2016/17 edition.
F. U.S. crude stocks denote monthly average of U.S. stocks of crude oil excluding strategic petroleum reserves. Oil price denotes average of Brent, Dubai, and West Texas Intermediate. Last observation is April 2017.

Among oil importers, activity is expected to improve. In Morocco and Tunisia, agricultural production (e.g., wheat) is projected to rebound under more normal weather. Egypt's growth is expected to remain near 4 percent in fiscal year 2017 and strengthen in the two years thereafter, supported by the gradual implementation of business climate reforms and improved competitiveness, although high inflation weighs on near-term activity. In many oil importers, depreciating currencies and rising food prices may dampen private consumption. A gradual recovery in growth is expected in Jordan as reforms progress, and in Lebanon as political stability is restored. Fiscal consolidation, including public spending cuts in some economies, and political uncertainty are the main headwinds to growth in this sub-region.

The pace of fiscal and external account adjustment is contingent upon the movement in oil prices. More than four-fifths of the region's economies are projected to have fiscal deficits in 2017. Several years of fiscal adjustment lie ahead for both oil exporters and importers. For economies with flexible exchange rates, current account balances are expected to improve as a result of depreciations. For economies with pegged exchange rates, external account balances are expected to be cushioned by fiscal consolidation and higher oil prices. Remittance flows to the MENA region, which contracted sharply in 2016, are expected to recover in 2017, supported by more stable exchange rate expectations in Egypt and robust activity in the Euro Area, a major source of remittance flows for several oil importers (World Bank 2017h).

Risks

The regional growth outlook faces three main risks: geopolitical conflicts, a lower-than-expected rise in oil prices, and political and social obstacles to reforms. Geopolitical risks in the region have persisted into 2017. The U.S. sanctions on the Islamic Republic of Iran imposed in early 2017 may deter foreign investors' confidence. Security tensions and conflict in Iraq and the Syrian Arab Republic are serious obstacles for these economies. Ongoing conflicts in the region have caused

destruction of capital, displacement of people and, in the case of the Republic of Yemen, famine. Fighting and instability in the Republic of Yemen limit its hydrocarbon production and have imposed human and physical costs (World Bank 2017i). The continued conflict in Syria contributes to regional instability, depressing business and consumer confidence while restraining private consumption and reducing investment inflows in neighboring countries, such as Jordan and Lebanon. In addition, the continued flow of refugees is causing strains on the public finances of these countries.

Deteriorating geopolitical tensions on a broader scale would shake investor confidence. Sovereign risk, as reflected in sovereign credit default swap spreads, has been declining in the GCC, but is vulnerable to conflict-driven uncertainty. In non-GCC MENA economies, business costs of terrorism are more elevated compared to other emerging and developing economies. Tourism, an important source of revenue for several oil importers, is at risk; the sector remains weak and has only recently begun to stabilize in Egypt and Morocco. Efforts to expand tourism through bilateral initiatives, such as Morocco's tourism-marketing initiative with China in 2016, may help cope with some of these risks. Heightened policy uncertainty in some advanced economies, and associated risks of increased protectionism and more stringent immigration restrictions, may adversely impact the region through reduced trade, remittance, and financial flows. The region is particularly reliant on the European Union for financial and trade flows, while the United States also contributes materially to foreign investment in some economies (IMF 2017c; World Bank 2017j).

A lower-than-expected rise in oil prices would likely diminish fiscal space in oil exporters and weigh on confidence (Husain et al. 2015). A number of forces could limit the price rise. One is the extent to which U.S. oil shale production and crude stocks can offset OPEC production cuts. News of record-high U.S. crude inventories in March pushed down oil prices from $55/bbl to $51/bbl over a four-day period, and inventories did not fall as much as expected in April. Second, compliance with OPEC production cuts may weaken. Weaker oil prices would contribute to a deterioration, or slower improvement, in external and fiscal balances. They would also impose strains on the non-oil sectors of the region, either directly from consolidation programs (e.g., reductions in public investment), or indirectly via strains on banking liquidity, which tends to be driven by public-sector deposits.

The implementation of comprehensive reforms could face challenges. The agreement on Lebanon's budget on March 27, the first in 12 years, marks a step toward political and economic stabilization but has prompted protests among citizens and firms who oppose higher taxes.

Protests over tax hikes have also occurred in parts of Algeria in 2017. Such developments could discourage further reform and prolong the period of adjustment. In Tunisia, where reforms had been previously delayed, the new government has agreed with the workers' union on a rescheduling of negotiated salary increases signed in 2015. This will help slow wage bill increases to 14.1 percent of GDP in 2017. To further contain the wage bill in 2018, the government has proposed two measures—a voluntary early retirement program and a negotiated departure program—both anchored in the IMF Extended Fund Facility program with coordinated technical support from the IMF and the World Bank.

TABLE 2.4.1 Middle East and North Africa forecast summary

(Real GDP growth at market prices in percent, unless indicated otherwise)

	2014	2015	2016 Estimates	2017	2018 Projections	2019	2016	2017	2018	2019
							(percentage point difference from January 2017 projections)			
EMDE MENA, GDP[a]	3.4	2.8	3.2	2.1	2.9	3.1	0.5	-1.0	-0.4	-0.3
(Average including economies with full national accounts and balance of payments data only)[b]										
EMDE MENA, GDP[b]	3.4	2.7	3.1	2.2	2.9	3.2	0.5	-0.9	-0.5	-0.3
GDP per capita (U.S. dollars)	1.4	0.8	1.3	0.6	1.4	1.8	0.4	-0.9	-0.6	-0.3
PPP GDP	3.5	2.6	3.3	2.4	3.0	3.3	0.5	-0.9	-0.6	-0.4
Private consumption	6.4	1.5	2.6	2.3	3.0	3.2	-0.2	-0.7	-0.4	-0.3
Public consumption	6.9	1.7	-1.0	1.0	1.6	1.6	-0.4	0.1	-0.5	-0.7
Fixed investment	5.8	3.3	0.1	2.9	4.6	5.6	1.5	-0.8	1.1	1.7
Exports, GNFS[c]	2.3	1.9	5.8	2.3	3.7	3.9	0.9	-2.9	-1.2	-1.1
Imports, GNFS[c]	7.0	0.0	2.1	3.0	3.0	3.4	1.3	-1.9	-2.2	-2.0
Net exports, contribution to growth	-1.7	0.9	1.9	0.0	0.6	0.5	-0.1	-0.6	0.3	0.2
Memo items: GDP										
Oil exporters[d]	3.4	2.6	3.2	1.8	2.5	2.8	0.5	-1.1	-0.6	-0.3
GCC countries[e]	3.2	3.8	1.9	1.3	2.3	2.5	0.3	-0.9	-0.3	-0.2
Saudi Arabia	3.7	4.1	1.4	0.6	2.0	2.1	0.4	-1.0	-0.5	-0.5
Iran, Islamic Rep.	4.3	-1.8	6.4	4.0	4.1	4.2	1.8	-1.2	-0.7	-0.3
Oil importers[f]	3.0	3.7	2.8	3.7	4.1	4.4	-0.2	-0.2	-0.1	-0.1
Egypt, Arab Rep.	3.7	4.4	4.1	4.3	5.0	5.3	-0.1	-0.1	-0.1	-0.1
Fiscal year basis[g]	2.9	4.4	4.3	3.9	4.6	5.3	0.0	-0.1	-0.1	-0.1

Source: World Bank.

World Bank forecasts are frequently updated based on new information and changing (global) circumstances. Consequently, projections presented here may differ from those contained in other Bank documents, even if basic assessments of countries' prospects do not differ at any given moment in time.

a. EMDE refers to emerging market and developing economy. GDP at market prices and expenditure components are measured in constant 2010 U.S. dollars. Excludes Libya, Syria, and the Republic of Yemen due to data limitations.

b. Aggregate includes all countries in notes d and f except Djibouti, Iraq, Qatar, and West Bank and Gaza, for which data limitations prevent the forecasting of GDP components.

c. Exports and imports of goods and non-factor services (GNFS).

d. Oil exporters include Algeria, Bahrain, Iraq, the Islamic Republic of Iran, Kuwait, Oman, Qatar, Saudi Arabia, and the United Arab Emirates.

e. The Gulf Cooperation Council (GCC) includes Bahrain, Kuwait, Oman, Qatar, Saudi Arabia, and the United Arab Emirates.

f. Oil importers include Djibouti, Egypt, Jordan, Lebanon, Morocco, Tunisia, and West Bank and Gaza.

g. The fiscal year runs from July 1 to June 30 in Egypt; the column labeled 2016 reflects the fiscal year ended June 30, 2016.

For additional information, please see www.worldbank.org/gep.

TABLE 2.4.2 Middle East and North Africa economy forecasts[a]

(Real GDP growth at market prices in percent, unless indicated otherwise)

	2014	2015	2016	2017	2018	2019	2016	2017	2018	2019
			Estimates	Projections			(percentage point difference from January 2017 projections)			
Algeria	3.8	3.8	3.5	1.8	1.0	1.5	-0.1	-1.1	-1.6	-1.3
Bahrain	4.4	2.9	3.0	1.9	1.9	2.3	1.0	0.1	-0.2	-0.1
Djibouti	6.0	6.5	6.5	7.0	7.0	7.2	0.0	0.0	0.0	0.2
Egypt, Arab Rep.	3.7	4.4	4.1	4.3	5.0	5.3	-0.1	-0.1	-0.1	-0.1
Fiscal year basis[b]	2.9	4.4	4.3	3.9	4.6	5.3	0.0	-0.1	-0.1	-0.1
Iran, Islamic Rep.	4.3	-1.8	6.4	4.0	4.1	4.2	1.8	-1.2	-0.7	-0.3
Iraq	0.7	4.8	10.1	-3.1	2.6	1.1	-0.1	-4.2	1.9	0.0
Jordan	3.1	2.4	2.0	2.3	2.6	3.0	-0.3	-0.3	-0.5	-0.4
Kuwait	0.5	1.8	2.9	0.2	2.7	2.9	0.9	-2.2	0.1	0.1
Lebanon	1.8	1.3	1.8	2.5	2.6	2.6	0.0	0.3	0.3	0.1
Morocco	2.6	4.5	1.1	3.8	3.7	3.6	-0.4	-0.2	0.2	0.0
Oman	2.5	5.7	2.2	0.9	2.4	2.9	-0.3	-2.0	-1.0	-0.7
Qatar	4.0	3.6	2.2	3.2	2.6	2.5	0.4	-0.4	0.5	1.2
Saudi Arabia	3.7	4.1	1.4	0.6	2.0	2.1	0.4	-1.0	-0.5	-0.5
Tunisia	2.3	1.1	1.0	2.3	3.0	3.5	-1.0	-0.7	-0.7	-0.5
United Arab Emirates	3.1	3.8	2.3	2.0	2.5	3.2	0.0	-0.5	-0.5	-0.1
West Bank and Gaza	-0.2	3.4	4.1	3.5	3.4	3.4	1.0	0.0	-0.1	-0.2

Source: World Bank.

World Bank forecasts are frequently updated based on new information and changing (global) circumstances. Consequently, projections presented here may differ from those contained in other Bank documents, even if basic assessments of economies' prospects do not significantly differ at any given moment in time.

a. GDP at market prices and expenditure components are measured in constant 2010 U.S. dollars. Excludes Libya, Syria, and Republic of Yemen due to data limitations.

b. The fiscal year runs from July 1 to June 30 in Egypt; the column labeled 2016 reflects the fiscal year ended June 30, 2016.

For additional information, please see www.worldbank.org/gep.

SOUTH ASIA

Growth in South Asia remains strong, with regional output projected to grow by 6.8 percent in 2017 and an average of 7.2 percent in 2018-19. Excluding India, growth is projected to average 5.8 percent in 2017-2019, with some cross-country variation. Robust domestic demand, an uptick in exports, and strong foreign direct investment inflows underpin this forecast. Domestic risks to the outlook include policy uncertainty related to upcoming elections and possible setbacks to reform progress. External risks include an increase in global financial volatility, a slowdown in remittances inflows, and rising geopolitical tensions.

Recent developments

Regional output expanded by an estimated 6.7 percent in 2016, despite temporary disruptions associated with the November withdrawal and replacement of large-denomination currency notes in India, the region's largest economy (Table 2.5.1). In general, South Asian economies benefited from an improvement in exports, low oil prices, infrastructure spending, and supportive macroeconomic policies last year. In India, activity was underpinned by favorable monsoon rains that supported agriculture and rural consumption, an increase in infrastructure spending, and robust government consumption (World Bank 2017k). In Pakistan, agricultural output rebounded following the end of a drought, while the successful completion of an IMF-supported program en-hanced macroeconomic conditions and foreign direct investment (FDI). Nepal's economy suffered from lingering effects of the 2015 earthquake and trade disruptions with India (World Bank 2017l). However, in some countries, activity in 2016 was set back by a sharp decline in remittances inflows (e.g., Bangladesh; World Bank 2016g), inclement weather conditions that reduced agricultural output (e.g., Sri Lanka), and security challenges (e.g., Afghanistan).

A pickup in regional growth is underway in 2017. In India, recent data indicate a rebound this year, with the easing of cash shortages and rising exports (World Bank 2017k). An increase in government spending in India, including on capital formation, has partially offset soft private investment. While manufacturing purchasing managers' indexes have generally picked up, industrial production has been mixed (Figure 2.5.1). In Pakistan, favorable weather and increased cotton prices are supporting agricultural production, and the China-Pakistan Economic Corridor infrastructure project, as well as a stable macroeconomic environment, is contributing to an increase in private investment.

Growth in Bangladesh has been supported by solid agricultural activity and robust services this year, despite ongoing security concerns. In Sri Lanka, a resumption of Chinese-funded investment and infrastructure projects such as the Colombo International Financial Centre has lifted private investment and FDI inflows; in addition, fiscal consolidation under an IMF program has helped improve investor sentiment. In Bhutan and Maldives, growth has continued to gain traction due to accommodative macroeconomic policies, as well as support from the energy and construction sectors. Nepal's growth has rebounded strongly following a good monsoon, reconstruction efforts, and normalization of trade across the southern border with India.

Note: This section was prepared by Temel Taskin and Boaz Nandwa. Research assistance was provided by Anh Mai Bui.

FIGURE 2.5.1 SAR: Recent developments

In India, the exchange of large-denominated currency in circulation in late 2016 weighed on investment, albeit temporarily. While purchasing managers' indexes across the region have generally improved in 2017, industrial production has been mixed.

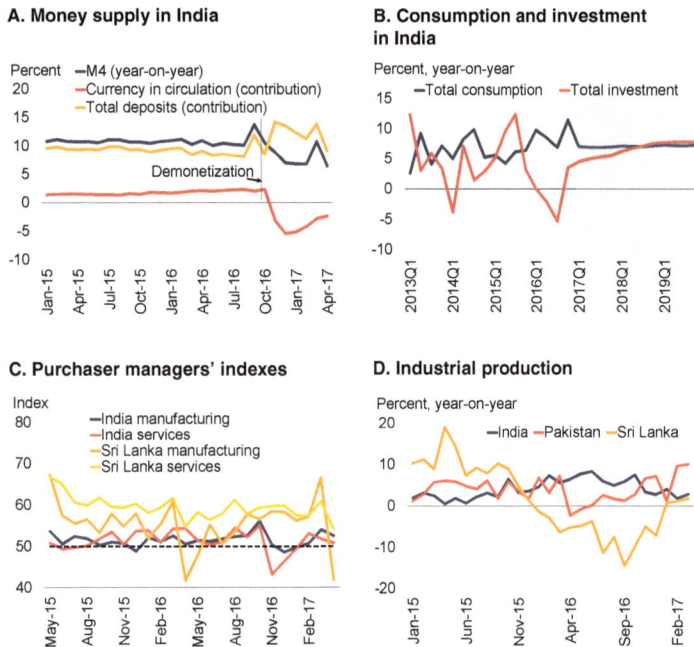

A. Money supply in India

B. Consumption and investment in India

C. Purchaser managers' indexes

D. Industrial production

Sources: Haver Analytics, World Bank.
Note: SAR stands for South Asia Region.
A. M4 stands for broad money supply. Last observation is April 2017.
B. Shaded areas are projections. Last observation is 2016 Q4.
C. Index values higher than 50 indicate expansion. Last observation is April 2017.
D. Last observation is March 2017.

Macroeconomic vulnerabilities continue to recede. Current account deficits are narrowing further amid stable oil prices and an uptick in exports. While remittances inflows declined in some countries (e.g., Bangladesh, India), foreign reserves increased and exchange rates remained stable, with rising FDI (e.g., India) and tourist arrivals (e.g., Nepal, Sri Lanka). Inflation has remained benign, hovering below target in Bangladesh, Pakistan, and India. Favorable weather (e.g., India, Pakistan) and lower oil prices have helped keep inflation low, and thereby made possible an accommodative monetary policy. Despite mixed progress with fiscal consolidation in the region, deficits generally declined.

Outlook

The regional forecast assumes that monetary policy across South Asia countries remains broadly accommodative, encouraging credit to the private sector; that fiscal policy tightens slightly to curb the increase in public debt; and that political tensions and insecurity abate. Regional growth is forecast to increase to 6.8 percent in 2017 and to strengthen to an average of 7.2 percent in 2018-19, reflecting a solid expansion of domestic demand and exports (Figure 2.5.2). Excluding India, regional growth will remain broadly stable at an average of 5.8 percent in 2017-19, as easing growth in Bangladesh and Nepal offset gains in Bhutan, Pakistan, and Sri Lanka.

India's growth is forecast to increase to 7.2 percent in FY2017 (April 1, 2017 - March 31, 2018) and accelerate to 7.7 percent by the end of the forecast horizon—slightly below previous projections. This outlook mainly reflects a more protracted recovery in private investment than previously envisaged. Nonetheless, domestic demand is expected to remain strong, supported by ongoing policy reforms, especially the introduction of the nationwide Goods and Services Tax (GST). Significant gains by the ruling party in state elections should support the government's economic reform agenda, which aims at unlocking supply constraints, and creating a business environment that is more conducive to private investment.

Pakistan's growth is expected to increase to 5.2 percent in FY2017 (July 1, 2016 - June 30, 2017) and remain strong over the forecast horizon, reflecting an upturn in private investment, increased energy supply, and improved security. The fiscal deficit should narrow further, as a result of revenue-led fiscal consolidation. Sri Lanka's growth is expected to pick up to about 4.7 percent in 2017 and accelerate to 5.1 percent by 2019, as the IMF-supported program helps improve macroeconomic resilience. Reforms initiated by the World Bank Development Policy Operation in 2016 are expected to reduce obstacles to private sector competitiveness in the medium-term and help attract FDI. Resumption of the Generalized System of Preferences Plus (GSP+) trading arrangement with the European Union will boost its export sector. Growth in Bangladesh is forecast to remain robust, averaging 6.6 percent during FY2018-FY2020. This reflects improving remittances as GCC economies recover, as well as rising business confidence and investment.

Risks

A number of downside risks continue to cloud the outlook. Setbacks to the assumed pace of structural reform would impede the unlocking of supply constraints, dampen productivity growth, and hold up integration into global value chains. This would hurt the business environment, reducing investment and FDI inflows to the region (IMF 2017d, 2017e). Security concerns in some countries (e.g., Afghanistan, Pakistan) could also hold back investment and business confidence. For several countries in the region, increased political or geopolitical tensions could pose major obstacles to economic and financial activity (e.g., Afghanistan, India, Pakistan). Upcoming elections in Nepal (between 2017 and 2019), Bangladesh and Pakistan (in 2018), and India (in 2019) could be accompanied by heightened policy uncertainty, and election results could surprise financial markets.

Despite progress in fiscal consolidation, public debt remains high across the region. In some cases debt is associated with investments that will pay for themselves (Bhutan), but in others there have been concerns about sustainability (e.g., Maldives) or about fiscal strains posed by an uneven repayment profile (e.g., Sri Lanka and, to some extent, Pakistan). In addition, contingent liabilities are building up, including from the debt of power utilities in Pakistan and prospects of debt write-offs for farmers in several states in India.

Compared to other EMDE regions, South Asia is less integrated into the global economy and, therefore, would be less affected by the materialization of a range of negative external shocks. However, two external risks remain a concern. First, weaker-than-expected recovery in external demand, or a widespread increase in trade protectionism in advanced economies, could weigh on exports (World Bank 2017n). In addition, an abrupt market reassessment about U.S. monetary policy tightening could lead to capital outflows, and hence to tighter domestic credit conditions (Rai and Suchanek 2014).

FIGURE 2.5.2 **SAR: Outlook and risks**

Regional growth is expected to rebound in 2017 and strengthen thereafter. Domestic demand and exports underlie this pickup. The outlook for remittances inflows is uncertain, as they could be affected by tighter immigration policies in some advanced economies and continued fiscal consolidation in GCC countries. Changing environmental patterns pose growing risks to the region, as natural events have affected an increasing number of people in recent years. An abrupt market reassessment about U.S. monetary policy tightening could lead to tighter domestic financial conditions, which have been benign of late.

A. GDP growth

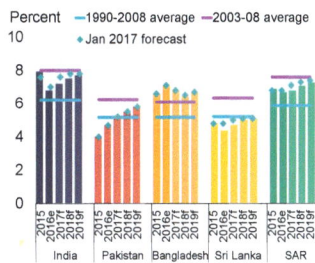

B. Contributions to growth in SAR

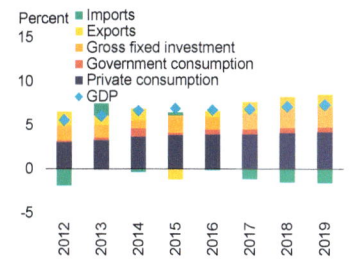

C. Growth in remittance inflows

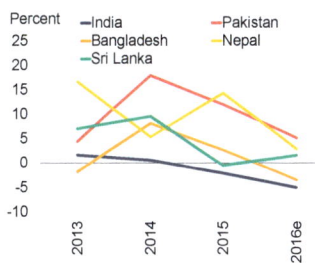

D. Sources of remittances, 2015

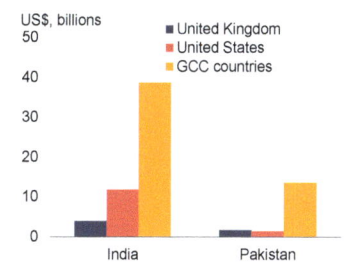

E. People affected by natural disasters

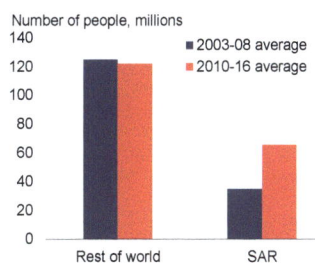

F. Sovereign bond spreads

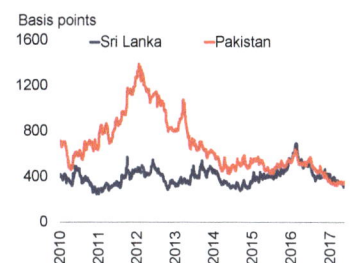

Sources: International Disaster Database, J.P. Morgan, World Bank.
Note: SAR stands for South Asia Region.
A.B. Shaded areas are projections.
E. Average annual number of people affected by disasters.
F. J.P. Morgan Emerging Market Bond Index. Last observation is May 23, 2017.

Second, the outlook for remittances is uncertain. The main risks would be from tighter immigration policies in advanced economies, especially in the United States and the United Kingdom, and continued fiscal consolidation in oil-exporting Gulf Cooperation Council (GCC) countries. Any substantial decline in remittances would dampen consumption and investment in major recipients (e.g., Bangladesh, Nepal).

Finally, changing environmental patterns pose growing risks. The number of people affected from extreme weather events has increased substantially in recent years (Figure 2.5.3). Natural disasters from extreme weather conditions often adversely affect agricultural output in the region, as recently experienced in India, Pakistan, and Sri Lanka (IMF 2016g).

TABLE 2.5.1 South Asia forecast summary

(Real GDP growth at market prices in percent, unless indicated otherwise)

	2014	2015	2016	2017	2018	2019	2016	2017	2018	2019
			Estimates	Projections			(percentage point difference from January 2017 projections)			
EMDE South Asia, GDP[a, b]	6.7	6.9	6.7	6.8	7.1	7.3	-0.1	-0.3	-0.2	-0.1
(Average including countries with full national accounts and balance of payments data only)[c]										
EMDE South Asia, GDP[c]	6.7	6.9	6.7	6.8	7.1	7.3	-0.1	-0.3	-0.3	-0.1
GDP per capita (U.S. dollars)	5.3	5.6	5.4	5.5	5.8	6.0	0.0	-0.2	-0.2	-0.1
PPP GDP	6.7	6.9	6.7	6.8	7.1	7.3	-0.1	-0.3	-0.3	-0.1
Private consumption	6.2	6.5	6.6	6.6	6.9	7.1	0.2	-0.1	-0.3	-0.3
Public consumption	8.9	2.6	5.5	5.8	5.8	5.8	-1.5	-1.4	-1.7	-1.8
Fixed investment	2.7	6.3	4.6	5.9	7.3	8.0	-1.9	-1.5	-0.1	0.7
Exports, GNFS[d]	5.4	-4.9	3.0	6.0	6.3	6.2	0.8	0.4	-0.8	-1.2
Imports, GNFS[d]	1.1	-1.0	0.4	4.4	5.9	6.3	-1.2	-0.7	-0.7	-0.6
Net exports, contribution to growth	1.0	-0.9	0.6	0.1	-0.2	-0.3	0.5	0.2	0.0	-0.1

Memo items: GDP[b]	14/15	15/16	16/17	17/18	18/19	19/20	16/17	17/18	18/19	19/20
South Asia excluding India	5.3	5.5	5.7	5.7	5.8	6.0	0.4	0.2	0.1	0.2
India	7.2	7.9	6.8	7.2	7.5	7.7	-0.2	-0.4	-0.3	-0.1
Pakistan (factor cost)	4.0	4.7	5.2	5.5	5.8	5.8	0.0	0.0	0.0	0.0
Bangladesh	6.6	7.1	6.8	6.4	6.7	7.0	0.0	-0.1	0.0	0.0

Source: World Bank.

World Bank forecasts are frequently updated based on new information and changing (global) circumstances. Consequently, projections presented here may differ from those contained in other Bank documents, even if basic assessments of countries' prospects do not differ at any given moment in time.

a. EMDE refers to emerging market and developing economy. GDP at market prices and expenditure components are measured in constant 2010 U.S. dollars.

b. National income and product account data refer to fiscal years (FY) for the South Asian countries, while aggregates are presented in calendar year (CY) terms. The fiscal year runs from July 1 through June 30 in Bangladesh and Pakistan, from July 16 through July 15 in Nepal, and April 1 through March 31 in India.

c. Sub-region aggregate excludes Afghanistan, Bhutan, and Maldives, for which data limitations prevent the forecasting of GDP components.

d. Exports and imports of goods and non-factor services (GNFS).

For additional information, please see www.worldbank.org/gep.

TABLE 2.5.2 **South Asia country forecasts**

(Real GDP growth at market prices in percent, unless indicated otherwise)

	2014	2015	2016	2017	2018	2019	2016	2017	2018	2019
			Estimates	Projections			(percentage point difference from January 2017 projections)			
Calendar year basis[a]										
Afghanistan	1.3	1.1	2.2	2.6	3.4	3.1	0.0	0.6	0.4	-0.5
Bhutan	5.7	6.5	6.8	6.8	7.7	10.5	-0.6	-3.1	-3.9	-1.2
Maldives	6.0	2.8	4.1	4.5	4.6	4.6	0.6	0.6	0.0	0.0
Sri Lanka	5.0	4.8	4.4	4.7	5.0	5.1	-0.4	-0.3	-0.1	0.0
	14/15	15/16	16/17	17/18	18/19	19/20	16/17	17/18	18/19	19/20
Fiscal year basis[a]										
Bangladesh	6.6	7.1	6.8	6.4	6.7	7.0	0.0	-0.1	0.0	0.0
India	7.2	7.9	6.8	7.2	7.5	7.7	-0.2	-0.4	-0.3	-0.1
Nepal	3.3	0.4	7.5	5.5	4.5	4.5	1.0	0.7	-0.2	-0.2
Pakistan (factor cost)	4.0	4.7	5.2	5.5	5.8	5.8	0.0	0.0	0.0	0.0

Source: World Bank.

World Bank forecasts are frequently updated based on new information and changing (global) circumstances. Consequently, projections presented here may differ from those contained in other Bank documents, even if basic assessments of countries' prospects do not significantly differ at any given moment in time.

a. Historical data are reported on a market price basis. National income and product account data refer to fiscal years (FY) for the South Asian countries with the exception of Afghanistan, Bhutan, Maldives, and Sri Lanka, which report in calendar year (CY). The fiscal year runs from July 1 through June 30 in Bangladesh and Pakistan, from July 16 through July 15 in Nepal, and April 1 through March 31 in India.

For additional information, please see www.worldbank.org/gep.

SUB-SAHARAN AFRICA

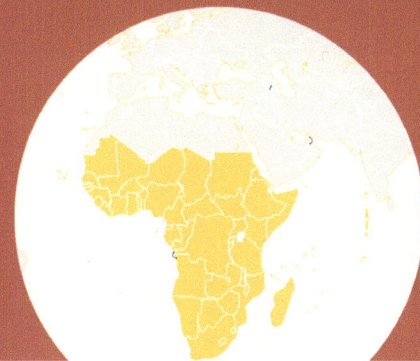

Growth in Sub-Saharan Africa is projected to recover to 2.6 percent in 2017 from the sharp deceleration to 1.3 percent in 2016, and to strengthen somewhat in 2018. The upturn reflects recovering global commodity prices and improvements in domestic conditions. Most of the rebound will come from Angola and Nigeria—the largest oil exporters. However, investment is expected to recover only very gradually, reflecting still tight foreign exchange liquidity conditions in oil exporters and low investor confidence in South Africa. Fiscal consolidation will slow the pace of recovery in metals exporters. Growth is expected to remain solid among non-resource-intensive countries. External downside risks to the outlook include stronger-than-expected tightening of global financing conditions, weaker-than-envisioned improvements in commodity prices, and the threat of protectionism. A key domestic risk is the lack of implementation of reforms that are needed to maintain durable macroeconomic stability and sustain growth.

Recent developments

After slowing sharply in 2016, growth in Sub-Saharan Africa (SSA) is recovering, supported by modestly rising commodity prices, strengthening external demand, and the end of drought in several countries. Despite recent declines, oil prices are 10 percent higher than their average levels in 2016. Metals prices have strengthened more than expected. Meanwhile, above-average rainfalls are boosting agricultural production and electricity generation in countries that were hit earlier by El Niño-related droughts (e.g., South Africa, Zambia). Security threats subsided in several countries. In Nigeria, militants' attacks on oil pipelines decreased. The economic recession in Nigeria is receding. In the first quarter of 2017, GDP fell by 0.5 percent (y/y), compared with a 1.7 percent contraction in the fourth quarter of 2016. The Purchasing Managers' Index for manufacturers returned to expansionary territory in April (Figure 2.6.1), indicating growth in the sector after contraction in the first quarter. Non-resource-intensive countries, including those in the West African Economic and Monetary Union (WAEMU), have been expanding at a solid pace.

Several factors are preventing a more vigorous recovery. In Angola and Nigeria, foreign exchange controls are distorting the foreign exchange market, thereby constraining activity in the non-oil sector. In South Africa, political uncertainty and low business confidence are weighing on investment. The previously delayed fiscal adjustment to lower oil revenues in the Central African Economic and Monetary Community (CEMAC) has started, restraining domestic demand. In Mozambique, the government's default in January and heavy debt burden are deterring investment. In contrast to oil and metals prices, world cocoa prices dropped, reducing exports and fiscal revenues in cocoa producers (e.g., Côte d'Ivoire, Ghana). In many countries, banks are seeking to limit credit risk by tightening lending standards and reducing credit to the private sector. Lastly, the drought in East Africa, which reduced agricultural production at the end of 2016, continued into 2017, adversely affecting activity in some countries (e.g., Kenya, Uganda), and contributing to famine in others (e.g., Somalia, South Sudan).

Current account deficits of oil and metals exporters are narrowing, helped by the pickup in commodity prices. Oil exports are rebounding in Nigeria on the back of an uptick in oil production from fields previously damaged by militants'

Note: This section was prepared by Gerard Kambou. Research assistance was provided by Xinghao Gong.

FIGURE 2.6.1 SSA: Recent developments

At the start of 2017, a modest pickup in activity was underway in the region's largest economies. Inflation began to ease, but was still high in oil-exporters. A drought in East Africa pushed up food prices in several countries. Current account and fiscal balances are improving somewhat among oil and metals exporters, helped by the increase in commodity prices. However, they remain under pressure in non-resource-intensive countries, reflecting the continued expansion in public investment.

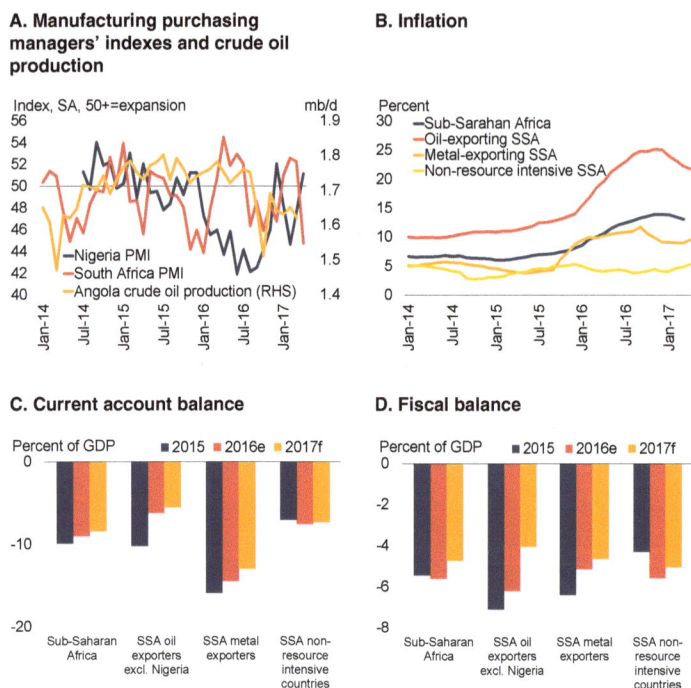

A. Manufacturing purchasing managers' indexes and crude oil production

B. Inflation

C. Current account balance

D. Fiscal balance

Sources: Central Bank of Nigeria, Haver Analytics, International Monetary Fund, World Bank.
Notes: SSA stands for Sub-Saharan Africa. Oil-exporting SSA consists of Angola, Ghana, and Nigeria; metal-exporting SSA consists of Botswana, Mozambique, Namibia, South Africa, and Zambia. Non-resource-intensive countries include agriculture-based economies and commodity importers.
A. SA stands for seasonally adjusted.
B.-.D. Unweighted average of available countries in the region.
C.D. e stands for estimate; f for forecast.

attacks. Mining companies across the region are resuming production and exports. In contrast, current account balances have remained under pressure in a number of non-resource-intensive countries. In these countries, capital goods imports have been strong, reflecting ambitious public investment programs. Capital inflows in the region are rebounding from their low level in 2016. Nigeria tapped the Eurobond market twice in the first quarter of 2017, followed by Senegal in May. Sovereign spreads have declined across the region from their November 2016 peak, with the notable exception of Ghana where they rose due to concerns about fiscal policy slippages. This trend reflects low financial market volatility, and a broader rebound in investor risk appetite for

emerging market and developing economies (EMDE) assets.

Regional inflation is gradually decelerating from its high level in 2016. Although a process of disinflation has started in Angola and Nigeria, inflation in both countries remains elevated, owing to a highly depreciated parallel market exchange rate. Inflation eased in metals exporters, reflecting stabilizing currencies after sharp depreciations, and lower food prices due to improved weather conditions (e.g., South Africa, Zambia). An exception is Mozambique, where inflation was still above 21 percent (y/y) in April, reflecting continued depreciation. Inflationary pressures increased in non-resource-intensive countries. In East Africa, drought led to a spike in food prices, notably in Kenya. However, in countries where the drought has been less severe, inflation has remained within central banks' targets. Low inflation in Tanzania, Uganda, and Zambia, and steadily falling inflation in Ghana allowed central banks to cut interest rates in early 2017.

Fiscal deficits remain elevated across the region. Oil and metals exporters are still running sizable fiscal deficits. Fiscal balances have deteriorated in several non-resource-intensive countries, reflecting a continued expansion in public infrastructure. Large fiscal deficits and, in some cases, steep exchange rate depreciations, have resulted in rising public debt ratios in the region (Box 2.6.1). A number of countries have embarked on fiscal consolidation to stabilize government debt (e.g., Chad, South Africa). In early April, S&P Global Ratings and Fitch downgraded South Africa's sovereign credit rating to sub-investment status on account of heightened political uncertainty.

Outlook

Growth in SSA is forecast to pick up to 2.6 percent in 2017, and average 3.4 percent in 2018-19, slightly above population growth (Figure 2.6.2). The recovery is predicated on moderately rising commodity prices and reforms to tackle macroeconomic imbalances. The forecasts are below those in January, reflecting a slower-than-anticipated recovery in several oil and metals exporters. Per capita output growth—which is

BOX 2.6.1 Deteriorating public finances in Sub-Saharan Africa

Public debt ratios have risen sharply, post-crisis. In several countries, government debt has increased by more than 10 percentage points of GDP between 2014 and 2016 and now exceeds 50 percent of GDP (World Bank 2017n). These include four commodity exporters (Angola, Mozambique, Republic of Congo, and Zambia) and two commodity importers (Burundi, Ethiopia).

Rising fiscal deficits have been the key driver of debt accumulation in most countries. Angola and the Republic of Congo, hit by a large drop in oil revenues, delayed or slowed fiscal consolidation. Both countries have run large fiscal deficits, which reached 17 percent of GDP in the Republic of Congo in 2016. Among metals exporters, Mozambique undertook large external borrowing through state-owned enterprises. Zambia's large fiscal deficits have been driven by elevated expenditure overruns. In non-resource-intensive countries, borrowing to finance large public investment projects underpinned the rise in public debt in Ethiopia.

Other contributory factors included exchange rate depreciation and civil conflict. Large exchange rate depreciations contributed to the increase in fiscal debt/GDP ratios in Mozambique and Zambia. Foreign currency debt accounted for 80 percent and 67 percent of total debt in Mozambique and Zambia, respectively, in 2016. Political instability and its adverse effects on growth have pushed up debt-to-GDP ratios in Burundi, where the government has continued to resort to central bank advances and the issuance of treasury bills to finance persistently high fiscal deficits.

Debt servicing costs have risen but remain sustainable for most countries. The rise in government debt, exchange rate depreciation, and increased recourse to non-concessional borrowing for infrastructure development have resulted in rising debt servicing costs. However, for most countries in the region, the interest-to-revenue ratio remains sustainable, helped by the high share of concessional borrowing. A notable exception is Nigeria, where the federal government's interest-to-revenue ratio rose from 33 percent in 2015 to 59 percent in 2016. In Mozambique, debt levels have increased sharply to an estimated 125 percent of GDP at end-2016, and the interest-to-revenue ratio has risen to above 15 percent, which is weighing on the ability of the government to meet debt service payments. As monetary policies in advanced economies continue to normalize, and global interest rates increase, pro-active public debt management will be needed to manage rollover risks in the region.

projected to increase from -0.1 percent in 2017 to 0.7 percent in 2018-19—will remain insufficient to achieve poverty reduction goals in the region if the constraints to more vigorous growth persist (Bhorat and Tarp 2016).

Growth in South Africa is projected to recover from 0.6 percent in 2017 to 1.5 percent in 2018-19. A rebound in net exports is expected to only partially offset weaker than previously forecast growth of private consumption and investment, as borrowing costs rise following the sovereign rating downgrade to sub-investment level. For Nigeria, growth is expected to rise from 1.2 percent in 2017 to 2.5 percent in 2018-19, helped by a rebound in oil production, as security in the oil-producing region improves, and by an increase in fiscal spending. In Angola, growth is projected to increase from 1.2 percent in 2017 to 1.5 percent in 2019, reflecting a slight pickup of activity in the industrial sector as energy supplies improve. The

subdued recovery in the region's largest economies reflects the slower-than-expected adjustment to low commodity prices in Angola and Nigeria, and higher-than-anticipated policy uncertainty in South Africa.

In other oil exporters, growth is expected to strengthen in Ghana as increased oil and gas production boosts exports and domestic electricity production. Growth will be weaker than previously projected in CEMAC, as larger-than-envisioned fiscal adjustment reduces public investment. In several metals exporters, high inflation and tight fiscal policy will be a greater drag on activity than previously expected.

Growth in non-resource-intensive countries should remain solid, on the basis of infrastructure investment, resilient services sectors, and the recovery of agricultural production. Ethiopia and Tanzania in East Africa, and Côte d'Ivoire and

FIGURE 2.6.2 **SSA: Outlook and risks**

Regional growth is expected to rebound to 2.6 percent in 2017, and to reach 3.5 percent in 2019, reflecting a modest recovery in Angola, Nigeria, and South Africa. Growth in non-resource-intensive countries is expected to remain solid, supported by domestic demand. Weaker-than-forecast commodity prices, worsening drought conditions, and cutbacks to U.S. official development assistance pose significant downside risks to the regional outlook.

A. GDP growth

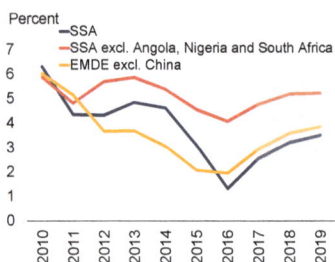

B. Growth forecasts

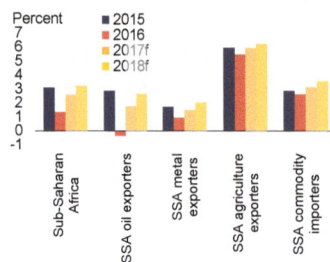

C. SSA countries affected by drought

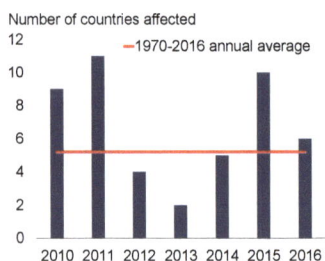

D. U.S. official development assistance

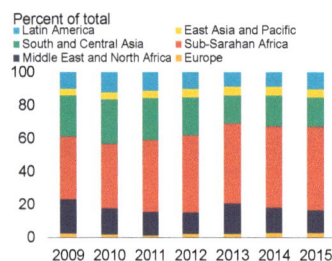

Sources: EM-DAT, OECD Geographical Distribution of Financial Flows to Developing Countries, The International Disaster Database, World Bank.
Notes: SSA stands for Sub-Saharan Africa. Non-resource-intensive countries include agricultural-based economies and commodity importers.
A. GDP-weighted averages.
C. Chart shows number of SSA countries experiencing at least one drought in any given year.
D. Regional assistance is not included.

Senegal in WAEMU will continue to expand at a robust pace on the back of public investment, although some countries (e.g., Ethiopia, Côte d'Ivoire) may not reach the high growth rates of the recent past. Many countries need to contain debt accumulation and rebuild policy buffers.

Risks

The regional outlook is subject to significant external risks. A sharp increase in global interest rates could discourage sovereign bond issuance, which has become a key financing strategy for governments in recent years, as they have increasingly looked to global markets for the funds to finance domestic investment (Papadavid 2016). If sustained, increases in global interest rates could further reduce the ability of governments in the region to access foreign bond markets. In addition, weaker-than-expected growth in advanced economies or in large emerging markets could reduce demand for exports, depress commodity prices, and curtail foreign direct investment in mining and infrastructure in the region (Chen and Nord 2017). Finally, the announcement of proposed cutbacks to U.S. official development assistance will be a source of concern for some of the region's smaller economies and fragile states.

On the domestic front, in countries where significant fiscal adjustments are needed, failure to implement appropriate policies could weaken macroeconomic stability and slow the recovery. This risk is particularly significant for Angola, CEMAC countries, Mozambique, and Nigeria. In addition, increased militants' activity (e.g., Nigeria), political uncertainty ahead of key elections (e.g., South Africa), and drought pose risks to the outlook. Weather-related risks are elevated in East Africa. Inadequate rainfalls have led to abnormal seasonal dryness in areas of Kenya, southern Ethiopia, South Sudan, and Uganda (Famine Early Warning Systems Network 2017). Worsening drought conditions will severely affect agricultural production, push food prices higher, and increase food insecurity.

TABLE 2.6.1 Sub-Saharan Africa forecast summary

(Real GDP growth at market prices in percent, unless indicated otherwise)

	2014	2015	2016	2017	2018	2019	2016	2017	2018	2019
			Estimates	Projections			(percentage point difference from January 2017 projections)			
EMDE SSA, GDP[a]	**4.6**	**3.1**	**1.3**	**2.6**	**3.2**	**3.5**	**-0.2**	**-0.3**	**-0.4**	**-0.2**
(Average including countries with full national accounts and balance of payments data only)[b]										
EMDE SSA, GDP[b]	4.6	3.1	1.3	2.6	3.2	3.5	-0.2	-0.3	-0.4	-0.2
GDP per capita (U.S. dollars)	1.9	0.4	-1.3	-0.1	0.6	0.9	-0.2	-0.3	-0.4	-0.2
PPP GDP	4.9	3.3	1.6	2.8	3.5	3.7	-0.1	-0.3	-0.4	-0.3
Private consumption	2.9	5.7	1.2	2.2	2.6	2.8	-0.3	-0.7	-0.8	-0.6
Public consumption	1.6	-3.3	2.0	2.5	2.7	2.8	-0.1	-0.2	-0.3	-0.2
Fixed investment	9.6	0.7	3.4	5.1	7.0	7.2	0.1	-0.3	0.0	0.1
Exports, GNFS[c]	7.0	2.4	1.1	2.7	3.0	3.3	-0.4	0.7	0.4	0.7
Imports, GNFS[c]	3.7	0.5	1.9	2.9	3.5	3.7	-0.4	-0.2	-0.2	-0.1
Net exports, contribution to growth	0.9	0.6	-0.2	-0.1	-0.2	-0.1	0.1	0.3	0.2	0.3
Memo items: GDP										
SSA excluding South Africa and Nigeria	5.3	4.3	3.5	4.3	4.7	4.8	-0.4	-0.6	-0.4	-0.4
SSA excluding South Africa, Nigeria, and Angola	5.4	4.5	4.1	4.8	5.2	5.2	-0.4	-0.6	-0.5	-0.6
Oil exporters[d]	5.4	2.9	-0.4	1.7	2.6	2.7	-0.2	-0.2	-0.3	-0.3
CFA countries[e]	5.5	4.0	2.8	3.6	4.1	4.3	-1.5	-1.2	-1.2	-1.2
South Africa	1.6	1.3	0.3	0.6	1.1	2.0	-0.1	-0.5	-0.7	0.2
Nigeria	6.3	2.7	-1.6	1.2	2.4	2.5	0.1	0.2	-0.1	0.0
Angola	4.8	3.0	0.0	1.2	0.9	1.5	-0.4	0.0	0.0	0.6

Source: World Bank.

World Bank forecasts are frequently updated based on new information and changing (global) circumstances. Consequently, projections presented here may differ from those contained in other Bank documents, even if basic assessments of countries' prospects do not differ at any given moment in time.

a. EMDE refers to emerging market and developing economies. GDP at market prices and expenditure components are measured in constant 2010 U.S. dollars. Excludes Central African Republic, São Tomé and Príncipe, Somalia, and South Sudan.

b. Sub-regional aggregate excludes Central African Republic, São Tomé and Príncipe, Somalia, and South Sudan, for which data limitations prevent the forecasting of GDP components.

c. Exports and imports of goods and non-factor services (GNFS).

d. Includes Angola, Cameroon, Chad, Democratic Republic of Congo, Gabon, Ghana, Nigeria, Republic of Congo, and Sudan.

e. Includes Benin, Burkina Faso, Cameroon, Central African Republic, Chad, Côte d'Ivoire, Equatorial Guinea, Gabon, Mali, Niger, Republic of Congo, Senegal, and Togo.

For additional information, please see www.worldbank.org/gep.

TABLE 2.6.2 Sub-Saharan Africa country forecasts[a]

(Real GDP growth at market prices in percent, unless indicated otherwise)

	2014	2015	2016	2017	2018	2019	2016	2017	2018	2019
			Estimates	Projections			(percentage point difference from January 2017 projections)			
Angola	4.8	3.0	0.0	1.2	0.9	1.5	-0.4	0.0	0.0	0.6
Benin	6.4	2.1	4.0	5.5	6.0	6.3	-0.6	0.3	0.7	1.0
Botswana[b]	4.1	-1.7	2.9	4.0	4.2	4.3	-0.2	0.0	-0.1	0.0
Burkina Faso	4.0	4.0	5.4	6.1	6.3	6.3	0.2	0.6	0.3	0.3
Burundi	4.7	-3.9	-0.6	1.5	2.0	2.6	-0.1	-1.0	-1.5	-0.9
Cabo Verde	0.6	1.5	3.9	3.3	3.7	3.7	0.9	0.0	0.2	0.2
Cameroon	5.9	5.8	4.5	3.9	4.4	4.6	-1.1	-1.8	-1.7	-1.5
Chad	6.9	1.8	-7.0	0.2	3.2	3.1	-3.5	0.5	-1.5	-3.2
Comoros	2.1	1.0	2.2	3.3	4.0	4.0	0.2	0.8	1.0	1.0
Congo, Dem. Rep.	9.0	6.9	2.2	4.7	4.9	4.9	-0.5	0.0	-0.1	-0.1
Congo, Rep.	6.8	2.6	-2.1	1.0	1.5	1.5	-6.7	-3.3	-2.2	-2.2
Côte d'Ivoire	8.5	9.2	7.8	6.8	6.5	6.3	0.0	-1.2	-1.6	-1.8
Equatorial Guinea	-0.7	-8.3	-7.3	-5.9	-7.0	-6.0	-1.6	-0.2	-0.4	0.6
Ethiopia[b]	10.3	9.6	7.5	8.3	8.0	7.9	-0.9	-0.6	-0.6	-0.7
Gabon	4.3	4.0	2.3	1.3	2.4	2.9	-0.9	-2.5	-2.2	-1.7
Gambia, The	0.9	4.1	2.1	2.5	3.8	4.0	1.6	1.7	1.2	1.4
Ghana	4.0	3.9	3.6	6.1	7.8	6.2	0.0	-1.4	-0.6	-2.2
Guinea	0.4	0.1	4.6	4.4	4.6	4.6	-0.6	-0.2	0.0	0.0
Guinea-Bissau	2.5	4.8	4.9	5.1	5.1	5.1	0.0	0.0	0.0	0.0
Kenya	5.3	5.7	5.8	5.5	5.8	6.1	-0.1	-0.5	-0.3	0.0
Lesotho	4.5	1.6	2.5	3.0	3.4	3.6	0.1	-0.7	-0.6	-0.4
Liberia	0.7	0.0	-1.2	3.0	5.3	5.7	-3.7	-2.8	0.0	0.4
Madagascar	3.3	3.8	4.4	3.5	6.4	4.7	0.3	-1.0	1.6	-0.1
Malawi	5.7	2.8	2.5	4.4	4.9	5.3	0.0	0.2	0.4	0.8
Mali	7.0	6.0	5.6	5.3	5.2	5.1	0.0	0.2	0.2	0.1
Mauritania	5.6	1.4	2.0	3.5	2.7	4.6	-2.0	-0.7	-1.1	0.8
Mauritius	3.7	3.5	3.5	3.4	3.5	3.3	0.3	-0.1	-0.3	-0.5
Mozambique	7.4	6.6	3.3	4.8	6.1	6.7	-0.3	-0.4	-0.5	0.1
Namibia	6.5	5.3	1.2	3.0	4.0	4.2	-0.4	-2.0	-1.4	-1.2
Niger	7.0	3.6	4.7	5.2	5.5	5.5	-0.3	-0.1	-0.5	-0.5
Nigeria	6.3	2.7	-1.6	1.2	2.4	2.5	0.1	0.2	-0.1	0.0
Rwanda	7.0	6.9	5.9	6.0	6.8	7.0	-0.1	0.0	-0.2	0.0
Senegal	4.3	6.5	6.6	6.7	6.9	7.0	0.0	-0.1	-0.1	0.0
Seychelles	3.3	3.5	4.4	4.2	3.8	3.5	0.6	0.7	0.3	0.0
Sierra Leone	4.6	-20.6	5.0	5.4	5.6	5.9	1.1	-1.5	-0.3	0.0
South Africa	1.6	1.3	0.3	0.6	1.1	2.0	-0.1	-0.5	-0.7	0.2
Sudan	2.7	4.9	4.7	4.1	3.9	3.9	1.2	0.4	0.2	0.2
Swaziland	2.7	1.9	-0.6	1.7	3.1	3.2	0.3	-0.2	0.0	0.1
Tanzania	7.0	7.0	6.9	7.2	7.2	7.4	0.0	0.1	0.1	0.3
Togo	5.9	5.4	5.0	4.6	5.5	5.5	-0.4	-0.4	0.0	0.0
Uganda[b]	5.6	5.6	4.8	4.6	5.2	5.6	0.2	-1.0	-0.8	-0.4
Zambia	5.0	2.9	3.3	4.1	4.5	4.7	0.4	0.1	0.3	0.5
Zimbabwe	3.8	0.5	0.7	2.3	1.8	1.7	0.3	-1.5	-1.6	-1.7

Source: World Bank.

World Bank forecasts are frequently updated based on new information and changing (global) circumstances. Consequently, projections presented here may differ from those contained in other Bank documents, even if basic assessments of countries' prospects do not significantly differ at any given moment in time.

a. GDP at market prices and expenditure components are measured in constant 2010 U.S. dollars. Excludes Central African Republic, São Tomé and Príncipe, Somalia, and South Sudan.

b. Fiscal-year based figures.

For additional information, please see www.worldbank.org/gep.

References

Bhorat, H., and F. Tarp. 2016. "The Pursuit of Long-Run Economic Growth in Africa." In *Africa's Lions: Growth Traps and Opportunities for Six African Economies*, edited by H. Bhorat and F. Tarp. Washington, DC: Brookings Institution.

BIS (Bank for International Settlements). 2017. "Statistical Bulletin." *BIS Quarterly Review* (March): 247–273.

Callen, T., R. Cherif, F. Hasanov, A. Hegazy, and P. Khandelwal. 2014. "Economic Diversification in the GCC: The Past, the Present, and the Future." IMF Staff Discussion Note 14/12, International Monetary Fund, Washington, DC.

Campanaro, A., and J. M. Masic. 2017. "Municipal Asset Management in China's Small Cities and Towns." Policy Research Working Paper 7997, World Bank, Washington, DC.

Chen W., and R. Nord. 2017. "A Rebalancing Act for China and Africa: The Effects of China's Rebalancing on Sub-Saharan Africa's Trade and Growth." African Department, International Monetary Fund, Washington, DC.

Crowley, M. A., H. Song, and N. Meng. 2016. "Tariff Scares: Trade Policy Uncertainty and Foreign Market Entry by Chinese Firms." CEPR Discussion Paper 11722, Centre for Economic Policy and Research, London.

Easterly, W., N. Fiess, and D. Lederman. 2003. "NAFTA and Convergence in North America: High Expectations, Big Events, Little Time." *Economia* 4 (1): 1–53.

EBRD (European Bank for Reconstruction and Development), European Investment Bank, and World Bank Group. 2016. *What's Holding Back the Private Sector in MENA? Lessons from the Enterprise Survey*. World Bank: Washington, DC.

Famine Early Warning System Network. 2017. "Rainfall Remains Well Below-average During Peak Rainy Season in the Horn of Africa." Global Weather Hazards Summary. April 21-27, 2017.

Husain, A. M., R. Arezki, P. Breuer, V. Haksar, T. Helbling, P. Medas, M. Sommer, and an IMF Staff Team. 2015. "Global Implications of Lower Oil Prices." Staff Discussion Note 15/15, International Monetary Fund, Washington, DC.

IADB (Inter-American Development Bank). 2017. "Routes to Growth in a New Trade World." Inter-American Development Bank, Washington, DC.

IMF (International Monetary Fund). 2016a. "Asia: Maintaining Robust Growth amid Heightened Uncertainty." Regional Economic Outlook Update series, International Monetary Fund, Washington, DC.

————. 2016b. Thailand Selected Issues. International Monetary Fund, Washington, DC.

————. 2016c. "China Spillovers. New Evidence from Time-Varying Estimates." Spillover Notes No. 7, International Monetary Fund, Washington, DC.

————. 2016d. "China's Footprint in Global Commodity Markets." Spillover Notes No. 6, International Monetary Fund, Washington, DC.

————. 2016e. "Spillovers from China: Financial Channels." Spillover Notes No. 5, International Monetary Fund, Washington, DC.

————. 2016f. "Spillover Implications of China's Slowdown for International Trade." Spillover Notes No. 4, International Monetary Fund, Washington, DC.

————. 2016g. "ASEAN-5 Cluster Report— Evolution of Monetary Policy Frameworks." International Monetary Fund, Washington, DC.

————. 2016h. "Asia and Pacific: Building on Asia's Strengths during Turbulent Times." Regional Economic Outlook series. April. International Monetary Fund, Washington, DC.

————. 2017a. "Indonesia, Staff Report for the 2016 Article IV Consultation." International Monetary Fund, Washington, DC.

_____. 2017b. *Regional Economic Outlook: Western Hemisphere*. Washington, DC: International Monetary Fund.

_____. 2017c. *Regional Economic Outlook: Middle East and Central Asia Update*. International Monetary Fund: Washington, DC.

_____. 2017d. "India, Staff Report for the 2016 Article IV Consultation." International Monetary Fund, Washington, DC.

_____. 2017e. "India Selected Issues." International Monetary Fund, Washington, DC.

_____. 2017f. "West African Economic and Monetary Union: Staff Report on Common Policies of Member Countries." Country Report No. 17/99, International Monetary Fund, Washington, DC.

Kose, A., F. Ohnsorge, L. Ye, and E. Islamaj. 2017a. "Weakness in Investment Growth: Causes, Implications and Policy Responses." CAMA Working Papers 2017-19, Centre for Applied Macroeconomic Analysis, Crawford School of Public Policy, The Australian National University.

Miyajima, K. 2017. "What Influences Bank Lending in Saudi Arabia?" Working Paper 17/31, International Monetary Fund, Washington, DC.

Papadavid, P. 2016. "Post-election Rises in U.S. Interest Rates: Rate Rises Could Hurt Africa's Access to Finance." Briefing papers. Macroeconomic impact series. Overseas Development Institute, International Economic Development Group.

Rai, V., and L. Suchanek. 2014. "The Effect of the Federal Reserve's Tapering Announcements on Emerging Markets." Working Paper: 2014-50, Bank of Canada.

Reinhart, C. M., and K. S. Rogoff. 2014. "Recovery from Financial Crisis: Evidence from 100 Episodes." *American Economic Review: Papers and Proceedings* 104 (5): 50-55.

Schiff, M., and Y. Wang. 2002. "Regional Integration and Technology Diffusion: The Case of NAFTA." World Bank, Washington, DC.

Schiffbauer, M., A. Sy, S. Hussain, H. Sahnoun, and P. Keefer. 2015. "Jobs or Privileges: Unleashing the Employment Potential of the Middle East and North Africa." MENA Development Report. World Bank, Washington, DC.

World Bank. 2014. *Turn Down the Heat: Confronting the New Climate Normal*. Washington, DC: World Bank.

World Bank. 2016a. "The Quest for Productivity Growth." Malaysia Economic Monitor. December. World Bank, Washington, DC.

_____. 2016b. "Aging Society and Economy." Thailand Economic Monitor. December. World Bank, Washington, DC.

_____. 2016c. *Global Economic Prospects: Spillovers amid Weak Growth*. Washington, DC: World Bank.

_____. 2016d. *East Asia and Pacific Economic Update: Reducing Vulnerabilities*. October. Washington, DC: World Bank.

_____. 2016e. *Europe and Central Asia Economic Update: Polarization and Populism*. November. Washington, DC: World Bank.

_____. 2016f. "Russia Economic Report." World Bank, Washington, DC.

_____. 2016g. "Bangladesh Development Update." October. World Bank, Washington, DC.

_____. 2017a. *East Asia and Pacific Economic Update*. (April issue). Washington, DC: World Bank.

_____. 2017b. "Staying the Course." Indonesia Economic Quarterly. March. World Bank, Washington, DC.

_____. 2017c. "Philippines Monthly Economic Developments." March. World Bank, Washington, DC.

_____. 2017d. *Global Economic Prospects: Weak Investment in Uncertain Times*. Washington, DC: World Bank.

_____. 2017e. "Russia Economic Report." World Bank, Washington, DC.

_____. 2017f. "Kazakhstan Economic Update: The Economy Has Bottomed Out: What is Next?" Spring 2017. World Bank, Washington, DC.

_____. 2017g. *Europe and Central Asia Economic Update.* Washington, DC: World Bank.

_____. 2017h. "Migration and Development Brief 27." World Bank, Washington, DC.

_____. 2017i. "Leaning Against the Wind: Fiscal Policy in Latin American and the Caribbean in a Historical Perspective." World Bank, Washington, DC.

_____. 2017j. "Global Compact on Migration." Migration and Development Brief 27. World Bank, Washington, DC.

_____. 2017k. "MENA Economic Monitor: The Economics of Post-Conflict Reconstruction in MENA." April. World Bank, Washington, DC.

_____. 2017l. "India Development Update." May. World Bank, Washington, DC.

_____. 2017m. "Nepal Development Update." March. World Bank, Washington, DC.

_____. 2017n. "South Asia Economic Focus: Globalization Backlash." Spring. World Bank, Washington, DC.

_____. 2017o. "Africa's Pulse." Volume 15, April 2017. World Bank, Washington, DC.

World Bank and Development Research Center of the State Council, the People's Republic of China. 2014. *Urban China: Toward Efficient, Inclusive, and Sustainable Urbanization.* Washington, DC: World Bank.

World Bank and Ministry of Planning and Investment of Vietnam. 2016. *Vietnam 2035: Toward Prosperity, Creativity, Equity, and Democracy.* Washington, DC: World Bank.

STATISTICAL APPENDIX

TABLE 1 Real GDP Growth

	Annual estimates and forecasts[a]						Quarterly growth[b]					
	2014	2015	2016e	2017f	2018f	2019f	15Q4	16Q1	16Q2	16Q3	16Q4	17Q1e
World	2.8	2.7	2.4	2.7	2.9	2.9	2.5	2.2	2.4	2.3	2.6	2.7
Advanced Economies	1.9	2.1	1.7	1.9	1.8	1.7	1.8	1.5	1.7	1.7	1.8	2.0
United States	2.4	2.6	1.6	2.1	2.2	1.9	1.9	1.6	1.3	1.7	2.0	2.0
Euro Area	1.2	2.0	1.8	1.7	1.5	1.5	2.3	1.7	2.2	1.7	1.4	1.7
Japan	0.3	1.1	1.0	1.5	1.0	0.6	0.9	0.5	0.9	1.1	1.7	1.6
United Kingdom	3.1	2.2	1.8	1.7	1.5	1.5	1.7	1.6	1.7	2.0	1.9	2.0
Emerging Market and Developing Economies	4.3	3.6	3.5	4.1	4.5	4.7	3.7	3.6	3.7	3.5	4.0	4.0
East Asia and Pacific	6.8	6.5	6.3	6.2	6.1	6.1	6.5	6.3	6.4	6.4	6.5	6.5
Cambodia	7.1	7.0	6.9	6.9	6.9	6.7	..	..	..	..	..	..
China	7.3	6.9	6.7	6.5	6.3	6.3	6.8	6.7	6.7	6.7	6.8	6.9
Fiji	5.6	3.6	2.0	3.7	3.5	3.3	..	..	..	..	..	..
Indonesia	5.0	4.9	5.0	5.2	5.3	5.4	5.2	4.9	5.2	5.0	4.9	5.0
Lao PDR	7.5	7.4	7.0	7.0	6.8	7.2	..	..	..	..	..	..
Malaysia	6.0	5.0	4.2	4.9	4.9	5.0	4.6	4.1	4.0	4.3	4.5	5.6
Mongolia	6.9	2.2	1.0	-0.2	1.9	8.0	-2.2	3.0	-0.3	-7.3	9.8	4.2
Myanmar	8.0	7.3	6.5	6.9	7.2	7.3	..	..	..	..	..	..
Papua New Guinea	7.4	6.8	2.4	3.0	3.2	3.4	..	..	..	..	..	..
Philippines	6.1	6.1	6.9	6.9	6.9	6.8	6.7	6.9	7.1	7.1	6.6	6.4
Solomon Islands	2.0	3.3	3.0	3.3	3.0	3.0	..	..	..	..	..	..
Thailand	0.9	2.9	3.2	3.2	3.3	3.4	2.7	3.1	3.6	3.2	3.0	3.3
Timor-Leste	5.9	4.3	5.1	4.0	5.0	6.0	..	..	..	..	..	..
Vietnam	6.0	6.7	6.2	6.3	6.4	6.4	7.0	5.5	5.6	6.6	6.8	5.1
Europe and Central Asia	2.3	1.0	1.5	2.5	2.7	2.8	1.4	1.6	2.0	0.3	2.1	..
Albania	1.8	2.6	3.2	3.5	3.5	3.8	1.8	3.3	3.4	3.1	4.0	..
Armenia	3.6	3.0	0.2	2.7	3.1	3.4	..	..	..	..	..	..
Azerbaijan	2.0	1.1	-3.8	-1.4	0.6	1.3	0.1	-2.9	-2.4	-2.3	-2.5	..
Belarus	1.7	-3.9	-2.6	-0.4	0.5	1.2	-4.5	-3.7	-1.5	-3.6	-1.9	..
Bosnia and Herzegovina	1.1	3.0	2.8	3.2	3.7	4.0	..	..	..	..	..	..
Bulgaria	1.3	3.6	3.4	3.0	3.2	3.3	3.6	3.6	3.5	3.2	3.5	3.4
Croatia	-0.4	1.6	2.9	2.9	2.5	2.6	1.8	2.7	2.8	2.9	3.4	..
Georgia	4.6	2.9	2.7	3.5	4.0	4.5	3.0	3.3	2.8	2.2	2.7	..
Hungary	4.0	3.1	2.0	3.7	3.7	3.0	3.4	1.1	2.8	2.2	1.6	4.1
Kazakhstan	4.2	1.2	1.0	2.4	2.6	2.9	1.0	-0.3	-0.3	1.5	2.5	..
Kosovo	1.2	4.1	3.6	3.9	4.2	4.4	..	..	..	..	..	..
Kyrgyz Republic	4.0	3.9	3.8	3.4	4.0	4.8	..	..	..	..	..	..
Macedonia, FYR	3.6	3.8	2.4	2.8	3.3	3.8	6.0	2.4	2.9	2.0	2.4	..
Moldova	4.8	-0.5	4.1	4.0	3.7	3.5	..	..	..	..	..	..
Montenegro	1.8	3.4	2.5	3.3	3.0	2.0	..	..	..	..	..	..
Poland	3.3	3.9	2.8	3.3	3.2	3.2	4.6	2.6	3.1	2.0	3.3	4.2
Romania	3.1	3.9	4.8	4.4	3.7	3.5	4.0	4.3	6.0	4.3	4.8	5.7
Russia	0.7	-2.8	-0.2	1.3	1.4	1.4	-3.2	-0.4	-0.5	-0.4	0.3	0.5
Serbia	-1.8	0.8	2.8	3.0	3.5	3.5	1.1	3.9	2.0	2.8	2.5	1.0
Tajikistan	6.7	6.0	6.9	5.5	5.9	6.1	..	..	..	..	..	..
Turkey	5.2	6.1	2.9	3.5	3.9	4.1	7.4	4.5	5.3	-1.3	3.5	..
Turkmenistan	10.3	6.5	6.2	6.3	6.5	6.5	..	..	..	..	..	..
Ukraine	-6.6	-9.8	2.3	2.0	3.5	4.0	-2.4	0.1	1.5	2.3	4.8	2.4
Uzbekistan	8.1	8.0	7.8	7.6	7.7	7.8	..	..	..	..	..	..

TABLE 1 Real GDP Growth

TABLE 1 Real GDP Growth *(continued)*

	Annual estimates and forecasts[a]						Quarterly growth[b]					
	2014	2015	2016e	2017f	2018f	2019f	15Q4	16Q1	16Q2	16Q3	16Q4	17Q1e
Latin America and the Caribbean	0.9	-0.8	-1.4	0.8	2.1	2.5	-1.2	-1.4	-0.8	-0.6	-0.2	..
Argentina	-2.5	2.6	-2.3	2.7	3.2	3.2	2.6	0.6	-3.7	-3.7	-2.1	..
Belize	4.1	1.0	-1.5	2.1	2.0	2.0	..	..	..	..	..	..
Bolivia	5.5	4.9	4.3	3.7	3.7	3.4	6.0	4.9	3.2	5.0	..	..
Brazil	0.5	-3.8	-3.6	0.3	1.8	2.1	-5.8	-5.4	-3.6	-2.9	-2.5	..
Chile	1.9	2.3	1.6	1.8	2.0	2.3	1.9	2.5	1.7	1.8	0.5	0.1
Colombia	4.4	3.1	2.0	2.0	3.1	3.4	3.4	2.7	2.5	1.2	1.6	1.1
Costa Rica	3.7	4.7	4.3	3.8	3.6	3.5	3.7	5.1	4.6	3.4	4.2	..
Dominica	3.9	2.2	0.6	3.0	2.1	2.1	..	..	..	..	..	..
Dominican Republic	7.6	7.0	6.6	5.3	5.0	4.8	..	..	..	..	..	..
Ecuador	4.0	0.2	-1.5	-1.3	-0.4	0.3	-2.0	-4.0	-2.1	-1.2	1.5	..
El Salvador	1.4	2.3	2.4	2.0	1.8	1.7	2.4	2.1	2.4	2.4	2.6	..
Guatemala	4.2	4.1	3.1	3.5	3.5	3.6	4.0	2.9	3.7	2.6	3.0	..
Guyana	3.8	3.1	3.3	3.5	3.6	3.7	..	..	..	..	..	..
Haiti[c]	2.8	1.2	1.4	0.5	1.7	2.3	..	..	..	..	..	..
Honduras	3.1	3.6	3.6	3.4	3.3	3.3	5.0	3.7	4.0	2.9	3.8	..
Jamaica	0.7	1.0	1.4	2.0	2.1	2.3	..	..	..	..	..	..
Mexico	2.3	2.6	2.3	1.8	2.2	2.5	2.5	2.2	2.6	2.0	2.3	2.8
Nicaragua	4.8	4.9	4.7	4.3	4.2	4.2	6.2	3.3	6.7	4.7	4.2	..
Panama	6.1	5.8	4.9	5.2	5.4	5.8	..	..	..	..	..	..
Paraguay	4.7	3.0	4.1	3.6	3.8	3.8	0.7	1.5	6.5	5.4	3.4	..
Peru	2.4	3.3	3.9	2.8	3.8	3.6	4.8	4.4	3.7	4.5	3.0	2.1
St. Lucia	0.5	1.6	0.8	0.5	0.7	0.7	..	..	..	..	..	..
St. Vincent and the Grenadines	-0.5	2.1	1.8	2.5	2.8	2.9	..	..	..	..	..	..
Suriname	0.4	-2.7	-10.4	0.9	2.2	1.2	..	..	..	..	..	..
Trinidad and Tobago	-0.6	-0.6	-5.1	0.3	3.4	3.3	..	..	..	..	..	..
Uruguay	3.2	0.4	1.5	1.6	2.4	3.4	-1.3	0.0	1.3	1.1	3.4	..
Venezuela, RB	-3.9	-8.2	-12.0	-7.7	-1.2	0.7	..	..	..	..	..	..
Middle East and North Africa	3.4	2.8	3.2	2.1	2.9	3.1	3.9	2.6	1.9	2.2	2.4	..
Algeria	3.8	3.8	3.5	1.8	1.0	1.5	..	..	..	..	..	..
Bahrain	4.4	2.9	3.0	1.9	1.9	2.3	2.8	4.5	2.5	3.9	1.1	..
Djibouti	6.0	6.5	6.5	7.0	7.0	7.2	..	..	..	..	..	..
Egypt, Arab Rep.[c]	2.9	4.4	4.3	3.9	4.6	5.3	4.0	3.6	4.5	3.4	3.8	..
Iran, Islamic Rep.	4.3	-1.8	6.4	4.0	4.1	4.2	..	..	..	..	..	..
Iraq	0.7	4.8	10.1	-3.1	2.6	1.1	..	..	..	..	..	..
Jordan	3.1	2.4	2.0	2.3	2.6	3.0	2.6	2.3	1.9	1.8	2.0	..
Kuwait	0.5	1.8	2.9	0.2	2.7	2.9	..	..	..	..	..	..
Lebanon	1.8	1.3	1.8	2.5	2.6	2.6	..	..	..	..	..	..
Morocco	2.6	4.5	1.1	3.8	3.7	3.6	..	..	..	..	..	..
Oman	2.5	5.7	2.2	0.9	2.4	2.9	..	..	..	..	..	..
Qatar	4.0	3.6	2.2	3.2	2.6	2.5	3.9	1.4	1.8	3.9	1.7	..
Saudi Arabia	3.7	4.1	1.4	0.6	2.0	2.1	4.3	2.6	0.9	1.2	2.2	..
Tunisia	2.3	1.1	1.0	2.3	3.0	3.5	0.7	0.6	1.1	1.3	1.2	..
United Arab Emirates	3.1	3.8	2.3	2.0	2.5	3.2	..	..	..	..	..	..
West Bank and Gaza	-0.2	3.4	4.1	3.5	3.4	3.4	..	..	..	..	..	..

TABLE 1 Real GDP Growth *(continued)*

	Annual estimates and forecasts[a]						Quarterly growth[b]					
	2014	2015	2016e	2017f	2018f	2019f	15Q4	16Q1	16Q2	16Q3	16Q4	17Q1e
South Asia	6.7	6.9	6.7	6.8	7.1	7.3	6.8	8.5	7.0	7.3	6.9	..
Afghanistan	1.3	1.1	2.2	2.6	3.4	3.1	..	..	..	..	..	..
Bangladesh[c d]	6.1	6.6	7.1	6.8	6.4	6.7	..	..	..	..	..	..
Bhutan	5.7	6.5	6.8	6.8	7.7	10.5	..	..	..	..	..	..
India[c d]	7.2	7.9	6.8	7.2	7.5	7.7	6.9	8.6	7.2	7.4	7.0	..
Maldives	6.0	2.8	4.1	4.5	4.6	4.6	..	..	..	..	..	..
Nepal[c d]	6.0	3.3	0.4	7.5	5.5	4.5	..	..	..	..	..	..
Pakistan[c d]	4.0	4.0	4.7	5.2	5.5	5.8	..	..	..	..	..	..
Sri Lanka	5.0	4.8	4.4	4.7	5.0	5.1	2.8	5.1	2.4	4.6	5.3	..
Sub-Saharan Africa	4.6	3.1	1.3	2.6	3.2	3.5	1.4	-0.2	-0.2	-0.5	-0.2	..
Angola	4.8	3.0	0.0	1.2	0.9	1.5	..	..	..	..	..	..
Benin	6.4	2.1	4.0	5.5	6.0	6.3	..	..	..	..	..	..
Botswana[c]	4.1	-1.7	2.9	4.0	4.2	4.3	-3.5	2.3	3.9	6.9	4.2	..
Burkina Faso	4.0	4.0	5.4	6.1	6.3	6.3	..	..	..	..	..	..
Burundi	4.7	-3.9	-0.6	1.5	2.0	2.6	..	..	..	..	..	..
Cabo Verde	0.6	1.5	3.9	3.3	3.7	3.7	..	..	..	..	..	..
Cameroon	5.9	5.8	4.5	3.9	4.4	4.6	..	..	..	..	..	..
Chad	6.9	1.8	-7.0	0.2	3.2	3.1	..	..	..	..	..	..
Comoros	2.1	1.0	2.2	3.3	4.0	4.0	..	..	..	..	..	..
Congo, Dem. Rep.	9.0	6.9	2.2	4.7	4.9	4.9	..	..	..	..	..	..
Congo, Rep.	6.8	2.6	-2.1	1.0	1.5	1.5	..	..	..	..	..	..
Côte d'Ivoire	8.5	9.2	7.8	6.8	6.5	6.3	..	..	..	..	..	..
Equatorial Guinea	-0.7	-8.3	-7.3	-5.9	-7.0	-6.0	..	..	..	..	..	..
Ethiopia[c]	10.3	9.6	7.5	8.3	8.0	7.9	..	..	..	..	..	..
Gabon	4.3	4.0	2.3	1.3	2.4	2.9	..	..	..	..	..	..
Gambia, The	0.9	4.1	2.1	2.5	3.8	4.0	..	..	..	..	..	..
Ghana	4.0	3.9	3.6	6.1	7.8	6.2	..	..	..	..	..	..
Guinea	0.4	0.1	4.6	4.4	4.6	4.6	..	..	..	..	..	..
Guinea-Bissau	2.5	4.8	4.9	5.1	5.1	5.1	..	..	..	..	..	..
Kenya	5.3	5.7	5.8	5.5	5.8	6.1	5.7	5.9	6.2	5.7	..	..
Lesotho	4.5	1.6	2.5	3.0	3.4	3.6	..	..	..	..	..	..
Liberia	0.7	0.0	-1.2	3.0	5.3	5.7	..	..	..	..	..	..
Madagascar	3.3	3.8	4.4	3.5	6.4	4.7	..	..	..	..	..	..
Malawi	5.7	2.8	2.5	4.4	4.9	5.3	..	..	..	..	..	..
Mali	7.0	6.0	5.6	5.3	5.2	5.1	..	..	..	..	..	..
Mauritania	5.6	1.4	2.0	3.5	2.7	4.6	..	..	..	..	..	..
Mauritius	3.7	3.5	3.5	3.4	3.5	3.3	..	..	..	..	..	..
Mozambique	7.4	6.6	3.3	4.8	6.1	6.7	..	..	..	..	..	..
Namibia	6.5	5.3	1.2	3.0	4.0	4.2	..	..	..	..	..	..
Niger	7.0	3.6	4.7	5.2	5.5	5.5	..	..	..	..	..	..
Nigeria	6.3	2.7	-1.6	1.2	2.4	2.5	1.8	-0.7	-1.6	-2.4	-1.6	-0.7
Rwanda	7.0	6.9	5.9	6.0	6.8	7.0	..	..	..	..	..	..
Senegal	4.3	6.5	6.6	6.7	6.9	7.0	..	..	..	..	..	..
Seychelles	3.3	3.5	4.4	4.2	3.8	3.5	..	..	..	..	..	..
Sierra Leone	4.6	-20.6	5.0	5.4	5.6	5.9	..	..	..	..	..	..

TABLE 1 Real GDP Growth *(continued)*

	Annual estimates and forecasts[a]							Quarterly growth[b]					
	2014	2015	2016e	2017f	2018f	2019f		15Q4	16Q1	16Q2	16Q3	16Q4	17Q1e
Sub-Saharan Africa (continued)													
South Africa	1.6	1.3	0.3	0.6	1.1	2.0		0.6	-0.6	0.3	0.7	0.7	..
Sudan	2.7	4.9	4.7	4.1	3.9	3.9		..	..	..	..	..	..
Swaziland	2.7	1.9	-0.6	1.7	3.1	3.2		..	..	..	..	..	..
Tanzania	7.0	7.0	6.9	7.2	7.2	7.4		..	..	..	..	..	..
Togo	5.9	5.4	5.0	4.6	5.5	5.5		..	..	..	..	..	..
Uganda[c]	5.6	5.6	4.8	4.6	5.2	5.6		..	..	..	..	..	..
Zambia	5.0	2.9	3.3	4.1	4.5	4.7		..	..	..	..	..	..
Zimbabwe	3.8	0.5	0.7	2.3	1.8	1.7		..	..	..	..	..	..

Sources: World Bank and Haver Analytics.

a. Aggregate growth rates calculated using constant 2010 U.S. dollars GDP weights.

b. Year-over-year quarterly growth of not-seasonally-adjusted real GDP, except for the United States, Ecuador, and Tunisia, where only seasonally-adjusted data are available.
Year-over-year quarterly growth in the United Kingdom is calculated using seasonally-adjusted real GDP.

Regional averages are calculated based on data from following countries.

East Asia and Pacific: China, Indonesia, Malaysia, Mongolia, Philippines, Thailand, and Vietnam.

Europe and Central Asia: Albania; Azerbaijan; Belarus; Bulgaria; Croatia; Georgia; Hungary; Kazakhstan; Macedonia, FYR; Poland; Romania; Russia; Serbia; Turkey; and Ukraine.

Latin America and the Caribbean: Argentina, Bolivia, Brazil, Chile, Colombia, Costa Rica, Ecuador, El Salvador, Guatemala, Honduras, Mexico, Nicaragua, Paraguay, Peru, and Uruguay.

Middle East and North Africa: Bahrain, Egypt, Jordan, Qatar, Saudi Arabia, and Tunisia.

South Asia: India and Sri Lanka.

Sub-Saharan Africa: Botswana, Kenya, Nigeria, and South Africa.

c. Annual GDP is on fiscal year basis, as per reporting practice in the country.

d. GDP data for Pakistan are based on factor cost. For Bangladesh, Nepal, and Pakistan, the column labeled 2017 refers to FY2016/17. For India, the column labeled 2016 refers to FY2016/17.

For additional information, please see www.worldbank.org/gep.

Global Economic Prospects: Selected Topics, 2015-17

Growth and Business Cycles

Low-income countries

Recent developments and outlook	June 2017, Box 1.1
Recent developments and outlook	January 2017, Box 1.1
Recent developments and outlook	June 2016, Box 1.1
Graduation, recent developments, and prospects	January 2015, Chapter 1

Regional perspectives

Recent developments and outlook	June 2017, Box 1.2
Recent developments and outlook	January 2017, Box 1.2
Recent developments and outlook	June, 2016, Box 1.2

Recent investment slowdown

Europe and Central Asia	January 2017, Box 2.2.1
Latin America and the Caribbean	January 2017, Box 2.3.1
Middle East and North Africa	January 2017, Box 2.4.1
South Asia	January 2017, Box 2.5.1
Sub-Saharan Africa	January 2017, Box 2.6.1

Regional Integration and spillovers

East Asia and Pacific	January 2016, Box 2.1.1
Europe and Central Asia	January 2016, Box 2.2.1
Latin America and the Caribbean	January 2016, Box 2.3.1
Middle East and North Africa	January 2016, Box 2.4.1
South Asia	January 2016, Box 2.5.1
Sub-Saharan Africa	January 2016, Box 2.6.1

Other topics

Investment developments and outlook: East Asia and Pacific	January 2017, Box 2.1.1
Weak investment in uncertain times: Causes, implications and policy responses	January 2017, Chapter 3
Implications of rising uncertainty for investment in EMDEs	January 2017, Box 3.2
Implications of the investment slowdown in China	January 2017, Box 3.3
Interactions between public and private investment	January 2017, Box 3.4
Quantifying uncertainties in global growth forecasts	June 2016, SF 2
Who catches a cold when emerging markets sneeze?	January 2016, Chapter 3
Sources of the growth slowdown in BRICS	January 2016, Box 3.1
Understanding cross-border growth spillovers	January 2016, Box 3.2
Within-region spillovers	January 2016, Box 3.3
Recent developments in emerging and developing country labor markets	June 2015, Box 1.3
What does weak growth mean for poverty in the future?	January 2015, Box 1.1
What does a slowdown in China mean for Latin America and the Caribbean?	January 2015, Box 2.2
How resilient is Sub-Saharan Africa?	January 2015, Box 2.4

Global Economic Prospects: Selected Topics, 2015-17

Commodity Markets	
From commodity discovery to production: Vulnerabilities and policies in LICs	January 2016, Chapter 1
After the commodities boom: What next for low-income countries?	June 2015, Chapter 1, SF
Low oil prices in perspective	June 2015, Box 1.2
Understanding the plunge in oil prices: Sources and implications	January 2015, Chapter 4
What do we know about the impact of oil prices on output and inflation? A brief survey	January 2015, Box 4.1

Globalization of Trade and Financial Flows	
Arm's-Length Trade: A Source of Post-Crisis Trade Weakness	June 2017, SF
The U.S. economy and the world	January 2017, Special Focus
Regulatory convergence in mega-regional trade agreements	January 2016, Box 4.1.1
Can remittances help promote consumption stability?	January 2016, Chapter 4
Potential macroeconomic implications of the Trans-Pacific Partnership Agreement	January 2016, Chapter 4
Regulatory convergence in mega-regional trade agreements	January 2016, Box 4.1.1
China's integration in global supply chains: Review and implications	January 2015, Box 2.1
What lies behind the global trade slowdown?	January 2015, Chapter 4

Monetary and Exchange Rate Policies	
Investment-less credit booms	January 2017, Box 3.1
Recent credit surge in historical context	June 2016, SF1
Peg and control? The links between exchange rate regimes and capital account policies	January 2016, Chapter 4
Negative interest rates in Europe: A glance at their causes and implications	June 2015, Box 1.1
Hoping for the best, preparing for the worst: Risks around U.S. rate liftoff and policy options	June 2015, SF1.1
Countercyclical monetary policy in emerging markets: Review and evidence	January 2015, Box 1.2

Fiscal Policy	
Debt Dynamics in Emerging Markets and Developing Economies: Time to Act?	June 2017, SF
Having fiscal space and using it: Fiscal challenges in developing economies	January 2015, Chapter 3
Revenue mobilization in South Asia: Policy challenges and recommendations	January 2015, Box 2.3
Fiscal policy in low-income countries	January 2015, Box 3.1
What affects the size of fiscal multipliers?	January 2015, Box 3.2
Chile's fiscal rule—An example of success	January 2015, Box 3.3
Narrow fiscal space and the risk of a debt crisis	January 2015, Box 3.4

Development Economics Prospects Group (DECPG): Selected Other Publications on the Global Economy, 2015-17

Commodity Markets Outlook	
Investment weakness in commodity exporters	January 2017, SF
OPEC in historical context: Commodity agreements and market fundamentals	October 2016, SF
Energy and food prices: Moving in tandem?	July 2016, SF
Resource development in an era of cheap commodities	April 2016, SF
Weak growth in emerging market economies: What does it imply for commodity markets?	January 2016, SF
Understanding El Niño: What does it mean for commodity markets?	October 2015, SF
How important are China and India in global commodity consumption	July 2015, SF
Anatomy of the last four oil price crashes	April 2015, SF
Putting the recent plunge in oil prices in perspective	January 2015, SF

High-Frequency Monitoring
Global Monthly
Global Weekly

ECO-AUDIT

Environmental Benefits Statement

The World Bank Group is committed to reducing its environmental footprint. In support of this commitment, we leverage electronic publishing options and print-on-demand technology, which is located in regional hubs worldwide. Together, these initiatives enable print runs to be lowered and shipping distances decreased, resulting in reduced paper consumption, chemical use, greenhouse gas emissions, and waste.

We follow the recommended standards for paper use set by the Green Press Initiative. The majority of our books are printed on Forest Stewardship Council (FSC)–certified paper, with nearly all containing 50–100 percent recycled content. The recycled fiber in our book paper is either unbleached or bleached using totally chlorine-free (TCF), processed chlorine–free (PCF), or enhanced elemental chlorine–free (EECF) processes.

More information about the Bank's environmental philosophy can be found at http://www.worldbank.org/corporateresponsibility.

www.ingramcontent.com/pod-product-compliance
Lightning Source LLC
Chambersburg PA
CBHW061152030426
42336CB00002B/19